Presented to:

_____

From:

_____

Dedicated to
Jack and Gerri McEntee
for showing me and many others the way of wisdom.

Published by Wisdom Hunters, LLC

Scripture taken from the Holy Bible, New International Version,® NIV® Copyright © 1973, 1978, 1984 by International Bible Society. Used by permission of Zondervan. All rights reserved.

Book design by Jeff Voeltner, www.jeffvoeltner.com, jvoeltner@gmail.com
Wisdom Hunters, LLC PO Box 800062, Roswell, GA 30075
Visit us at www.WisdomHunters.com
The Wisdom Hunters name and logo are trademarks of Wisdom Hunters, LLC.

ISBN: 978-0692216439

ACKNOWLEDGEMENTS

Thanks to my wife Rita for being a constant voice of wisdom for me and our children.

Thanks to Rebekah Coons whose big idea for Wisdom Hunters was birthed 2010 in Cape Town, South Africa.

Thanks to Bethany Thoms for your extraordinary management of this book project.

Thanks to our faithful and friendly servant leadership team: Rita Bailey, Bethany Thoms, Susan Fox, Gwynne Maffett, Max Prince and Rachel Prince.

Thanks to our Wisdom Hunters Board of Directors: Scott Melby, Deb Ochs, Jack McEntee, Andrew Wexler, Cliff Bartow, John Hightower, and Advisory Board: Jack Alexander, Johnny Hunt, Pete Ochs, Gerri McEntee, Chris Gardner, Aaron Farley, Gary Nieber, Todd and Rebekah Coons

Thanks to Susan Fox and Jim Armstrong for your professional and precise editing and proofing.

Thanks to Jeff Voeltner for your incredible book cover and interior design creativity.

Thanks to the daily Wisdom Hunters daily devotional readers who give generously and who write how their faith has grown, as a result of a regular time with God in His word the Bible.

Thanks to my heavenly Father for loving me well and for extending His grace and favor through the power of His Spirit and the gift of His son Jesus. Everyday is sweeter than the day before!

Love in Christ,
Boyd Bailey, Roswell, GA

INTRODUCTION

———◦●◦———

I guide you in the way of wisdom and lead you along straight paths. Proverbs 4:11, NIV84

We follow the way of wisdom by understanding and applying the ways of God.

When I was thirty-one years old, a friend described to me his wisdom journey. I listened intently because his life was worth emulating. He was the spiritual leader of his family, a respected businessman, and a student of the Scriptures. Astonishingly, for ten years he had read daily a chapter in Proverbs based on the day of the month. For example, on May 3 he read the third chapter of Proverbs and meditated on its meaning for his life.

I felt the Holy Spirit prompting me to accept that same challenge; so from age thirty-one to age forty-one, I read a chapter in Proverbs based on the day of the month. It was uncanny how what I was learning mirrored my life experiences. Everything from the wise management of money to avoiding sexual temptation transformed my behavior. Ideas about parenting, marriage, and relationships began to strongly motivate my selfless service to others. The way of wisdom works.

Wisdom can be defined as having experience, sound judgment, and common sense. However, for our discussions wisdom is doing the right thing as God defines right. It is following the Lord's will for our life. The way of wisdom is Jesus Christ's ecosystem for life that integrates our mind, will, emotions, and spirit. A humbling reality: We are not wise, but there is a way of wisdom we can develop into a lifestyle. Yes, we check our ego at the door before entering wisdom's house!

By God's grace, through the Holy Spirit's teaching and by knowing Christ, we begin to discern the way of wisdom. Often on the surface of our thinking there is a way that seems right, but it is a distraction, even destructive (Proverbs 14:12). It harms relationships, leads to financial bondage, and in some cases causes death. In contrast the way of wisdom brings healing to the hurting, life to relationships, peace to the suffering, faith to families, and help to the unfortunate.

Wisdom is about God. Since it is all about Him, it makes sense to seek out His way of wisdom. Since there is always more to learn, becoming

wise requires an ongoing system of searching out His insights. In all my 54 years, I do not recall anyone ever saying they had arrived in their need for wisdom. Thus, the wise diligently stay on the path of seeking understanding from Christ. We are all an unfinished wise work in process. As with humility, I am not wise if I think I am!

I began this journey of wisdom hunting as an older teenager. Unfortunately, my youthful indiscretions led me to the way of foolishness. Fortunately, I've been blessed by a group of men and women who chose the way of wisdom. They unselfishly invested their time in my life and influenced me by their behavior, words, and writings. My mom, wife, grandmother, neighbor, boss, pastor, maintenance man, farmer, and educators all dispensed wisdom at significant stages in my life. People prodded me (and still prod me!) to learn the way of wisdom.

Above all, Holy Scripture has been my primary resource in my exploration for wisdom. The Bible is like an endless mine of riches waiting to be discovered by a humble heart in search of insight. In each new life season the Word of God has given me wisdom for marriage, parenting, work, finances, relationships, and health. Wisdom regularly reminds me how to trust and obey the Lord.

I'll confess, I have not always been a diligent student of wisdom. I struggle with bad thinking from past hurts and sinful behaviors that contribute to inaccurate assumptions in the present. My mind is in need of daily renewal, as the Spirit scrubs away lies and replaces them with truth. So, join me as a fellow wisdom seeker, and let's humbly search out the wisdom of God… Jesus Christ!

"Christ the power of God and the wisdom of God" (1 Corinthians 1:24).

JANUARY

And so, from the day we heard, we have not ceased to pray for you, asking that you may be filled with the knowledge of his will in all spiritual wisdom and understanding, so as to walk in a manner worthy of the Lord, fully pleasing to him, bearing fruit in every good work and increasing in the knowledge of God.

Colossians 1:9-10

INFERIOR WISDOM

Now this is our boast: Our conscience testifies that we have conducted ourselves in the world, and especially in our relations with you, with integrity and godly sincerity. We have done so, relying not on worldly wisdom but on God's grace.
2 Corinthians 1:12

———————

Worldly wisdom has a way of reducing heaven's wisdom to an afterthought. It's usually after first using our worldly wisdom—and finding that our ways don't work—that we pray and seek to discern the Lord's ways. It's tempting to rely on what seems to work instead of asking what are the principles we should live by based on God's economy. Worldly wisdom is not only inferior, it is also a competitor with God's grace.

The Lord sees the world's wisdom as foolishness, and the world sees His wisdom as foolishness. Some who embrace the wisdom of the world say there is no personal God, but God says in His wisdom that this thinking flows from a fool. The fool says in his heart, "There is no God" (Psalm 14:1). Sadly, the world's wisdom has no room for Jesus.

"For since in the wisdom of God the world through its wisdom did not know him, God was pleased through the foolishness of what was preached to save those who believe"
(1 Corinthians 1:21).

Related Readings: Job 5:13; Jeremiah 8:9; Isaiah 29:14;
1 Corinthians 1:17; 2:1-16; 3:19

SUPERIOR WISDOM

Where is the wise person? Where is the teacher of the law?
Where is the philosopher of this age? Has not God made
foolish the wisdom of the world? 1 Corinthians 1:20

Do not try to outsmart your Savior Jesus Christ with intelligence
void of humility and the fear of God. Academics, without an
infusion of faith in almighty God, lead down a reckless path of
disconnection from Deity. However, wise is the man or woman
who is full of the grace of God, and who studies truth long and
hard for the glory of God.

Faith in Jesus Christ as the Son of God is not a leap into the
dark; rather, it is a step into the light. Christian belief is based on
the historical fact of His death on the cross and His resurrection
from the dead. For some the Lord's wisdom wins out over theirs,
and they begin to seek out those people and places that possess
His knowledge.

"I saw that wisdom is better than folly, just as light is better than
darkness" (Ecclesiastes 2:13).

Related Readings: Matthew 7:24; Luke 2:52; 2 Peter 3:15;
James 1:5, 3:13-18

JANUARY 3

CHRIST IS WISDOM

We preach Christ crucified: a stumbling block to Jews and foolishness to Gentiles, but to those whom God has called, both Jews and Greeks, Christ the power of God and the wisdom of God. 1 Corinthians 1:23-24

———————◆◆◆———————

Christ is the wisdom of God, so to know Him is to know and understand godly wisdom. The life of Jesus illustrates for us wisdom while His teaching educates us in wisdom. It's in relationship with God the Son that Christians are able to grow in godly wisdom. The source of wise counsel is found in Christ—like pure water bubbles from the crevice of a remote mountain rock, so God's living water of truth flows from the heart of Jesus.

Because wisdom starts with Jesus, it's necessary to first enter into a personal relationship with Christ. The Holy Scriptures declare a Savior who is looking to love all those who come to Him in faith and repentance. Salvation in Jesus Christ is the first step to qualification for His wisdom. Fear of God leads to faith in God—that faith can access the wisdom of God. So, have you placed your faith in Jesus Christ? If so, you are very wise.

"Holy Scriptures, which are able to make you wise for salvation through faith in Christ Jesus" (2 Timothy 3:15b).

Related Readings: Romans 16:27; 1 Corinthians 1:30; Ephesians 1:17; Colossians 1:28

WISDOM IS CHARACTER

Who is wise and understanding among you? Let them show it by their good life, by deeds done in the humility that comes from wisdom… But the wisdom that comes from heaven is first of all pure; then peace-loving, considerate, submissive, full of mercy and good fruit, impartial and sincere.

James 3:13, 17

Wisdom is much more than knowledge—it is character. In fact, someone can be smart, clever, and insightful, but without character there is an absence of authentic wisdom. This heavenly wisdom is marked with the residue of righteousness. Thus, a wise person prays that their character keeps up with their growing wisdom. Integrity validates godly insight.

A wise person of character is pure in motive and peace loving in relationships. The wise defer to the needs of others, submit to authority, initiate empathy, bear the fruit of the Spirit, gather all the facts before making a decision, and are genuine in their concerns. Wisdom and character are prayer partners in their faith journey. Leave only your fingerprints of faith on wise advice, and trust God to conform others into the image of His Son Jesus.

"Now this is our boast: Our conscience testifies that we have conducted ourselves in the world, and especially in our relations with you, with integrity and godly sincerity. We have done so, relying not on worldly wisdom but on God's grace" (2 Corinthians 1:12).

Related Readings: Daniel 12:3; 10; Hosea 14:9; Matthew 24:45; 1 Corinthians 3:18

WISDOM IS LEARNED

The proverbs of Solomon son of David, king of Israel: for gaining wisdom and instruction; for understanding words of insight; for receiving instruction in prudent behavior, doing what is right and just and fair. Proverbs 1:1-3

———————

There is a definite educational element to wisdom. It does not happen in a spiritual vacuum or without intellectual effort. Those who excel in becoming wise learn how to educate themselves in the ways of wisdom. They read the Bible and other writings that define wisdom with a filter of faith in God. There are wise sayings outside of Holy Writ, but beyond the context of Christ, worldly wisdom drifts into a cheap imitation of godly wisdom.

Therefore, for wisdom to be the most meaningful, it must incubate and grow in a teachable and humble heart. A seed of corn does not germinate on the surface of dry, hard soil. In a similar ecosystem, seeds of wisdom bring life and insight to a cultivated heart moistened by heaven's righteous rain. Lifetime learners understand the need to always gain wisdom. Moses, upon a foundation of faith, was educated in wisdom in preparation to be God's leader.

"Moses was educated in all the wisdom of the Egyptians and was powerful in speech and action" (Acts 7:22).

Related Readings: Proverbs 11:2; Jeremiah 49:7; Luke 2:52; Ephesians 1:8

COMFORT IN LOSS

And many Jews had come to Martha and Mary to comfort
them in the loss of their brother. John 11:19

———————◆◈◆————————

Have you lost someone or something close to your heart—a
baby, a spouse, a friend, a job, or an opportunity? A great loss
requires great grace or the pain is unbearable. Why do some
expectant mothers have a stillborn child and others don't? We
can't truly understand these puzzling matters until we get to
heaven and are able to ask, "Why, Lord, why?"

Where is God when emotions run raw and a great hole of hurt
pierces the heart? We don't always understand the ways of
God, but we can always count on Christ's comfort. The Lord
lingers long close to those caught in the pain of great loss. What
others cannot totally understand, your heavenly Father fully
comprehends. Grace soothes aching hearts. Christ's comfort
nurses like cool water flowing down a dry, thirsty throat.

"For just as we share abundantly in the sufferings of Christ, so
also our comfort abounds through Christ" (2 Corinthians 1:5).
The Lord's comfort is limitless in its capacity to cure.

Related Readings: Job 42:11; Psalm 86:17, 119:76; John 14:1;
2 Corinthians 7:6-7

WISE DATING

Do not be unequally yoked together with unbelievers. For what fellowship has righteousness with lawlessness? And what communion has light with darkness?
2 Corinthians 6:14 NKJV

What relational path honors the Lord and honors my dating? Ask objectively; is there agreement in faith, family, and values? Dating relationships that honestly ask heartfelt questions flush out communication and prepare a couple for success, as God defines success. Wise dating waits for God's best and is not suddenly smitten by surface feelings. If, for example, an older teenager, college student, or single adult is "in love" with someone who does not practice faith in Jesus Christ, then the probability of a successful long-term relationship is very low.

It's hard enough to work through personality differences, diverse family backgrounds and character development without adding disagreement in the foundational issue of faith in God and obedience to Him. Start with belief in Jesus Christ and love for Him as your beginning point for being together in a dating relationship; only then do you have a good base to build upon. Like a beautiful house with a cracked concrete foundation are two pretty people who aren't both disciples of Jesus. Committed Christian relationships are not perfect, but they persevere.

"Jesus is 'the stone you builders rejected, which has become the cornerstone.' Salvation is found in no one else, for there is no other name under heaven given to mankind by which we must be saved" (Acts 4:11-12).

Related Readings: Genesis 24: 3-4; Psalm 24:3-5; 1 Corinthians 3:16-17; Ephesians 6:1-3

TRUTH OR LIES

Jesus answered, "I am the way and the truth and the life." John 14:6a; When he lies, he speaks his native language, for he is a liar and the father of lies. John 8:44b

———◆———

Truth flows from the "Truth"—Jesus—and lies from the "father" of lies—the devil. So, truth tellers side with the Lord and liars side with Satan. With whom do we align? Lying is so short-term focused. We are afraid we will lose something if we don't lie. We may lose someone's respect, but when we are found to be a liar, it compounds into humiliation. We may lose money, but when indiscretions are exposed over time, we lose more in compromised credibility. Better to lose a little with honesty than a lot with lies.

The devil is an expert in luring us away from the Lord's desires by offering a short-term solution—lying, which leads to long-term, destructive consequences. Liars are unable to remember their inconsistencies, so when confronted they sheepishly say, "I don't remember," or "I can't recall what I said." Children who chronically lie seem oblivious—they continue to fib until the painful consequences of not telling the truth causes them to change.

"If we claim to have fellowship with him and yet walk in the darkness, we lie and do not live out the truth" (1 John 1:6).

Related Readings: Proverbs 12:17, Jeremiah 9:3; Romans 1:25; 1 John 2:21

THE LORD PROVIDES

But the Lord provided a great fish to swallow Jonah, and
Jonah was inside the fish three days and three nights.
Jonah 1:17, NIV84

The Lord provides. He provides because this is His heart's
desire. By His very nature He is a provider. It is impossible for
Him not to provide. It gives Him great pleasure to provide. Just
as an earthly father delights in providing for his children, so
does your heavenly Father. "If you then, though you are evil,
know how to give good gifts to your children, how much more
will your Father in heaven give the Holy Spirit to those who ask
him!" (Luke 11:13).

When you fear, He provides peace. When you feel lonely, He
provides companionship. When you suffer loss, He provides
comfort. When you become proud, He provides humility.
When you lack the necessities of life, He provides your needs.
When you struggle with insecurity, He gives you little victories
to gain back much needed confidence. Your confidence grows
out of your trust in Him. He gives you strength.

"If anyone serves, they should do so with the strength God
provides, so that in all things God may be praised through Jesus
Christ. To him be the glory and the power for ever and ever.
Amen" (1 Peter 4:11b).

Related Readings: Job 36:26-31; Psalm 111:5;
Matthew 6:25-34; Acts 14:16-17

THE LORD'S REQUIREMENTS

He has showed you, O man, what is good. And what does the LORD require of you? To act justly and to love mercy and to walk humbly with your God. Micah 6:8, NIV84

God has expectations for His children: Justice, mercy, and humility are three of His requirements. These are not electives for the student of God's Word, but three virtuous attributes that are required. Furthermore, the Lord does not ask His followers to behave in any fashion that He has not already modeled before them. He acts justly, He loves mercy, and He walks humbly. He does not expect any behavior from His followers that He has not already exhibited. His justice is sure, right, and fair. His mercy is fresh, deep, and everlasting. His humility is authentic, tranquil, and service oriented. Jesus came to earth from heaven to give us a picture of God's glory.

For Christ followers, He is your life, and as you walk with Him that realization becomes more apparent. You cannot walk with God and not change—you become like the one with whom you walk. When you walk with the Lord you begin to grow in justice, mercy, and humility. When you walk with God, you are transformed into the image of His Son Jesus.

"For those God foreknew he also predestined to be conformed to the image of his Son, that he might be the firstborn among many brothers and sisters" (Romans 8:29).

Related Readings: Genesis 5:22-24; Joshua 22:5; Luke 24:1-35; 1 John 1:7

RAISING DAUGHTERS

Love is patient, love is kind. 1 Corinthians 13:4a

Raising daughters requires God's grace, loving patience and wisdom. Indeed, wise are parents of daughters who regularly partner in prayer for their special gifts from the Lord.

Daughters who love Jesus desire moms who set the example of being adorned with inner beauty and are not obsessed by outward beauty, which eventually fades away. Daughters need moms they can proudly emulate. Indeed, a discerning mom is a listening friend to her little girl—and a loving, but firm disciplinarian when necessary.

Raising daughters is not a passive role for fathers. On the contrary, dads are available to provide, protect, and care for their sensitive girls. Some daughters won't demand attention, but inside they still crave compassion and conversation. Wise is the father who takes the time to regularly date his daughter with acceptance and for understanding.

Furthermore, help your daughter find her identity in Christ and not in the culture. Society tells her she must look and act a certain way to be accepted, but a godly parent teaches her that acceptance comes from being a daughter of King Jesus. He loves her unconditionally, just as He made her. True identity comes from trusting Christ and His plan for her life.

"The king is enthralled by your beauty; honor him, for he is your lord" (Psalms 45:11, NIV84).

Related Readings: Ruth 2:22-23; Esther 2:15-18; Luke 8:41-42; Ephesians 6:1-4

RAISING SONS

Listen, my son, to your father's instruction and do not forsake
your mother's teaching. Proverbs 1:8

———— ◆◆◆ ————

Raising sons requires intentionality from a parent or parents.
Wise are the father and mother who have a plan to teach their
son how to make God-honoring choices and to lead like Jesus.
Yes, being an excellent example is fundamental, but it takes
more than modeling—sons need to understand why, what, and
how.

For example, they need life preparation in how to: become a
Christian, pray, and study the Bible. Take them through the book
of John to love Jesus, the book of Ephesians to grasp grace, and
the book of Proverbs to embrace wisdom. Boys and young men
who grow up fearing God are prepared to persevere through
adversity, success, marriage, and parenting.

"Listen to your father, who gave you life, and do not despise
your mother when she is old. Buy the truth and do not sell it—
wisdom, instruction and insight as well" (Proverbs 23:22-23).

Related Readings: Proverbs 23:15-16; 31:2; Philippians 2:22;
James 2:21

SIBLING RIVALRY

Now Israel loved Joseph more than any of his other sons, because he had been born to him in his old age; and he made an ornate robe for him. When his brothers saw that their father loved him more than any of them, they hated him and could not speak a kind word to him. Genesis 37:3-4

———————

Do you outwardly favor one of your children over another? Have you used a phrase like, "I wish you were more like your sister; she always gets an A on her tests"? If so, you are in danger of creating an environment that fosters rivalry between your children. Sad is a child who thinks they have to live up to a sister's or brother's unreachable standard.

Jealousy jabs at the heart and causes a child to react angrily toward the other object of their parent's affection. Since they don't feel like they measure up, they try to discredit the favored sibling, or they create chaos to draw attention to themselves. It is disheartening to see even grown children remain in a state of fierce competition. Cruelty needs to be replaced with calmness and anger with forgiveness.

"Anger is cruel and fury overwhelming, but who can stand before jealousy? Better is open rebuke than hidden love" (Proverbs 27:4-5).

Related Readings: Job 42:11; Luke 14:26; Acts 13:45; 2 Corinthians 12:20

GOD IS GOOD

The Lord is good, a refuge in times of trouble. He cares for those who trust in him. Nahum 1:7

———◆———

God is good. He is good when times are bad. He is good all the time. Do not relegate God to the bad side of the ledger just because you are experiencing bad times. Focus on the goodness of God, for He is good. His goodness is a refuge for you in times of trouble. Your security is in the safe environment His goodness provides. God's goodness is the standard by which people measure goodness. No person's goodness exceeds God's goodness. Your goodness is but a reflection of His, because apart from the Lord there resides in us no good thing. His goodness is foundational for all goodness.

Thus, Christ dwelling in you by faith allows the goodness of God to flourish. It is one of the wonders of grace. Indeed, faith in Jesus unleashes the goodness of God in your life. Good works without the goodness of God are just good works for the temporal. But good works, motivated by the goodness of God, reap eternal benefits. The Lord is good.

"I say to the LORD, 'You are my Lord; apart from you I have no good thing.'" (Psalm 16:2).

Related Readings: Luke 16:25; Hebrews 6:4-6;
2 Thessalonians 1:11; Titus 1:15

STAY IN PROCESS

I planted the seed, Apollos watered it, but God has been making it grow. So neither the one who plants nor the one who waters is anything, but only God, who makes things grow.
1 Corinthians 3:6-7

Are you struggling to stay in the process? It may be the engagement process—he or she cannot make up their mind on a date, time and location for the wedding. Perhaps you feel trapped in the process of a job search—a promising door opens and then closes just as quickly. The process at work is a challenge, because the project never seems to be completed on time and is not up to standard.

Or, for years you have prayed for the salvation of a loved one and they seem further away from the Lord than when you first started petitioning for their soul. It's in the process that God purifies our heart and gets our attention to go deeper with Him. The process may not seem perfect, but it is necessary to draw us near to Jesus in utter dependence.

"For this reason, since the day we heard about you, we have not stopped praying for you. We continually ask God to fill you with the knowledge of his will through all the wisdom and understanding that the Spirit gives, so that you may live a life worthy of the Lord" (Colossians 1:9-10a).

Related Readings: Jeremiah 29:4-6; Proverbs 25:4-5; Matthew 13:23; James 1:2-4

AVAILABLE GRANDPARENTS

After this, Job lived a hundred and forty years; he saw his children and their children to the fourth generation. And so Job died, an old man and full of years. Job 42:16-17

God gives grandparents the opportunity to be available for their grandchildren. It can be the most fulfilling season of life, because of the joy that comes from seeing the third generation follow the Lord with wholehearted commitment. Grandchildren need their grandparents for fun, support, encouragement, wisdom, security, and a loving legacy. Do you have a plan to be intentional in your grandchildren's lives?

Grandparents who take the time to be with their grandchildren invest in the next godly generation. Do you want to be remembered for being available to those who desire you the most, or for being busy doing good things for people who probably won't attend your funeral? Bless your grandchildren with your faithfulness to them and the Lord—pray for His will in their lives. Grandchildren need their grandparents' blessing.

"When Israel saw the sons of Joseph, he asked, 'Who are these?' 'They are the sons God has given me here,' Joseph said to his father. Then Israel said, 'Bring them to me so I may bless them'" (Genesis 48:8-9).

Related Readings: Proverbs 16:31; Isaiah 46:4; Titus 2:1-5

UNHOLY ACCOLADES

Woe to you when everyone speaks well of you, for that is how their ancestors treated the false prophets. Luke 6:26

Authentic teachers and preachers of the Bible will have some who disagree with, even dismiss, their proclamations of truth. If a spokesperson for the Lord is not criticized by some, there is need to worry that they are watering down God's Word. Churches are not created to make everyone feel good but to lead them to faith in Christ and holy living.

Furthermore, it is important how the messenger delivers the message—not with a holier-than-thou disposition but in a spirit of compassion and humble boldness. Followers of Jesus are not out to intentionally offend and attack those who embrace untruth or a worldly way of living. However, we are to speak the truth in love and trust God with how people will respond. Has a vocal minority unfairly criticized your stand on marriage? Do some of your family members think you are strange because of the way you raise your children in Christ? If so, do not be ashamed that some do not speak well of you; sometimes we are best known by our enemies.

"So do not be ashamed of the testimony about our Lord or of me his prisoner. Rather, join with me in suffering for the gospel, by the power of God" (2 Timothy 1:8).

Related Readings: 2 Chronicles 6:34-35; Jeremiah 14:14; Matthew 7:15; 1 Peter 4:2-4

RACIAL HEALING

You are all sons of God through faith in Christ Jesus, for all of you who were baptized into Christ have clothed yourselves with Christ. There is neither Jew nor Greek, slave nor free, male nor female, for you are all one in Christ Jesus.
Galatians 3:26-28, NIV84

Christianity is color blind. The foot of the cross is level and provides acceptance for all who embrace faith in Jesus Christ. Man erects barriers, but belief in Christ tears them down. Man makes himself superior and treats others as inferiors. However, our superior savior, Jesus, makes humble followers of the Lord significant.

Your devotion to Christ is meant to dissolve distrust toward those who differ from you. In fact, it is out of the beauty of diversity that your beliefs are made real. Faith untested by inclusiveness is indeed inferior. Belief in God equalizes egos and checks pride. Our Christian "brand promise" is love for one another because He first loved us.

"From one man he made all the nations, that they should inhabit the whole earth; and he marked out their appointed times in history and the boundaries of their lands. God did this so that they would seek him and perhaps reach out for him and find him, though he is not far from any one of us. 'For in him we live and move and have our being'" (Acts 17:26-28a).

Related Readings: Exodus 12:48-49; Ezekiel 17:23; Matthew 23:8; Acts 10:28-47

PEACEFUL PROTEST

The king's heart is like channels of water in the hand of the LORD; He turns it wherever He wishes. Every man's way is right in his own eyes, but the LORD weighs the hearts. To do righteousness and justice is desired by the LORD more than sacrifice. Proverbs 21:1-3 NASB

There is a reaction associated with conflicting opinions—it can be a peaceful protest, or it can become a violent outburst. Mental illness can drive a man mad with murderous intent, but those of sound mind must not be driven by vicious rage. The most productive process in expressing disagreement initiates civil discourse and is redemptive in its motive.

As followers of Jesus we are wise not to take matters into our own hands but to leave them in the hands of our Lord. We appeal to a higher power—almighty God, to intervene in injustice. Like the king who gave Nehemiah everything he requested and more, so the Lord can direct the heart of authorities to change laws and resource righteous causes.

"The king said to me, 'What is it you want?' Then I prayed to the God of heaven, and I answered the king, 'If it pleases the king and if your servant has found favor in his sight, let him send me to the city in Judah where my ancestors are buried so that I can rebuild it'" (Nehemiah 2:4-5).

Related Readings: Isaiah 32:17; Psalm 35:20; Luke 6:29; 1 Timothy 2:2

LIFE IS PRECIOUS

For you created my inmost being; you knit me together in my mother's womb. I praise you because I am fearfully and wonderfully made; your works are wonderful, I know that full well. Psalm 139:13-14

Why does a mom—even a dad—travel hundreds of miles to be at the bedside of their daughter or daughter-in-law as they deliver their grandbaby? When an infant enters the room in their mother's arms, why do people stop, stare, and adore the little one? Because life means something—it is a gift from God that reminds humans of His glory and goodness.

When we look at a newborn's feet, we see the faithfulness of our heavenly Father. When we hold his hand and count her fingers, we feel the comfort of the Holy Spirit. And when we look deep into their innocent eyes, we see the love of our Lord Jesus Christ reminding us of His infinite existence. God's glory glows through His divine handiwork. Almighty God's creation begins at conception, where He instructs in wisdom and desires faithfulness.

"Surely I was sinful at birth, sinful from the time my mother conceived me. Yet you desired faithfulness even in the womb; you taught me wisdom in that secret place" (Psalm 51:5-6).

Related Readings: Psalm 71:6; Isaiah 49:4-6; Jeremiah 1:5; Galatians 1:14-16

FRIEND OF GOD

And the scripture was fulfilled that says, "Abraham believed God, and it was credited to him as righteousness," and he was called God's friend. James 2:23

What does it mean to be a friend of God? It's like a child who becomes an adult and begins to relate to their dad or mom as a friend but still treats them with honor and respect. So it is with your heavenly Father—in the infant stages of faith you cannot fathom friendship until you mature through the elementary application of submission to God, trust in God, obedience to God, fear of God, and love of God and people.

Once we relate to our heavenly Father in holy surrender, dependence, and belief, we are in a position to appreciate engaging Him as a friend. But this friend relationship cannot bypass His Lordship in our lives. Candidates for friendship with God first have to first travel down the path of perseverance, brokenness, and character development. Friendship comes with a history of faithful service to Jesus, not with a flippant attitude but with one of awe. Jesus extends friendship to His faithful disciples.

"I no longer call you servants, because a servant does not know his master's business. Instead, I have called you friends, for everything that I learned from my Father I have made known to you" (John 15:15).

Related Readings: Exodus 33:11; 2 Chronicles 20:7; Luke 5:20, 34; 12:4-5

SHARE GOD STORIES

When they [Paul and Barnabas] came to Jerusalem, they were welcomed by the church and the apostles and elders, to whom they reported everything God had done through them.
Acts 15:4

―――――◄◆►―――――

Can a follower of Jesus contain the great works God does in and through them? Or, are they compelled to communicate Christ's faithfulness, forgiveness, healing, answered prayers, and salvation stories? Joy and gratitude to God cannot be contained in a life surrendered to the Lord. God waits for His works to be openly shared for His glory.

The grace of God causes a man or woman to glow under its influence. Discerning Christians look at a soul captivated by Christ and they know they have been with Jesus. So, we humbly tell of how the Lord is meeting financial needs, delivering a friend from addiction, growing disciples, and how He healed a fractured family relationship. A soul might explode unless it shares God's faithfulness.

"Since my youth, God, you have taught me, and to this day I declare your marvelous deeds" (Psalm 71:17).

Related Readings: Job 37:5; Psalm 86:10; Matthew 21:42; Acts 15:12

FAITH LIVING

For we live by faith, not by sight. 2 Corinthians 5:7

———————⟡———————

Faith living is focused on God living. It is the road less traveled. Even for believers in Jesus Christ, faith living is not always predominant. Why settle for anything less? If we limit ourselves to our efforts, our logic and what we can see, then we only tip God with our faith. He is calling us beyond the honeymoon stage of our faith to mature faith. A faith that only thinks of the past is anemic and stunted. Faith alive is focused on God's vision for the future. It is caught up in the possibilities of today with no fear of tomorrow.

Faith living enjoys God's ability to create. For example, He can create resourceful relational opportunities, as He is the connector par excellence. By faith He can be trusted to lead you to just the right people, people you can serve and people who can join you to accomplish God's will. Determine ways to bring value to the other person. It is not about what you can get from them. It is all about how you can serve them.

"By faith Abraham, when called to go to a place he would later receive as his inheritance, obeyed and went, even though he did not know where he was going" (Hebrews 11:8).

Related Readings: Habakkuk 2:4; Romans 1:17; Galatians 2:20; 3:11; Hebrews 10:38

DISCONNECT TO RECONNECT

After leaving them, he [Jesus] went up on a mountainside to
pray. Mark 6:46

Is your life hurried and full of busyness? If so, consider coming
away with Christ in quiet communion. A neglected soul
needs the nurturing of a still spot. Like the body needs food,
water, and sleep, so the soul needs Scripture, prayer, and rest.
Disconnection from distractions allows for connection with
Christ. Be still and know God in deep intimacy.

"He says, 'Be still, and know that I am God; I will be exalted
among the nations, I will be exalted in the earth'" (Psalm
46:10).

Stillness positions us to see the Lord with eyes of faith. He longs
to love His children with unlimited and unconditional love. A
heart loved by heaven cannot help but love others on earth. When
your heavenly Father holds you in His warm embrace, you are
able to serve others with care and compassion. God's grace
infuses a hungry heart for Him. Indeed, loving relationships
happen in the margin of life. It requires trust to disconnect
from important activities and meaningfully connect with Christ
and people. Faith facilitates intimacy. For example, let go of
uncertainties at work and let God and others bear that burden.
You avoid burnout and have the emotional energy to give at
home. Your family needs your full attention in order to feel like
you understand their needs. You disconnect to reconnect.

Related Readings: Psalm 28:7; 37:4-6; Matthew 4:1-17;
Acts 14:23

DIRECTIONS FROM GOD

When Pharaoh let the people go, God did not lead them on the road through the Philistine country, though that was shorter. For God said, "If they face war, they might change their minds and return to Egypt." So God led the people around by the desert road toward the Red Sea. Exodus 13:17-18a

———————

The Lord's path for His people is not always a straight line from point A to point B. In His wisdom He may allow us to go through the wilderness before we arrive at the Promised Land. He knows preparation precedes the blessing of the destination. He desires that we learn to trust in Him along the way to where He wants us to go. It's when the Lord's will is a nonlinear route that we begin to doubt and wonder why He has led us through a desert experience.

However, if life were that easy we could easily take credit for our successes and grow demanding and proud, rather than grateful and humble. Thank the Lord that He has you in a process that requires intense prayer and faith. He knows what's best to grow your faith so you are able to handle His blessings.

"Trust in the LORD with all your heart and lean not on your own understanding; in all your ways submit to him, and he will make your paths straight" (Proverbs 3:5-6).

Related Readings: Proverbs 12:28; Isaiah 55:8-9, 64:5; Jeremiah 32:19; Hebrews 3:8

FAMOUS FATHER

LORD I have heard of your fame; I stand in awe of your deeds, O LORD. Renew them in our day, in our time make them known; in wrath remember mercy. Habakkuk 3:2, NIV84

Most are not famous, but God is the most famous—His fame is from everlasting to everlasting. He is famous now—He was famous in the past—He will be famous in the future. No one person or event is more famous than God. He is the famous One. God's name is inscribed on the heavenly walk of His stars.

His fame stretches from universe to universe. Its expanse is from galaxy to galaxy. No amount of light years can capture the fame of God. His fame is beyond time. The fame of the Lord God Almighty covers the earth. It races from sea to shining sea. God is famous. He is on center stage as Creator, Savior, and Lord. God is our heavenly hero.

"I will set a sign among them, and I will send some of those who survive to the nations—to Tarshish, to the Libyans and Lydians (famous as archers), to Tubal and Greece, and to the distant islands that have not heard of my fame or seen my glory. They will proclaim my glory among the nations" (Isaiah 66:19).

Related Readings: Joshua 9:9; 1 Kings 10:1; Ruth 4:14

GOD'S FAVOR

When his master saw that the LORD was with him and that the LORD gave him success in everything he did, Joseph found favor in his eyes and became his attendant. Potiphar put him in charge of his household, and he entrusted to his care everything he owned. Genesis 39:3-4

The Lord's favor rests on His followers who remain faithful to Him. It is humbling to know that God extends wisdom and grace to those who go hard after Him. Though someone is separated from loved ones by a long distance, the Lord is nearby to impart His calming presence. Rest assured, Jesus brings success to souls who submit to His will.

Moreover, favor with God leads to favor with man. A heart connection on earth takes place when there has been a heart connection in heaven. People of influence are on the lookout for those they can trust. It is not a small thing to delegate management and leadership responsibilities—hence those with character are entrusted with more. Therefore, stay faithful in your responsibilities as a servant leader at work and home.

"Whoever can be trusted with very little can also be trusted with much, and whoever is dishonest with very little will also be dishonest with much" (Luke 16:10).

Related Readings: 1 Chronicles 28:19; Isaiah 62:3; Luke 1:66; 1 John 2:8-10

SOURCE OF PRESIDENTIAL POWER

"Do you refuse to speak to me?" Pilate said. "Don't you realize I have power either to free you or to crucify you?" Jesus answered, "You would have no power over me if it were not given to you from above." John 19:10-11a

A God-blessed nation is built around leaders who understand their roles as wise stewards. Our country rose in global influence because of this and will decline without it. Leadership cannot dismiss its responsibility to lead by the rule of law and its accountability to almighty God. The Lord gives leaders power to fulfill His agenda.

Leadership is a stewardship given by God. This is true on a micro level in the home, and on the macro level in government. A councilman, mayor, state legislator, governor, congressman, Supreme Court justice, and president all eventually answer to almighty God. It is the fear of the Lord and respect for His commands that lead leaders to become great. Humility, honesty, and submission to holy God allow governments to govern well.

"I urge, then, first of all, that requests, prayers, intercession and thanksgiving be made for everyone—for kings and all those in authority, that we may live peaceful and quiet lives in all godliness and holiness" (1 Timothy 2:1-2, NIV84).

Related Readings: Exodus 3:19-20; Psalm 21:1-7; Acts 13:21-22; 1 Peter 2:13-17

SUPPORT WEARY SERVANTS

When Moses' hands grew tired, they took a stone and put it under him and he sat on it. Aaron and Hur held his hands up—one on one side, one on the other—so that his hands remained steady till sunset. Exodus 17:12

When people grow tired they need the support of sensitive friends. Their fatigue may flow from trials and tribulations out of their control. They may be worn down by ongoing financial challenges. A rebellious child finds them spent emotionally or a newborn keeps them in a chronic state of physical exhaustion. Do you know someone who is overwhelmingly tired? Who needs your hands-on support?

Indeed, fatigue weakens faith. When we extend a little bit of encouragement, it may be a lifeline that leads someone to the Lord. Well-timed encouragement is eternal medicine for a suffering soul. Each day, life extracts courage from a hurting heart, so we come alongside to give courage with a kind word, a little cash or a faith-filled prayer. Few complain of too much loving support.

"He died for us so that, whether we are awake or asleep, we may live together with him. Therefore encourage one another and build each other up, just as in fact you are doing" (1 Thessalonians 5:10-11).

Related Readings: Romans 11:18; 2 Corinthians 13:11; 1 Thessalonians 4:18; Hebrews 3:13

INSPECT WHAT'S EXPECTED

Moses inspected the work and saw that they had done it just as the LORD had commanded. So Moses blessed them.
Exodus 39:43

———◄•◊•►———

Excellent work requires regular inspection. We all do better when others are watching, especially when it's the Lord and those we respect. Work is an expression of the worker, so it's imperative the work is intentional and completed with integrity. If we resist someone looking over our shoulder to verify our efforts then we miss out on much needed accountability.

Do you have clarity in what's expected of you in your role at work? If not, seek out your supervisor and confirm his or her expectations and make sure they align with your understanding. Like a team sport, you want to make sure you are both playing the same game and executing the same plays. Excellent execution requires alignment of expectations. Be grateful you have a boss who cares to look closely at what you do.

"Be sure you know the condition of your flocks, give careful attention to your herds" (Proverbs 27:23).

Related Readings: Genesis 43:16; Luke 16: 1-14; Hebrews 2:1; 1 Peter 4:10

PRIORITY LIVING

Now this is what the LORD Almighty says: "Give careful thought to your ways." Haggai 1:5

Priority living is based on what God deems necessary and important. He deserves our very best. Followers of Christ are honored to not give the Lord the first fruits, not the leftovers. First fruits giving and living means Jesus receives the best of everything about us. We give Him the best of our time and money. Priority living is defining priorities as God defines them, then planning our actions, goals and living around these priorities.

Without intentionally living out God's priorities, we default to reactionary living. Whatever comes our way becomes our default for living. This may take less thinking and praying, but it is no way to honor the Lord. Priority living asks the question, "Am I defining priorities as God defines priorities, and am I living these out for His glory?" Once His priorities are defined, the goal is to execute His priorities for His glory. Priority living is prayerful living. It is aligning with God's heart the best you know how and then trusting Him with your time and money. Priority living is giving God first and foremost what He deserves and expects from His children.

"But seek first his kingdom and his righteousness, and all these things will be given to you as well" (Matthew 6:33).

Related Readings: Psalm 86:12; Matthew 7:12; Philippians 4:8; 1 Peter 2:12

FEBRUARY

But grow in the grace and knowledge of our Lord and Savior Jesus Christ. To him be the glory both now and to the day of eternity.

Amen.

2 Peter 3:18

BOND SERVANT

The Lord's bond-servant must not be quarrelsome, but be kind to all, able to teach, patient when wronged, with gentleness correcting those who are in opposition, if perhaps God may grant them repentance leading to the knowledge of the truth.
2 Timothy 2:24-25, NASB

———◆◆◆———

We are all servants to something—either servants to the light or servants to the darkness. Satan is served or the Lord and Savior Jesus Christ is served—there is no middle ground. The wise and humble servant serves the Lord with a grateful heart. It is much better to be bound by the grace of God than enslaved by the lies of the devil.

"I am sending you to them to open their eyes and turn them from darkness to light, and from the power of Satan to God, so that they may receive forgiveness of sins and a place among those who are sanctified by faith in me" (Acts 26:17b-18).

What does it mean to be a bond-servant of Christ? It means owned by God. The lost stand on the slave block of sin waiting to be auctioned to the highest bidder. Hallelujah that heaven came down to the cross of Christ and purchased, through His shed blood, all who would believe. Purchase means possession—He is Master of all or not Master at all.

Related Readings: Deuteronomy 32:36; Psalm 116:16; Galatians 1:10; Revelation 15:3

LORD HELP ME

The woman came and knelt before him. "Lord, help me!" she said. Matthew 15:25

———————

A life lived well requires help from the Lord. Life is like a ship on open sea: we navigate through calm waters, rough waters, uncertain waters and beautiful waters—but all the time trusting its Creator. The source of our strength must be Christ, or we grow chronically tired. Faith in the Lord triumphs over fear and frustration—this is especially true when someone we love suffers severely and all we can do is lift them up to Jesus.

Indeed, His help comes to those who kneel in humble dependency and cry out to Jesus, "Lord help me!" When the body writhes in pain, we cry for help. When a critical word crushes our spirit, we cry for help. When unanswered questions stalk our mind, we cry for help. When relational conflict emaciates our emotions, we cry for help. Help from heaven gives hope, healing, and the energy to push through tough times and trust Him.

"The LORD is my strength and my shield; my heart trusts in him, and he helps me. My heart leaps for joy, and with my song I praise him" (Psalm 28:7).

Related Readings: Psalm 30:2, 10; 33:20; Isaiah 41:13-14; Acts 20:35; Hebrews 13:6

SPIRIT-LED LIVING

So he said to me, "This is the word of the Lord to Zerubbabel. Not by might nor by power, but by my Spirit," says the LORD Almighty. Zechariah 4:6

The Holy Spirit is God's fuel for living. He leads, convicts, comforts, and gives courage. On the other hand the world promotes power and might. The world's approach is forceful: If the door is closed, knock it down. If you have the power and authority, use it to make things happen. Lack of faith can panic and prematurely force unrighteous results.

On the contrary, Spirit-led living is about dependence. It is dependence on God rather than any other form of reliance. Money, might, and power are cheap imitations of God dependence. These temporal fortresses are fleeting. When all is said and done, they are undependable. Money, control, and your title can be here today and gone tomorrow. But, the Spirit of God wants you to grow in His awareness and follow His lead. Like a hurricane that gains strength as time passes, so does God's Spirit. You cannot accomplish His best without the leadership and empowerment of the Holy Spirit. He may even lead you to places of discomfort, as His desire is to place you in positions of dependence.

"The Spirit gives life; the flesh counts for nothing. The words I have spoken to you—they are full of the Spirit and life" (John 6:63).

Related Readings: Exodus 31:3; John 3:34; Acts 4:25-31; 2 Timothy 1:7

FEBRUARY 4

VALUE OTHERS MORE

Do nothing out of selfish ambition or vain conceit. Rather, in
humility value others above yourselves, not looking to your
own interests but each of you to the interests of the others.
Philippians 2:3-4

The value of something or someone determines their importance.
For example, if a hobby is highly valued it gets attention, even
to the exclusion of relational investments in a needy child. It's
easier to get lost in leisure than to face the reality of a broken
relationship. Predetermining a high appraisal of someone keeps
them a high priority in hard times.

Indeed, there is a tension between our own interests and the
interests of others. After all, doesn't the Lord want us to take
care of ourselves? Of course He does—but it is not hiding
behind our own issues and ambitions to the exclusion of placing
others above ourselves. Humility esteems the good in others
while recognizing its own struggles.

"For by the grace given me I say to every one of you: Do not
think of yourself more highly than you ought, but rather think
of yourself with sober judgment, in accordance with the faith
God has distributed to each of you" (Romans 12:3).

Related Readings: Ruth 1:16-18; Matthew 23:11;
Luke 9:46-48; 22:27-30

UNINTENTIONAL SIN

If the entire Israelite community sins by violating one of the LORD's commands, but the people do not realize it, they are still guilty. Leviticus 4:13, NLT

———◆◆◆———

Unintentional sin still has very real consequences. For example, I can forget to report extra income to the Internal Revenue Service, but I still owe the taxes and penalty on the overdue obligation. Or, I can make a flippant remark to my spouse or children as a weak attempt at humor and not realize how badly I hurt their feelings. My good intentions can mean well, however the consequences of sinful actions still need genuine forgiveness.

It's not enough to say, "I didn't mean to" or "That's not what I meant." Inadvertent actions that bruise relationships, question our integrity, or violate the Lord's commands require a response of confession and repentance. It's woefully inadequate to blame memory loss or ignorance on behavior that assumes things are OK—when sin is present. Indeed, intentional actions that create clarity and accountability impede unintentional sinning.

"In the past God overlooked such ignorance, but now he commands all people everywhere to repent" (Acts 17:30).

"Would not God have discovered it, since he knows the secrets of the heart" (Psalm 44:21).

Related Readings: Psalm 90:8; Ezekiel 45:20; Matthew 7:21-23; Hebrews 9:7

PERSISTENCE PAYS OFF

Then Jesus told his disciples a parable to show them that they should always pray and not give up. Luke 18:1

Has rejection caused you to give up on an opportunity or a person? Are you tired of trying to do the right thing, without experiencing positive results? It is precisely at this point of frustration and fear that God calls us to persevere in prayer and continue to graciously engage individuals and circumstances. Those who give up—give up on God.

Like an oscillating fan, your faith may waver back and forth between confidence and uncertainty, so hit the button of belief and stay focused on the Lord. Go forward by faith to love an estranged relationship. Call the company who went with a competitor and see how you might still serve them. Reach out until your requests are not ignored anymore.

A faithful man or woman in the hands of God has the attention of heaven and earth. When you are on His assignment, rejection has to first go through almighty God's agenda. It's not the individual full of energy at the outset who outlasts others, it's the wise ones who conserve their vigor over the long haul—strengthened by their Savior's stamina.

"Rejoice always, pray continually, give thanks in all circumstances; for this is God's will for you in Christ Jesus" (1 Thessalonians 5:16-18).

Related Readings: Numbers 14:38; Daniel 6:10; Acts 20:22-25; Romans 2:7

DILIGENTLY OBEY

This will happen if you diligently obey the Lord your God.
Zechariah 6:15b

Diligent obedience to the Lord is a command for the follower of Jesus Christ. We have the responsibility, the opportunity, and the obligation to obey. What a joy to receive marching orders from Jesus. He is the Commander in Chief. What He says and expects matters dearly, as obedience can be a matter of joy or despair and life or death.

Our obedience facilitates God's will for our life and for the lives of those around us. We cannot handle the blessings of God if we are not obedient to the commands of God. He blesses our hard work when we apply our skills and gifts well. However, what keeps us successful and credible is our character. When we sow obedience, we reap character. When we sow disobedience, we become a character. Thus, diligently obey the Lord.

"Do not be deceived: God cannot be mocked. A man reaps what he sows. Whoever sows to please their flesh, from the flesh will reap destruction; whoever sows to please the Spirit, from the Spirit will reap eternal life" (Galatians 6:7).

Related Readings: 2 Kings 22:13; Jeremiah 11:4-7; Matthew 8:27; Hebrews 4:2

FEBRUARY 8

PURE MOTIVES

Ask all the people of the land and the priests, "When you
fasted and mourned in the fifth and seventh months for the past
seventy years, was it really for me that you fasted?"
Zechariah 7:5

Pure motives are sometimes hard to distinguish. Especially
difficult are motives related to religion. Why do we serve
God? If gratitude and love are the reasons for our service, then
our motives are right, but it is not always that easy or clear.
Sometimes as committed Christians the lines of pure-hearted
motivation are blurred. Service for Christ is not to make us
feel better about ourselves; rather, our service is to glorify our
Savior Jesus.

Indeed, service for God with wrong motives can easily lead
to burnout, disappointment, and disillusionment. An act of
service—on behalf of Christ—is not conditional. You hold it
with an open hand, and with a pure heart you offer your time
and money. Your expectations are at peace, knowing you
have followed the example of Jesus. Your motive is to please
and obey Him—it is not for your fame but for your heavenly
Father's name.

"It will be revealed with fire, and the fire will test the quality of
each person's work" (1 Corinthians 3:13).

Related Readings: Proverbs 30:12; 1 John 3:3;
Revelation 19:8, 14

STRENGTH IN THE LORD

"I will strengthen them in the Lord and in his name they will walk," declares the Lord. Zechariah 10:12, NIV84

The Lord is strength for the journey of life. Fatigue and discouragement can assault us like a bandit on a deserted dirt road. Life is constantly swinging its bruising punches. Before long we can become beaten down with no energy to continue. We know in our head we are a child of the King, but our heart feels no royal resilience. Fatigue requires faith.

Weariness is an opportunity for the Lord to strengthen you. He uses His people to energize and encourage one another. We are all needy, and it is just a matter of time before we all have to learn how to receive. The Lord wraps His strength around the gift of a prayer warrior—someone who storms heaven on your behalf is a strength giver.

Do not let divorce, death, or disappointment exclude you from the Lord's strength. Work will get you down. People will let you down. Failure will knock you down. Your greatest fears may cause you to wake up in the middle of the night in a cold sweat. Fight fear with fear—the fear of God. Let it strengthen you, fortifying your faith in Him.

"Teach me your way, LORD, that I may rely on your faithfulness; give me an undivided heart, that I may fear your name" (Psalm 86:11).

Related Readings: Psalm 105:4; Isaiah 12:2; Luke 10:27; 1 Thessalonians 3:13

FEBRUARY 10

AFFECTION AND ACCEPTANCE

Then people brought little children to Jesus for him to place his hands on them and pray for them. But the disciples rebuked them. Jesus said, "Let the little children come to me, and do not hinder them, for the kingdom of heaven belongs to such as these." Matthew 19:13-14

Jesus was tender and tough. He took the time to love little children, but He was also bold to confront greed in the face of businessmen using God for personal gain. However, most of the time Jesus modeled affection toward those who could and those who could not reciprocate—and acceptance toward those who had experienced rejection. He graciously extended both.

Do you daily receive the affection and acceptance of almighty God? Have you begun to comprehend the depth and breadth of His magnificent love? Oh, what a Savior and lover of your soul! A close friend may give you a cold shoulder, but Jesus warmly embraces your cares and concerns. Perhaps a fellow Christian rejected you for your indiscretions, but Jesus accepts you despite your failures and lifts you up to walk faithfully with Him.

"Jesus straightened up and asked her, 'Woman, where are they? Has no one condemned you?' 'No one, sir,' she said. 'Then neither do I condemn you,' Jesus declared. 'Go now and leave your life of sin'" (John 8:10-11).

Related Readings: Deuteronomy 10:15; Acts 15:8; Romans 14:1-3; Philippians 1:8

TRIAL BY FIRE

This third I will bring into the fire; I will refine them like silver and test them like gold. They will call on my name and I will answer them. Zechariah 13:9a

---

A trial by fire purifies. We normally do not invite this or look forward to it as a tool of God's purification. It is a call to intimacy and dependence on our heavenly Father. Satan's desire is to drive us from God during our adversity, but God's heart is to draw us unto Him as life heats up. Indeed, fiery trials seem to never let up or give up.

One after another trials crash against our faith. Like hurricane-force gales and floods, they wear us down and sometimes breach life's levees. Anguish and pain may currently overwhelm you. Life is not fun right now. People you trusted let you down. Your health is fragile. Your job is in jeopardy. You are in a trial and you feel you're on trial. However, the refining fires of heaven burn away pride and replace it with humility. God removes anxiety and replaces it with His peace. Like Daniel's three Hebrew friends, there is a fourth one with you in the fire—Jesus.

"He said, 'Look! I see four men walking around in the fire, unbound and unharmed, and the fourth looks like a son of the gods'" (Daniel 3:25).

Related Readings: Deuteronomy 7:19; Luke 22:28; 1 Thessalonians 3:3; James 1:2

FEBRUARY 12

ABUNDANT FORGIVENESS

Then Peter came to Jesus and asked, "Lord how many times shall I forgive my brother when he sins against me? Up to seven times?" Jesus answered, "I tell you, not seven times, but seventy-seven times." Matthew 18:21-22, NIV84

Sin's offense hurts. There is no doubt about it. Sin wounds indiscriminately. It is no respecter of persons. Sin builds walls. It ravages relationships and it separates. Sin is a sorry excuse for wrong behavior. Just the sound of the word elicits negative emotion. Sin is deceptive, carnal, and Christ-less. Sin is unfair, sad, and sometimes sadistic.

Sin follows a process of desire, conception, birth, maturity, and death. James describes its diabolical development. "Then, after desire has conceived, it gives birth to sin; and sin, when it is full-grown, gives birth to death" (James 1:15). So sin is not to be taken lightly. Certainly its infliction of pain cannot be ignored for long. It can kill relationships.

Nonetheless, when you are sinned against, you are to forgive. When someone's sin assaults your attitude, you are to forgive them. When someone's sin berates your work, you are to forgive them. When someone's sin violates your trust, you are to forgive them. When someone's sin steals your joy, you are to forgive them.

"Jesus said, 'Father, forgive them, for they do not know what they are doing'" (Luke 23:34a).

Related Readings: Genesis 50:17; Psalm 130:4; Luke 17:3; Ephesians 4:32

DIALOGUE DAILY

Gracious words are a honeycomb, sweet to the soul and healing to the bones. Proverbs 16:24

———————

Busyness is the uncaring culprit of inconsistent communication in marriage. Couples exhausted from a calendar of frantic activity have no emotional energy at the end of the day to engage in meaningful conversation. Like two silent ships they pass through the night unaware of the other's tattered soul. However, hearts that dialogue daily are intentional with intimacy. It may be only 30 minutes of focused conversation after dinner, but wise couples stay verbally connected.

Often women starve for words and men lack language. So, husbands, make sure you unselfishly express yourself to your sweetheart. Ask the Lord to give your conversation clarity, compassion and depth. And wives, be patient with your man, who wants to share his heart. Remember, his speech needs a safe environment for expression. Your respect and approval frees him to speak freely. Daily dialogue gives couples emotional connection that facilitates trust, security, and love.

"Set an example for the believers in speech, in conduct, in love, in faith and in purity" (1 Timothy 4:12b).

Related Readings: Proverbs 22:11; Malachi 3:16; 1 Corinthians 13:1; Ephesians 4:15

DATE WEEKLY

I delight to sit in his shade, and his fruit is sweet to my taste.
Song of Songs 2:3b

Couples who calendar weekly dates understand that they shouldn't take themselves and life too seriously. A night of romance and fun is a surefire way to keep the flames of marriage burning brightly. Work and children are put on pause during this window of intimacy so emotions can lovingly engage. A date is meant to be free from distractions (no electronics) and mental clutter. Indeed, weekly dates recalibrate a husband and wife's relationship around love and laughter.

When you sit in the shade of your spouse's tree of trust, you find acceptance and affirmation. No one can give you more meaningful approval than your best friend. If he or she seeks approval elsewhere, you are in danger of emotional estrangement. Yes, dating gives you an excuse to pursue your precious marriage partner with romantic anticipation. You clean up and dress up just for them. Perhaps you take turns planning the date experience so that it stays fresh and exciting.

Date night can require a financial commitment, so budget accordingly. There is a cost, but you can't afford not to invest in your most important relationship. Focused time with your sweetheart honors them and honors the Lord. Plan to date weekly.

"Arise, come, my darling; my beautiful one, come with me" (Song of Songs 2:13b).

Related Readings: Song of Songs 1:4; 1 Samuel 1:19; 1 Corinthians 7:3; 1 Peter 3:7

FEBRUARY 15

DIVISIONS DOWNFALL

Jesus knew their thoughts and said to them, "Every kingdom divided against itself will be ruined, and every city or household divided against itself will not stand."
Matthew 12:25

———————

Division weakens, cripples, and eventually causes a downfall. It is internal erosion that cannot stand up to conflicting turmoil from within. The greatest threat to a nation, an organization, a home, or an individual comes from the inside out. For example, an implosion of unbelief can bring down a religious person. He or she wants God, but the intellectual conflict cannot be resolved, and outside of faith in Christ it will not be.

The same can be said for a church. The church can become its own worst enemy. If the basic tenets of the Christian faith are watered down, then there is nothing substantial left to believe. If Christ's deity, miracles, and resurrection are in question, then the church is set up for division and ultimately a slow but sure death. However, principles and values based on God's truth will stand—and whoever embraces them and lives for them will stand together. Our goal as followers of Jesus Christ is to unite around faith in Him.

"And I, when I am lifted up from the earth, will draw all people to myself" (John 12:32).

Related Readings: Genesis 2:24; Daniel 2:43; John 3:14; Acts 15:30-35

48

FEBRUARY 16

NATURAL DISASTER

The priests are in mourning, those who minister before the
LORD. The fields are ruined, the ground is dried up; the grain
is destroyed, the new wine is dried up, the oil fails.
Joel 1:9b-10

A natural disaster may or may not be judgment from God. One
thing is for sure, it is evidence of God. It is a wake-up call. The
extreme devastation is from forces uncontrived by mankind.
The wind, the water, and the floods are the result of heaven's
fury. This arrest in activity is an opportunity to look up. It is
a time to take the attention from ourselves and ask God what
He is up to. He is in control. He does have a plan, and He does
have His way of doing things. He has a purpose in this troubling
event we define as a natural disaster.

Certainly it is a time to seek God, and secondly, it is an opportunity
to serve people. Basic needs like food, clothing, and shelter are
wanting. God's people have the prime-time chance to shine for
Jesus. Natural disasters are gargantuan ministry opportunities. A
natural disaster should lead us to a supernatural sense of God's
wonder. The Lord is large and in charge.

"He causes his sun to rise on the evil and the good, and sends
rain on the righteous and the unrighteous" (Matthew 5:45b).

Related Readings: Psalm 82:5; Isaiah 24:19; Acts 16:26;
Revelation 6:13

FEBRUARY 17

DOUBLE-MINDED

But when you ask, you must believe and not doubt, because the one who doubts is like a wave of the sea, blown and tossed by the wind. That person should not expect to receive anything from the Lord. Such a person is double-minded and unstable in all they do. James 1:6-8

Double-mindedness comes from doubt. Doubt about being in the right career. Doubt related to investing in the right relationships. Doubt in the Almighty's ability to handle the circumstances or the people. Chronic doubt is a detriment to faith and hope, because it causes instability and insecurity. Has doubt and double-mindedness frozen your faith?

Do you feel torn between two people? Has your divided loyalty at work created conflict and confusion? Does your lack of conviction cause you to react like a whipsaw to the latest advice? Like a ship without a rudder or sail, you are tossed back and forth by the winds of change and conflict. Without confidence from Christ there is confusion.

"I am confident in the Lord that you will take no other view. The one who is throwing you into confusion, whoever that may be, will have to pay the penalty" (Galatians 5:10).

Related Readings: Isaiah 41:29; 50:7; Matthew 6:22-23; 1 Peter 1:13

MENTALLY ENGAGED

We demolish arguments and every pretension that sets itself up against the knowledge of God, and we take captive every thought to make it obedient to Christ. 2 Corinthians 10:5

———⊷⊶⊷———

Are you mentally engaged with eternal thinking? The world's cares can be so demanding that they can cause us to disengage from capturing our thoughts for Christ. Like an AWOL soldier, our thinking can wander into enemy territory and fall into false reasoning. Instead, the Lord desires that His children proactively capture every thought and make it obedient to Christ. Mentally engaged Christians are conscious to actively think well.

Thoughts can be fleeting and flirt with sin, or they can be disciplined as becomes a disciple of Jesus Christ. Indeed, intentional intellectual engagement with God's Word instructs us in integrity. It's those who pay the price not to resign their thoughts to the trends of society that grow in their conviction to not compromise their character in Christ. A mind full of Christ's thoughts has no room for knowledge that's against Him. Thus, allow your master Jesus to mold your thinking into His thinking, and you will gladly act accordingly.

"For who has known the mind of the Lord that he may instruct him? But we have the mind of Christ" (1 Corinthians 2:16, NIV84).

Related Readings: Psalms 10:4; 139:17; Romans 7:25; 12:2; 1 Corinthians 1:10

51

SERVANT LEADERSHIP

Whoever wants to become great among you must be your servant, and whoever wants to be first must be your slave—just as the Son of Man did not come to be served, but to serve, and to give his life a ransom for many. Matthew 20:26b-28

***

Servant leadership is service to others. It is not jockeying for position, nor is it politicking for power. Instead, it is posturing for the opportunity to serve. This does not bode well for the insecure soul in need of abundant attention. Servant leaders avoid the limelight and serve in ways that often go unnoticed. The little things are what make a servant leader. It may be taking out the trash at home or making the coffee at work.

No task is too menial for the servant leader; there is something bigger than behavior that distinguishes a servant leader. It is an attitude of how to make others successful. He or she knows that if those around them are successful, then there is a good chance they will experience success. They are wise to want what's best for others. Jesus served for the glory of God. His ultimate service was laying down His life in love.

"If your first concern is to look after yourself, you'll never find yourself. But if you forget about yourself and look to me, you'll find both yourself and me" (Matthew 10:39, The Message).

Related Readings: Exodus 18:26; Zephaniah 3:9; Ephesians 6:9; 1 Peter 4:10

EMOTIONALLY LOVE GOD

Jesus replied, "Love the Lord your God with all your heart."
Matthew 22:37a

———◆◆◆———

Emotionally love God, for faith has feelings: feelings of gratitude for God's grace, feelings of joy for friendship with Jesus, and feelings of hope for a heavenly home. Emotions are meant to engage eternity, not be wed to the world. Worry can wreck a life, especially if a heart is consumed with what it can't control. So, trust Jesus with your feelings.

Because the heart is the seat of emotions, we are wise to guard our hearts. Wisdom appoints the sentinels of grace and truth to protect feelings by grounding them in faith. Pride makes promises to your heart it cannot keep. For example, it may capture your emotions with selfish ambition, only to ruin relationships. Humility, on the other hand, handles your heart with tender care. It leads it into unselfish service and true fulfillment.

Release your emotions to Christ and He will channel your energy into productive activity. Emotionally love the Lord and He will empower you for eternity's agenda. Lovers of God are known by God and are able to radically receive His love and give it liberally.

"Above all else, guard your heart, for everything you do flows from it" (Proverbs 4:23).

Related Readings: Joshua 22:5; Proverbs 24:12;
2 Corinthians 9:7; Philippians 4:7

FEBRUARY 21

DISCERNING GOD'S WILL

Do not conform to the pattern of this world, but be transformed by the renewing of your mind. Then you will be able to test and approve what God's will is—his good, pleasing and perfect will. Romans 12:2

———◄●►———

God's will is the goal of every sincere seeker of the Lord. His will is not elusive, but attainable to His children—it is good and acceptable. But, discernment is a process of testing and approving so that a Christian's faith and character grows and Christ's best is clarified. Discerning God's will is a spiritual exercise in divine due diligence.

God's will does not contradict God's Word. For instance, the Lord does not lead couples to live together outside of marriage. Men and women are meant to come together in marriage. It is the commitment of "becoming one" that God blesses. Indeed, the general principles for living are already outlined in the Bible—to know Him is to know His will.

"I keep asking that the God of our Lord Jesus Christ, the glorious Father, may give you the Spirit of wisdom and revelation, so that you may know him better" (Ephesians 1:17).

Related Readings: Isaiah 53:10; Acts 21:14; 1 Thessalonians 4:3; James 4:15

FORGIVEN PEOPLE FORGIVE

And be kind to one another, tenderhearted, forgiving one another, even as God in Christ forgave you.
Ephesians 4:32, NKJV

Forgiven people forgive, because they are eternally grateful for the grace of God's forgiveness in their heart. They are keenly aware that outside of Christ, they are cursed to a cycle of unforgiveness—lost in their sins. Thus, the Lord raised them up forgiven so they in turn can forgive. Forgiveness on earth flows from forgiveness in heaven. It is something to be passed on today, not to be stored away for some unique future occasion.

Unforgiveness encroaches on the health of our relationships. Its cancerous effect eats away at our enjoyment of God, family, and friends. Suddenly, without advance notice, we lash out at those we love—because of someone we don't love. Unforgiveness, like an inactive but rumbling volcano, waits to explode at any moment of disappointment. The embers of sin smolder and will erupt when pressure shakes its foundation. Love and kindness tear down walls of anger—grace and forgiveness build bridges of hope. Satan's destructive deception is exposed and destroyed in the face of your forgiveness.

"And what I have forgiven—if there was anything to forgive—I have forgiven in the sight of Christ for your sake, in order that Satan might not outwit us. For we are not unaware of his schemes" (2 Corinthians 2:10b-11).

Related Readings: Micah 7:18; Jeremiah 33:8; Luke 7:47; Hebrews 8:12

PERFECT PEACE

You will keep in perfect peace those whose minds are steadfast, because they trust in you. Trust in the LORD forever, for the LORD, the LORD himself, is the Rock eternal.
Isaiah 26:3-4

The world offers imperfect peace. It is temporary at best, as it comes in the form of materialism, a person, a pill, or a bottle. This caricature of peace prolongs pain and leads to long-term disappointment and disillusionment. Artificial peace restricts or rejects the peace of almighty God, only to eventually come back and seek out what's real.

Are you able to sleep peacefully at night? Do you have an assurance deep down in your soul that Christ is in control and can be trusted? If not, let loose of the idols of worry and pride—and redirect your energies to eternal solutions. Answers from above bring peace that's within. Where there is trust in the Lord, there is rest from fighting the enemy. The perfect peace of God cuts through confusion and keeps your mind and heart on Jesus.

"Grace and peace be multiplied to you in the knowledge of God and of Jesus our Lord, as His divine power has given to us all things that pertain to life and godliness, through the knowledge of Him who called us by glory and virtue" (2 Peter 1:2-3, NJKV).

Related Readings: 1 Chronicles 22:9; Psalm 85:8; Acts 10:36; Romans 14:17

PATIENT PEOPLE WAIT

I waited patiently for the LORD; he turned to me and heard
my cry. Psalm 40:1

———◆◆◆———

Patient people wait on God's best. "God things" happen to those
who are patient—those who wait. Patience is a virtue, but it is
also a vehicle in which the Lord delivers His blessings. Like a
loyal wife waiting for the gift of her husband's return from war,
so those who love Jesus wait on Him to return soon. Patience
waits on God to rain down His favor.

However, as we wait, we pray and we prepare. We pray for
patience—knowing that Jesus Christ is completely trustworthy.
Waiting is also the Lord's time to prepare our character. Our
character has to keep up with our success for us to remain
successful. Patience is the fruit of the Spirit—it resides with
God and is available for His children. So, seek the fullness of
the Holy Spirit each day. Wait for and anticipate good gifts
from your heavenly Father. Christ manages the clock of life, so
rest and regroup during His timeouts.

"Therefore be patient, brethren, until the coming of the Lord.
See how the farmer waits for the precious fruit of the earth,
waiting patiently for it until it receives the early and latter rain"
(James 5:7).

"And so after waiting patiently, Abraham received what was
promised" (Hebrews 6:15).

Related Readings: Psalm 27:14; 37:7; Micah 7:7;
Romans 8:25; Jude 1:21

TAKE AND GIVE

Take the talent from him and give it to the one who has ten talents. Matthew 25:28, NIV84

God has the prerogative to take and give. He can take what He has given us and give it to someone else. He can execute this transaction with or without our knowledge or understanding. Just because we enjoy His blessing today does not guarantee His blessing tomorrow. There is a direct correlation to our faithfulness and His blessing.

So, our obedience does matter. It does determine our level of responsibilities within God's Kingdom. Faithfulness allows us to enjoy God's blessings. If we are not faithful with God's blessings, He may take them from us and entrust them to someone else. It may be resources, relationships, opportunities, or skills. Thus, this responsibility of managing His blessings is not to be taken lightly. What is not used for God's purposes could very well be lost for good. If you have lost something, leave behind your disappointment. Reinvigorate your faithfulness. Let the Lord restore the joy of your salvation. What He took He may give back, so pray for His restoration.

"Restore to me the joy of your salvation and grant me a willing spirit, to sustain me" (Psalm 51:12).

Related Readings: Genesis 40:21; 2 Samuel 9:7;
2 Corinthians 13:9; 1 Peter 5:10

MEANINGFUL MEMORIES

Aware of this Jesus said to them, "Why are you bothering this woman? She has done a beautiful thing to me.... I tell you the truth, wherever this gospel is preached throughout the world, what she has done will also be told, in memory of her."
Matthew 26:10, 13, NIV84

How do you want to be remembered? How will your obituary read? Will it point to God? We will all have memories that reflect our life. Our past experiences may be pint-sized—built around us. Or they may be bigger than life because they are built around Christ. Your defining moments are building a memorial that will extend into the future.

There are spectators watching you assemble this life memorial. Your family is watching. Your friends are watching. Your acquaintances are watching. The world is watching. Most importantly, God is watching. Your memorial may consist of paying for the Christian education of your grandchildren. It may be funding initiatives and projects that leverage evangelism and discipleship in a country outside of your own. Whatever you do, do it as unto the Lord. Our Lord and His faithful followers do not dismiss memories and memorials for His glory.

"Cornelius stared at him in fear. 'What is it, Lord?' he asked. The angel answered, 'Your prayers and gifts to the poor have come up as a memorial offering before God'" (Acts 10:4).

Related Readings: Joshua 4:7; Isaiah 56:5;
1 Thessalonians 1:3; 2 Peter 1:15

EMOTIONAL FAITHFULNESS

You have heard that it was said, "You shall not commit adultery." But I tell you that anyone who looks at a woman lustfully has already committed adultery with her in his heart.
Matthew 5:27-28

There is a constant allure for emotional connection between a woman and a man. A pure motive of care for someone other than your spouse can easily turn into emotional unfaithfulness. An emotionally needy woman at work will give signs to seeking men who are unfulfilled at home. It seems exciting and inviting, but in the end—it wrecks homes.

Married couples are meant to fulfill their emotional needs within their marriage experience. This is why it's imperative to process past and present pain in a healthy manner. Then communication and care can flourish and feed your emotional desires. Invite the Holy Spirit to jointly instruct your minds and to knit your humble hearts together in love and kindness. Seek out other married couples to learn from who are good models of emotional faithfulness.

"That their hearts may be encouraged, being knit together in love, and attaining to all riches of the full assurance of understanding, to the knowledge of the mystery of God, both of the Father and of Christ, in whom are hidden all the treasures of wisdom and knowledge" (Colossians 2:2¬3, NKJV).

Related Readings: Genesis 2:18a; Proverbs 15:1; 29:11; Matthew 7:1; 2 Corinthians 1:3-7

PURSUIT OF WISDOM

If any of you lacks wisdom, you should ask God, who gives generously to all without finding fault, and it will be given to you. But when you ask, you must believe and not doubt.
James 1:5-6a

———————

Pursuit. It is what we all experience. We pursue dreams, we pursue jobs, we pursue opportunities, we pursue a husband or a wife, we pursue hobbies, we pursue friends, we pursue adventure, we pursue good health, we pursue success, we pursue significance, and we pursue happiness—to name a few of our positive pursuits. Indeed, what we pursue becomes the focus of what we do.

Pursuit is stated clearly as a priority in the United States Declaration of Independence: "Life, liberty and the pursuit of happiness." Over the course of history, the human race as a whole, would agree that the pursuit of good things is an inalienable right of individuals. Conversely, we can choose to chase after unhealthy pursuits like: greed, lust, power, and pride. Wise pursuits facilitate good outcomes, while foolish pursuits produce bad results.

"The wise inherit honor, but fools get only shame"
(Proverbs 3:35).

Related Readings: Job 28:27-28; Ecclesiastes 4:13; 10:12; 1 Corinthians 3:18

MONEY'S DISTRACTION

Jesus looked at him and loved him. "One thing you lack," he said. "Go, sell everything you have and give to the poor, and you will have treasure in heaven. Then come, follow me."
Mark 10:21

It is easy for money to become a distraction. Just the making and management of money takes effort and focus. Indeed, money becomes a subtle master if it is not held in check. Our affections gravitate toward what we think about. If the majority of our waking moments are consumed by the thought of making more money, then we are distracted.

Yes, we need to do our work with excellence as unto the Lord. However, if making money becomes our consuming focus, then its devotion competes with God. Billions of people wake up every day to make money, but are they making money or is money making them? If my life is consumed by money, very little is left for a life well spent.

"No one can serve two masters. Either you will hate the one and love the other, or you will be devoted to the one and despise the other. You cannot serve both God and money" (Luke 16:13).

Related Readings: Deuteronomy 15:10; Job 22:23-25; Luke 11:41; 1 Timothy 3:3

MARCH

"Blessed are those who hunger and thirst for righteousness, for they shall be satisfied."

Matthew 5:6

MARCH 1

BEST EFFORT

She did what she could. She poured perfume on my body
beforehand to prepare for my burial. Mark 14:8

———————•✦•———————

God expects our best, nothing more, nothing less. Our best plus
God's best is a productive combination. Indeed, we can fall into
the false belief that God will take care of everything without
our effort. Or, we take on the unnecessary stress of believing
everything depends on us, without thoroughly trusting in the
Lord. Neither is healthy nor right—He simply expects our
best—He understands our limitations.

Your stage of life, giftedness, experience, availability and
wisdom all determine your capacity. The ability of others will be
more or less than your own, so let the Lord define what you can
or cannot do. There will always be opportunities, but measure
each engagement alongside your ability to give it your best. Do
not commit under duress knowing that your ability to deliver is
sorely limited. Instead, have confidence in God to say "no" now
in preparation for a "yes" later.

Indeed, when you have given it your best, this is all that is
required of God. You have done what you could. Do your best,
trust God with the rest, and rest in Him.

"Everyone was amazed and gave praise to God. They were filled
with awe and said, 'We have seen remarkable things today'"
(Luke 5:26).

Related Readings: 1 Chronicles 29:6; Proverbs 25:14;
Luke 9:13; Romans 12:6

WISE INVESTMENT

And the things you have heard me say in the presence of many
witnesses entrust to reliable people who will also be qualified
to teach others. 2 Timothy 2:2

People are a priority for God—they are on His heart. Jesus died
and rose from the grave for people. The earth is filled with people
and heaven is populated with people. God created people in His
image, and they are a product of His grace. The Lord's affection
and holy desire is to enjoy and bless His people forever. People
matter much to Christ.

Thus, as an image bearer of almighty God, our prerogative is to
love people. When we love the Lord, we love what He loves. Oh
what a privilege to pour into people on behalf of Jesus Christ.
Yes, we are all a work in progress, and the road of relational
investing can be bumpy and disappointing—but how rewarding
to see faithful people flourish. Train faithful men and women
who can train others in the art of godly living. It is messy and
sweaty but sweet in its outcome. Pray for reliable disciples who
will reproduce righteous living.

"No discipline seems pleasant at the time, but painful. Later on,
however, it produces a harvest of righteousness and peace for
those who have been trained by it" (Hebrews 12:11).

Related Readings: Daniel 1:5; Acts 22:3; Ephesians 6:4;
Hebrews 5:14

SOUL FOOD

I am the bread of life… Here is the bread that comes down from heaven, which anyone may eat and not die. I am the living bread that came down from heaven. Whoever eats this bread will live forever. John 6:48, 50-51a

---

The human soul hungers for food that only comes through faith in Jesus Christ. There are other competing condiments from the culture, but only Christ can give life on earth and for eternity. His bread is baked in the oven of brokenness and comes out hot and satisfying. Man's manna only leads to death, but the Lord's nourishment is forever.

Why do we waste time feeding at the trough of distrust, when our Savior has prepared a feast for the faithful? A soul shrivels for lack of attention, but a soul is satisfied with eternal sustenance. Like a luscious grape feeds from the life-giving vine, so we stay connected to Christ—for His nutrients are not of this world. Your soul smells the freshly baked bread of Jesus—its delicious aroma is like homemade bread right out of the oven. Spread on your heavenly buttermilk biscuit some butter of belief—add some jelly of joy and oh how tasty is your Lord's love, acceptance, and holiness.

"I have come that they may have life, and that they may have it more abundantly" (John 10:10b, NKJV).

Related Readings: Exodus 16:4; Isaiah 55:1; Psalm 34:8; 1 Corinthians 11:26

TRIUMPH OVER TRAGEDY

Who shall separate us from the love of Christ? Shall trouble or hardship or persecution or famine or nakedness or danger or sword?… No, in all these things we are more than conquerors through him who loved us. Romans 8:35, 37

———————

Tragedy can strike life like the touching down of a tornado or the detonation of a terrorist bomb. Famines, earthquakes, volcanic eruptions, and tsunamis all gain momentum in the last days. There are wars and rumors of wars. Indeed, hardship does not discriminate between the righteous and the unrighteous.

What happens to our faith when circumstances come crashing down around us like the collapse of the walls in our home? Do we persevere through the floundering of our finances and the relational wreckage left behind in the wake of a divorce? It's easy to be a Christian when life is on cruise control, but real life has twists and turns that requires trust.

Thanks be to God—nothing can separate us from the love of Christ! His love is a bridge over troubled waters, His love is a ladder out of the pit of pride, His love is the resilience to rise above the pain of rejection, His love leads us peacefully through the valley of the shadow of death— indeed the love of Christ conquers all circumstances!

"May the Lord direct your hearts into God's love and Christ's perseverance" (2 Thessalonians 3:5).

Related Readings: Ephesians 3:17-18; 2 Corinthians 5:14; 13:14; 1 John 3:23

MARCH 5

EVIL EXPOSED

Everyone who does evil hates the light, and will not come into the light for fear that their deeds will be exposed. But whoever lives by the truth comes into the light, so that it may be seen plainly that what they have done has been done in the sight of God. John 3:20-21

———————

Evil lurks in places like the dark crevices of a compassionless living compound. It schemes to suck life from those who give life. Evil can endure for a season in seclusion, but eventually it will be exposed along with its hellish intentions. A corrupt character thinks it can get away with obstruction of justice; however, payday does come one day.

Evil not only is an incubator for sinful deeds, but it attacks others with its vile consequences. It is consumed with conquering righteousness with unrighteous actions. However, evil cannot stand in the presence of almighty God. Satan, the evil one, has been defeated—the roaring lion has been defanged by the Word of God living in us. Hence, humility walks with Christ on His lighted path. Walk in the light, as He is the light, and have fellowship with one another.

"Because you are strong, and the word of God lives in you, and you have overcome the evil one" (1 John 2:14b).

Related Readings: Job 29:3; Psalm 89:15; Matthew 13:19; 1 John 1:7

VALUE HIGHLY

The Pharisees, who loved money, heard all this and were sneering at Jesus. He said to them, "You are the ones who justify yourselves in the eyes of others, but God knows your hearts. What people value highly is detestable in God's sight."
Luke 16:14-15

God's value system contrasts with man's value system. Man values money over relationship—God values relationship over money. Man values gaining power—God values giving power. Man values temporal possessions—God values eternal rewards. Man values recognition—God values anonymity. What God values—brings value.

Indeed, ascribed value prescribes behavior. So, what do you value highly? Perhaps in the past it was the voice of people's praise that you pursued, but now you understand the futility of this vain pursuit. It's the caring affirmation from almighty God that brings peace, fulfillment, and security. People's praise is fickle, but Christ's is consistent and valid. You live in quiet confidence when the acceptance of Jesus is what you value highly.

"Having predestined us to adoption as sons by Jesus Christ to Himself, according to the good pleasure of His will, to the praise of the glory of His grace, by which He made us accepted in the Beloved" (Ephesians 1:5-6, NKJV).

Related Readings: 1 Samuel 26:24; Proverbs 10:2, 20; Matthew 13:46; Luke 7:2

HUMBLE LEADER

Rejoice greatly, O Daughter of Zion! Shout, Daughter of Jerusalem! See, your king comes to you, righteous and having salvation, gentle and riding on a donkey, on a colt, the foal of a donkey. Zechariah 9:9, NIV84

———————

Jesus modeled humble leadership. There were no airs—pretension was absent from His personality. Christ could be gentle and aggressive at the same time. He led, but He led with sensitivity and prayerful obedience to His heavenly Father. A humble leader refrains from public pomp and defers to a modest manner. Humble led is humble bred.

A humble leader does not get too far ahead of his followers. Indeed, he takes the time to get them up to speed. He makes sure there is understanding of the overall goals of the organization. He provides for the team the teaching, training, and coaching necessary to serve with excellence. He or she sets a high standard of character with their own example, but they are patient to work with people at all levels of maturity.

So, by God's grace stay humble and serve the team for His glory. They will follow you wherever He leads. Indeed, humble leaders look to serve. It bears repeating: Humble led is humble bred.

"He [Jesus] poured water into a basin and began to wash his disciples' feet, drying them with the towel that was wrapped around him" (John 13:5).

Related Readings: Exodus 10:3; 2 Chronicles 36:12; Psalm 147:6; Luke 14:11

UNRESOLVED PAIN

He longed to fill his stomach with the pods that the pigs were eating, but no one gave him anything. When he came to his senses, he said, "How many of my father's hired servants have food to spare, and here I am starving to death!" Luke 15:16-17

Everyone is a product of pain, because we live in a world of pain—there is no utopia this side of heaven. Furthermore, unresolved past hurt produces present pain. Conversion to Christ does not automatically wipe away all our pain, but He does give us the tools—grace and truth—to heal hurts and to bring about wholeness in our hearts.

What is the source of your pain? Maybe, your rebellious child went to the faithless far country to find themselves—and hopefully in the process they will die to self. They left home thinking they had missed out, but pray that once in the cold, inhospitable world, they will miss the security, acceptance, and love at home. Selfish children create recurring pain. So, apply the balm of God's grace to your broken heart. Rest in the compassionate embrace of your sympathizing Savior Jesus. He who suffered in pain on the cross—to heal pain—ultimately resolves your pain.

"Then I would still have this consolation—my joy in unrelenting pain—that I had not denied the words of the Holy One" (Job 6:10).

Related Readings: Proverbs 15:1; Jeremiah 15:18; Matthew 4:24; 1 Peter 2:19

FINANCIAL ACCOUNTABILITY

We want to avoid any criticism of the way we administer this
liberal gift. For we are taking pains to do what is right, not
only in the eyes of the Lord but also in the eyes of man.
2 Corinthians 8:20-21

Financial accountability is first and foremost in the eyes of
an organization with integrity. This especially applies to gifts
made in the name of the Lord to a church or ministry. There is
a high standard of fiduciary responsibility for those who name
the name of Christ in how they handle cash. It's conscientious
money managers—not cavalier ones—who steward resources
well.

What checks and balances does your church have in place to
protect you from fraud? Do the ministries you support have an
audit by an outside firm to assure impartial oversight? These are
basic, bottom-line best practices that protect everyone involved.
Naïve trust without accountability—as it relates to money—can
lead to mismanagement of funds. Wise money management
doesn't do just enough to get by, but it goes the extra mile to
avoid any criticism in the handling of funds. Organizations that
highly value stewardship go to great pains to put in place leaders
of integrity who manage money with integrity.

"Well done, good and faithful servant! You have been faithful
with a few things; I will put you in charge of many things"
(Matthew 25:23a).

Related Readings: Judges 17:2; Amos 8:5; 1 Corinthians
16:1-4; Matthew 27:3-5

MARCH 10

INTIMACY TRUSTS

Those who know your name trust in you, for you, LORD, have never forsaken those who seek you. Psalm 9:10

Intimacy trusts and lack of intimacy distrusts. It is through the process of knowing God and understanding His heart that trust grows. There is nothing to be learned about the Lord that causes distrust. On the contrary, the more we get to know Jesus—the more we trust Jesus. The unusual affection of almighty God becomes evident once we engage deeply with Him. Trust buds at salvation—but over time it blossoms with intimacy.

The name of Jesus has no peer or "trusted brand" that comes even close, because its purity is without rival. Even the most trusted names you know can never approach the value of the name Jesus. Wise Christians are the ones who really get to know and trust the Savior of their soul. Jesus Christ is their trusted advisor, because of the intimate knowledge they have of Him.

"LORD Almighty, blessed is the one who trusts in you" (Psalm 84:12).

Related Readings: Proverbs 16:20; Isaiah 12:2; Galatians 6:2; Ephesians 4:31-32

MARCH 11

LOVED TO LOVE

We love because he first loved us. 1 John 4:19

Almighty God loves with an incredible love. His love has no boundaries or bias. The love of Jesus is limitless in the extent to which He will go with His grace. His love goes behind the enemy's lines of deceit and rescues those lost in their loveless state of mind. Christ's love looks for the unloved and offers comfort, care, compassion, and forgiveness.

The love of God is not without benefits. Those cloaked in the love of Christ have great boldness on the Day of Judgment—indeed, His great love covers all sin for those who have appropriated His salvation. Moreover, fear is cast out of the peace-loving presence of the Lord's love. Fear and love can't coexist where the love of Jesus fills humble hearts.

Therefore, take time to regularly receive the love of Jesus into your life. Commune with Christ, the lover of your soul, and you will experience His peace and security. Your rested spirit is positioned to be a robust lover for another hungry heart. Enter into God's eternal love, so you can deploy it on earth. The Lord loves you, so you can love others.

"There is no fear in love. But perfect love drives out fear" (1 John 4:18a).

Related Readings: John 14:23; 15:9-13; Romans 12:10; Galatians 5:13

MARCH 12

AVOIDABLE PAIN

The wisdom of the prudent is to give thought to their ways, but the folly of fools is deception. Proverbs 14:8

———————————

Pain is inevitable in life—but some pain can be avoided with proper preparation. There is no need to add unnecessary pain to relationships with unwise decisions and foolish behavior. For example, in marriage it takes much more than a grand wedding to create a great marriage. Promises need the backing of preparation to carry out commitments.

Wise couples get beyond the emotion of romantic love and become students of each other. They truly accept one another for who they are, believe the best of their intentions, and understand how to best communicate with their spouse. Pre-marriage preparation is a prescription for a productive and healthy life of marital maturity. Ignoring past pain, however, causes present pain. Avoid compounding pain by being healed of past relational hurt.

"Therefore confess your sins to each other and pray for each other so that you may be healed. The prayer of a righteous person is powerful and effective" (James 5:16).

Related Readings: 1 Chronicles 4:10; Job 2:13; 1 Peter 5:10-12; Revelation 21:4

MOM'S GODLY EXAMPLE

Turn to me and have mercy on me; show your strength in behalf of your servant; save me, because I serve you just as my mother did. Psalm 86:16

Moms who serve the Lord are a gift from the Lord. Like a cool breeze over a warm sweaty brow, they quietly refresh those under their watch. Instinctively, they discern a wounded heart and offer words of comfort. This sensitive servant of Jesus listens for the real meaning behind the spoken words entrusted to their confidence. They have attractive moral authority because they model The Way. Moms under the influence of Christ relationally influence others for Christ.

Are you a mom who loves Jesus? Do you celebrate the fruit of your faithful life? Give yourself permission to enjoy the character of Christ that continues to grow in those whom you have invested all these years. Behind most godly leaders, parents, pastors, teachers, diplomats, executive assistants, custodians, chauffeurs, caregivers and athletes is a praying mom. Because you model Jesus, your child wants to be like Jesus. God gives strength to those who serve Him like momma.

"Truly I am your servant, Lord; I serve you just as my mother did; you have freed me from my chains" (Psalm 116:16).

Related Readings: 2 Kings 14:3; John 2:5; 13:15; 1 Corinthians 4:16, 11:1; Philippians 3:17

HONOR AGING PARENTS

"**H**onor your father and mother"—which is the first
commandment with a promise. Ephesians 6:2

Aging parents are a gift from almighty God. How many
children have the opportunity to grow old with their mom and
dad? Some see disease or an accident snatch away their mother
or father before they become elderly. It is a blessing to support
those who may have supported us over the years. To serve and
honor our parents is to serve and honor Jesus. Yes, caring for
them is a picture to a lost world of how our heavenly Father
cares for us. Aging parents are God's excuse to love.

How can we help our aging parents in a way that honors them?
What if they don't want assistance, but find themselves in a very
needy situation? Build up relational equity with your mother
and father before their bodies begin to break down. Don't wait
until they really slow down before you start your service to
them. Dignify the aging process by honoring them along the
way. They'll feel more comfortable as you continue your care,
as mentally they are less aware. Caring for aging parents is not
about our convenience—it's about their honor.

"Stand up in the presence of the aged, show respect for the
elderly and revere your God. I am the LORD" (Leviticus
19:32).

Related Readings: Malachi 1:6; Matthew 15:5-7;
Romans 13:7; 1 Timothy 5:1-2; Titus 2:2-3

LUST FOR LUXURY

I will tear down my barns and build bigger ones, and there I will store my surplus grain. And I'll say to myself, "You have plenty of grain laid up for many years. Take life easy; eat, drink and be merry." Luke 12:18-19

Lust for luxury is the natural progression of a cultural craze for more stuff. This materialistic addiction is never satisfied—it always wants just a little bit more. Relationships are patronized, sacrificed, and neglected for the purpose of material gain. Image, not intimacy, is what's valued by those unable to be content. Insecurity drives a vain notion of security that's unachievable.

Bigger is not always better, because bigger brings complexity, not simplicity. Bigger requires added cost for upkeep and attention. What starts out as a desire for something nice can get out of hand and become a hindrance instead of a help. A bigger bank account, a bigger house, and a bigger car can become distractions. Soul fulfillment comes from building the Kingdom of God.

"But godliness with contentment is great gain. For we brought nothing into the world, and we can take nothing out of it. But if we have food and clothing, we will be content with that. Those who want to get rich fall into temptation and a trap and into many foolish and harmful desires that plunge people into ruin and destruction" (1 Timothy 6:6-9).

Related Readings: Jeremiah 17:11; Psalm 49:17; Romans 14:17; Hebrews 12:28

SUCCESS IS STRESSFUL

Then Jesus said to his disciples, "Whoever wants to be my disciple must deny themselves and take up their cross and follow me. For whoever wants to save their life will lose it, but whoever loses their life for me will find it." Matthew 16:24-25

Success as God defines success is stressful. To deny self, bear a cross for Christ, and follow Him is not a passive process. There is a weight of responsibility that comes to those who wholeheartedly follow Jesus. The resume of a disciple is full of stressful experiences that engage the Lord's faithfulness. Success brings stress, but God provides rest.

Furthermore, it's out of these seeds of stress that the Lord grows His kingdom. Hearts are made whole, marriages mature, children are parented with truth and grace, the hungry are fed, jobs are completed, giving is generous, churches are planted, the lost are saved, and God is glorified. Without stress there would be no babies born, buildings built, or battles fought. God's will is not stress-free living. It's when stress becomes distress that we have transitioned to distrust in the Lord. So, success sees stress as an opportunity for intimacy with Jesus Christ.

"And the God of all grace, who called you to his eternal glory in Christ, after you have suffered a little while, will himself restore you and make you strong, firm and steadfast" (1 Peter 5:10).

Related Readings: Job 1:10; Psalm 40:4; James 5:11; Revelation 2:3

THE ULTIMATE SACRIFICE

Greater love has no one than this: to lay down one's life for one's friends. You are my friends if you do what I command.
John 15:13-14

———————

Why do some brave souls volunteer to defend their nation and give their life if necessary for people they have never met? Why do these same soldiers beat their bodies into submission at boot camp, sharpen their minds through maneuvers, and toughen their emotions in simulated engagements? Why do these courageous comrades care so much to fight for freedom? Love is the initiator of those who represent a country founded on faith.

Men and women with moral authority from almighty God sacrifice because of love. Love of country causes them to proudly defend a nation built on belief in their Creator. Love of family brings back meaningful memories of home as they are hunkered down in a foxhole. Love of Christ reminds them of His ultimate sacrifice on their behalf. Those filled with faith gaze on God and give their all for the sake of the call to protect freedom.

"Fixing our eyes on Jesus, the pioneer and perfecter of faith. For the joy set before him he endured the cross, scorning its shame, and sat down at the right hand of the throne of God. Consider him who endured such opposition from sinners, so that you will not grow weary and lose heart" (Hebrews 12:2-3).

Related Readings: 1 Samuel 17:47; 2 Samuel 10:12; Psalm 144:1; 1 Timothy 6:12

FAILURE IS NOT FINAL

For though the righteous fall seven times, they rise again, but the wicked stumble when calamity strikes. Proverbs 24:16

———————

Failure is not final for the faithful—it is a stepping stone to success. The sense of failure is an opportunity for faith to flourish and for pride to be humbled. An extreme letdown allows the Lord to lift up the downhearted and hold them close for comfort. Failure facilitates a crystal clear focus on God and His game plan. It is a bridge to blessing.

Have you failed to be a good provider? Communicate caringly? Follow through with your commitments? Find a job? Love well? Become a consistent Christian? If so, join the club of everyone who breathes. We all struggle from time to time with unholy habits that drag us down and try to keep us down. But, by God's grace, we will stand up, firm in Him. A faith untested is only fragile and weak, but a faith forged out of failure is stable and strong.

"Do not be afraid. Stand firm and you will see the deliverance the LORD will bring you today" (Exodus 14:13a).

Related Readings: Proverbs 11:8; 28; Isaiah 45:8; Luke 18:9; 1 John 5:4

MARCH 19

A DIVINE SECRET

But about that day or hour no one knows, not even the angels in heaven, nor the Son, but only the Father. Matthew 24:36

———————

No one knows when Jesus will return—we know He will, but we don't know when. He came the first time as a suffering Servant to save the world from their sin, and He will come a second time as the reigning King over all. He ascended from the world in a blaze of glory, while promising to descend one day in that same glory. Jesus' estimated time of arrival is a divine secret reserved for the Lord God Almighty.

In fact, Jesus will return when we do not expect Him to return. The Almighty's ambiguity about the second coming of Christ is meant to move us to faith and action. It is vain to speculate about something that we are incapable of knowing. Instead, this mystery is a test of our faithfulness until He comes, or until we go to be with Him. Predicting the date of Christ's return distracts foolish prognosticators whose pride misses the point.

"Command certain people not to teach false doctrines any longer… Such things promote controversial speculations rather than advancing God's work—which is by faith" (1 Timothy 1:3b, 4b).

Related Readings: Zechariah 9:14; 1 Corinthians 15:52; 1 Thessalonians 5:1-11

REASSURING WORDS

Be assured that my words are not false; one who has perfect knowledge is with you. Job 36:4

————————◆◆◆————————

God made His children to need reassuring words like: I love you—I am here for you—I am committed to you no matter what—I am extremely grateful for you—You are beautiful—I admire you—Your work is outstanding—You are a special friend—We will not go into debt— We will thoroughly pray before any major decision—God is with you.

Reassuring words ratchet up the value of a relationship, because it is not enough just to think or feel committed. Verbalized care creates confidence and security. Ambiguity feeds insecure illusions and false fantasies. Pride thinks it can keep quiet and somehow communicate care, while humility can't help but speak words of comfort and affection. See your speech as a mouthpiece for God. He calls His children to be conduits of good conversation. Reassurance brings emotional rest. Listen to the Lord's loving words to you, and by faith you will receive His righteous reassurance.

"If anyone speaks, they should do so as one who speaks the very words of God. If anyone serves, they should do so with the strength God provides, so that in all things God may be praised through Jesus Christ" (1 Peter 4:11a).

Related Readings: 1 Samuel 17:18; Esther 9:30; Acts 20:2; Hebrews 10:22

TRUE LOVE MARRIES

On the third day a wedding took place at Cana in Galilee. Jesus' mother was there, and Jesus and his disciples had also been invited to the wedding. John 2:1-2

————◆◆◆————

True love transitions from the thought of living together—to the commitment of living together forever in marriage. It is not a man-centered conditional love, but a Christ-centered unconditional love. There is fidelity of focus on faith in God and faith in each other. Couples experiencing true love see marriage as a reflection of their relationship with Jesus.

Marriage is much more than a contract between couples; it is a covenant before the Almighty. It is a solemn agreement between two God-fearing souls who honor heaven with vows of commitment on earth. Marriage is sacred to your Savior Jesus, because it communicates His love through the most intimate love between a husband and a wife. True love trusts God first, then trusts the one who has given themselves to Christ in holy commitment. Jesus blesses weddings that honor Him and people who honor each other in unconditional love.

"As a young man marries a young woman, so will your Builder marry you; as a bridegroom rejoices over his bride, so will your God rejoice over you" (Isaiah 62:5).

Related Readings: Jeremiah 29:6; Malachi 2:14; Luke 20:34; Hebrews 13:4

MARCH 22

WISDOM IS AWARE

Whoever is wise let him heed these things and consider the great love of the LORD. Psalm 107:43, NIV84

Wisdom is being aware of the works of almighty God. It understands the context of what Christ has done over the centuries in people's lives and through the church. Wise are the men and women who appreciate the Lord's work in history and learn from "His story." The Bible is pregnant with stories of God's faithfulness and gives birth to great faith for those who apply its principles to their life. Wisdom invites the observations of the eye to affect the heart.

When you see God sustain someone under deep distress and severe affliction, your own faith becomes flush with fierce tenacity. Therefore, watch the Lord labor through a mom and dad who unselfishly love and care for their handicapped child. Observe God's work in the business or ministry leader who is more concerned with the welfare of his or her people than their next career move. Be aware of God's work around you, apply its lessons, and you will become the wiser. Wisdom is aware.

"For you are great and do marvelous deeds; you alone are God" (Psalm 86:10).

Related Readings: Nehemiah 1:5; Ecclesiastes 9:1; Ephesians 2:4; 1 John 3:1

LEVERAGED BY GOD

Others, like seed sown on good soil, hear the word, accept it, and produce a crop—some thirty, some sixty, some a hundred times what was sown. Mark 4:20

———•◆•———

Leverage in man's economy is debt owed to an individual or an institution with specific results required. Leverage in the Lord's economy is an obligation of faith and obedience to God's call, with nothing but eternal upside. Weak faithed followers of Jesus give in to culture's cry for immediate results and sacrifice waiting on God to give a 100 times return.

What does the Lord want to leverage in your life for His glory? Your business—so it becomes a conduit for doing good for God? Your church—so it lays aside all earthy encumbrances and totally embraces an eternal agenda of unconditional love and service, while proclaiming the gospel of Jesus Christ? Your time and money—so your most valued assets become an influential tool in the hand of the Almighty for His Kingdom's agenda?

"For day after day they seek me out; they seem eager to know my ways, as if they were a nation that does what is right and has not forsaken the commands of its God. They ask me for just decisions and seem eager for God to come near them" (Isaiah 58:2).

Related Readings: : 2 Chronicles 7:14; Isaiah 6:1-6; Matthew 28:19-20; Philippians 2:1-7

TEARS SPEAK VOLUMES

Jesus wept. Then the Jews said, "See how he loved him!"
John 11:35-36

———————

There is a non-verbal language of love that is communicated through compassionate tears. Empathy engages the heart at levels that verbal exchanges may not be able to penetrate. It is when emotion responds to emotion that a grieving soul senses they are cared for and understood. Tears quietly create the aura that "I feel your pain—I hurt because you hurt."

We mourn with those who mourn, so they are not alone. Desperation feeds at the table of aloneness, but security and peace preoccupy the person comforted by a community. It starts with a patient spouse or friend and spills over to sincere souls who believe in Jesus to bring wholeness and healing. Tears shed in love terminate isolation and invite intimacy.

Comfort is the first step in seeking to serve another's pain. Refrain from truth telling until the heart receives proper care. Fear and anger have to be flushed from a hurting heart before facts can be appropriately applied and comprehended. It's from a context of love and acceptance that people trust and receive. Tears become a conduit for Christ's care.

"This is what the LORD, the God of your father David, says: I have heard your prayer and seen your tears; I will heal you" (2 Kings 20:5b).

Related Readings: Job 16:20; Psalm 126:5; Acts 20:19; 2 Timothy 1:4

GOT YOUR BACK

But you will not leave in haste or go in flight; for the LORD will go before you, the God of Israel will be your rear guard.
Isaiah 52:12

———————

God's got your back—there is no need to panic and flee; stand firm by faith. His righteous rear guard is a godly garrison against an ever-scheming enemy. Unbelief will assault your blind side, but do not surrender to fear's facade. Release your inhibitions to intimacy with Jesus and trust Him to guide you in His ways. A believer backed by God can be bold to carry on.

The glory of God has your back. His glory not only illuminates your path going forward, but it also leads you backwards into needed retreats for renewal. A soul cannot be sustained by good activity but requires solace and solitude with its Savior Jesus. Spiritual armor—the sword of the Spirit, the breastplate of righteousness, and the helmet of salvation—cover your front, but your heavenly Father's glory covers your back. He protects your vulnerable areas.

"Then your light will break forth like the dawn, and your healing will quickly appear; then your righteousness will go before you, and the glory of the LORD will be your rear guard" (Isaiah 58:8).

Related Readings: Numbers 10:9; 1 Samuel 7:10; Psalm 24:7-9; Proverbs 21:31

WORRY IS WEARISOME

An anxious heart weighs a man down, but a kind word cheers him up. Proverbs 12:25, NIV84

———————◆◆◆▸————————

Worry is wearisome. It is fatigue to our emotions like physical exhaustion is to our bodies. Worry can trigger stomachaches, high blood pressure, headaches, anxiety disorders, and depression. It is an enemy to executing a joy-filled and productive life. Worry can so weigh you down that you are immobilized for lack of energy and because of fear. Your family tree may have borne the fruit of worry over generations, but you can purge an obsession with negative thinking through trust in the Lord. Exercised trust energizes the weary.

Your personality may lend itself to worry. You can see it in your furrowed brow, or in your brooding countenance. You worry about the economy and its effect on your retirement. You wring your hands over relational wars and wonder if they will ever end. You are stressed out over work because of situations and people you are unable to change. Anxiety may have paralyzed you as a parent because you don't feel qualified to carry out your responsibilities. Ask God for faith, patience, wisdom, and courage. Prayer is your time-tested prescription for worry.

"Do not be anxious about anything, but in everything, by prayer and petition, with thanksgiving, present your requests to God" (Philippians 4:6, NIV84).

Related Readings: Luke 1:37; 5:1; 11:28; Acts 13:7; Ephesians 6:17

HUGS OF HEALING

But while he was still a long way off, his father saw him and was filled with compassion for him; he ran to his son, threw his arms around him and kissed him. Luke 15:20b

———◆◆◆———

Do not be afraid to hug at home, because hugs bring healing. Sons and daughters need the secure embrace of their dad and the comforting caress of their mom. A child may be conflicted by a feeling of inadequacy or a fear of public embarrassment. It's in this state of uncertainty that a kind hug communicates care and concern. Shed stoic aloofness for emotional expression.

A heart full of compassion can't help but hug. When you feel the need to physically communicate acceptance and love—you hug. Pure affection should not be a hugger's way to get his or her own needs met, rather it is an unselfish act to meet another's need for comfort and love.

There is no need to conceal a need for affection—these desires come from your divine design. God made you with a tender heart that needs the heartfelt connection of another. Affectionate desires require a touch on the arm, holding hands, a kiss on the check, a pat on the back or a loving hug. Arms are meant to extend often, just as the Lord's arms extend toward His needy children.

"My hand will sustain him; surely my arm will strengthen him" (Psalm 89:21).

Related Readings: John 12:38; Romans 16:16; 2 Peter 1:7; James 5:11

SHREWD AND DISCERNING

I am sending you out like sheep among wolves. Therefore be as shrewd as snakes and as innocent as doves. Matthew 10:16

It is a temptation for followers of Jesus Christ to drift into naïve living. There can be disengagement with life that becomes irresponsible; but Jesus said, "My prayer is not that you take them out of the world but that you protect them from the evil one" (John 17:15). It is engagement in the world that gives Christians relational equity with unbelievers. Indeed, we are called to trust others but to simultaneously verify their words and actions.

Parents do this with their children when they confirm their homework assignments are complete. Adolescents have to be reminded to take their backpacks to their bedrooms, and warned not to snack before dinner. Loving moms and dads keep an eye out for their child (sometimes from the back of their heads, it seems), as they have one trusting eye of encouragement, and one somewhat skeptical eye of accountability. Jesus commends shrewdness that is Spirit led; so seek to apply the wisdom of God in your finances, family, business dealings, and relationships.

"The master commended the dishonest manager because he had acted shrewdly. For the people of this world are more shrewd in dealing with their own kind than are the people of the light" (Luke 16:8).

Related Readings: 2 Samuel 13:3-4; 22:27; Proverbs 22:3; 1 Corinthians 2:14

SOBER SELF-ASSESSMENT

For by the grace given me I say to every one of you: Do not think of yourself more highly than you ought, but rather think of yourself with sober judgment, in accordance with the measure of faith God has given you. Romans 12:3, NIV84

A proper perspective of oneself fosters sound judgment, and this begins with surrender and submission to Jesus. However, an enlarged ego clouds our judgment, like an early morning drive over a fog-covered bridge. We have a limited, even skewed, view of reality. If we speed up, we are destined to an unpleasant outcome. It is when we see our capacity larger than the Lord sees our capacity that we tend to follow the temptation of trusting in our abilities over faith in Him.

Ego forgets God's Word and foolishly embraces counsel contrary to Christ. We make decisions based on our limited emotional view without inviting the wisdom of two or three objective advisors who know our situation—and us—well. Unsound judgment seeks only the answer it is looking for, ignoring wise warnings. Indeed, an enlarged ego entangles itself with insecure thinking and feels the need to be the center of attention. Sound judgment comes by surrender to your Savior Jesus. By God's grace, have a modest self-assessment of your gifts and abilities.

"If anyone thinks they are something when they are not, they deceive themselves" (Galatians 6:3).

Related Readings: Deuteronomy 29:29; Psalms 131:1-2; 2 Corinthians 10:13-15; Colossians 2:18

STEADFAST HEART

My heart is steadfast, O God; I will sing and make music with all my soul. Psalm 108:1, NIV84

———————

A steadfast heart is secure in Christ, and not even the devil can drive it from its devotion to the Lord. Indeed, you can be steadfast because your Savior is steadfast. Markets may crumble and economies erupt in uncertainty, but a steadfast heart stays fixed on the faithfulness of its heavenly Father.

A steadfast heart understands its sufficiency is in Christ, so it goes there first by faith. Sometimes you climb to praise God by the ladder of prayer. At other times you bless the Lord for the past, prayerfully pleading by faith to Him in the present. The Holy Spirit seizes your steadfast heart, enabling you to pray your way up to praise or helping you to patiently praise the Lord until you are ready for prayer. When your faith begins to flicker, go to God and He will ignite its bright flame. Christ creates a steadfast heart and He blesses a steadfast heart. Indeed, your soul sings praises over steadfast security in your Savior!

"And the God of all grace, who called you to his eternal glory in Christ, after you have suffered a little while, will himself restore you and make you strong, firm and steadfast" (1 Peter 5:10).

Related Readings: Psalm 51:10; 57:7; 112:7; Proverbs 4:26; Isaiah 26:3; Philippians 4:1

PEACEFUL SLEEP

Without warning, a furious storm came up on the lake, so that the waves swept over the boat. But Jesus was sleeping. The disciples went and woke him, saying, "Lord, save us! We're going to drown!" Matthew 8:24-25, NIV84

Emotional and physical exhaustion may be the result of restless sleep. The storms of life can produce in us an insecure state of mind. We toss and turn with a tortured soul and a preoccupied brain. Indeed, peaceful sleep can seem elusive for those overwhelmed by the responsibilities of life. Bills, budgets, broken promises, health issues, and relational conflicts can disrupt and damage our nighttime bliss.

The results of sleepless nights are rude: You can't think straight, your countenance screams fatigue, you are impatient, and your learning retention is diminished. Brain cells fire erratically for lack of sleep, so your moral judgment may lapse and you can become reckless with your choices. Without rest you become emotionally fragile and physically vulnerable to infection, diabetes, heart disease, and obesity. A body without rest leads to an unhealthy and unsettling life.

Sleep is your Savior's way to get your undivided attention. It is a time of rest and a time to reconnect with Christ. You can rest peacefully and securely in the presence and protection of God. Yes, trust Jesus and take a nap!

"I will lie down and sleep in peace, for you alone, O LORD, make me dwell in safety" (Psalm 4:8, NIV84).

Related Readings: Isaiah 54:11; John 11:4; Acts 2:21; 12:6

APRIL

Blessed is the man who walks not in the counsel of the wicked, nor stands in the way of sinners, nor sits in the seat of scoffers; but his delight is in the law of the Lord, and on his law he meditates day and night. He is like a tree planted by streams of water that yields its fruit in its season, and its leaf does not wither. In all that he does, he prospers. Psalms 1:1-3

APRIL 1

CAREER CHALLENGES

Whatever you do, work at it with all your heart, as working
for the Lord, not for men. Colossians 3:23, NIV84

———◄◆►———

Career challenges are meant to keep us close to Christ, not
drive us through default to our own determination. These
occupational hazards come as a result of economic downturns,
or when a recession rears its ugly head. The fear of layoffs,
downsizing, and restructuring can linger over life like a
bad dream. Our confidence is shaken as we wonder if we
will continue to receive a paycheck. We may feel extremely
vulnerable, because our industry is caught up in change and
consolidation.

However, these down cycles are your opportunity to remain a
dependable employee, partner, investor, or boss. For instance,
make sure your attitude aligns around the Almighty's big
picture for your life. This season of service has been a gift from
your Savior, going forward you are a much better person than
before. Use these days of uncertainty to stay engaged in your
job. Remain an asset rather than a liability to your company.
Your work is for the Lord first, so labor with passion, focus,
and diligence.

"Do you see a man skilled in his work? He will serve before
kings; he will not serve before obscure men" (Proverbs 22:29,
NIV 84).

Related Readings: 2 Chronicles 34:12; Nehemiah 5:15;
Psalm 127:1; 1 Timothy 4:10

APRIL 2

POWER OF NO

Then Jesus told his disciples a parable to show them that they should always pray and not give up. Luke 18:1

The power of being told "no" comes when, instead of becoming discouraged, we use it as a lesson in determination. "No" is sometimes necessary to get our attention and give us the perspective we would have missed rushing through life. If everything were a "yes," we could certainly take people and things for granted and run the risk of our faith becoming flabby. It is when we exercise discipline, creativity, and prayer that we encounter God.

For example, you may want to spend money right now, but your budget shouts back "no" because money is tight. Instead of circumventing your circumstances with credit, become creative. Perhaps you can help someone steward one of their assets better by allowing you to use their beach or mountain home. Or, as a parent your "no" to your child is for their protection. It is better for them to suffer the minor pain of disappointment now than significant, life-altering harm in the future. Most importantly, a "no" is meant to move you toward knowing God. His "no" is your heavenly attention getter.

"Consider it pure joy, my brothers, whenever you face trials of many kinds, because you know that the testing of your faith develops perseverance" (James 1:2-3, NIV84).

Related Readings: 2 Samuel 22:7; Psalm 57:2; Luke 18:7; Hebrews 10:36; 11:27

PRODUCTIVE PAIN

Then God said, "Take your son, your only son, Isaac, whom you love, and go to the region of Moriah. Sacrifice him there as a burnt offering." Genesis 22:2a, NIV84

Pain is synonymous with suffering, anguish, trials, tribulation, adversity, trouble, and hard times. It affects our emotions, mind, body, soul, spirit, and will, for it is indiscriminate in its affliction. And, there are times God will ask His children to walk through extremely difficult situations. Indeed, there is probably no greater pain in life than to be willing to inflict pain on someone you love; yet this is what God asked Abraham to do with Isaac.

Pain was their teacher to bring them into alignment with almighty God's agenda. It was a moment to trust God, or trust their instinct of self-preservation. Fortunately, it was faith in their heavenly Father that fostered obedience. They allowed pain to replace self-sufficiency with strength in God. Productive pain finds solutions in obedience to God. Pain is a process of growing in grace, as we experience Christ in the middle of His suffering.

"Not only so, but we also rejoice in our sufferings, because we know that suffering produces perseverance; perseverance, character; and character, hope. And hope does not disappoint us, because God has poured out his love into our hearts by the Holy Spirit, whom he has given us" (Romans 5:3-5, NIV 84).

Related Readings: Psalm 69:29; Galatians 1:15-16; Hebrews 11:17; 1 Peter 1:7

TIME OF NEED

Let us then approach God's throne of grace with confidence, so that we may receive mercy and find grace to help us in our time of need. Hebrews 4:16

Everyone has a time of need. There are intense times, coming through death, divorce, and distress; and there are daily times, caused by temptation, fear, and frustration. The time of need may produce gratitude, because of experiencing the Lord's bountiful blessing. It may be the need for discretion with finances or modesty when speaking of a gifted and accomplished child. Whatever the need requires, there is an ever-accessible throne of grace to approach.

The throne of God's grace is good. It is not a throne of condemnation, but a throne of forgiveness. It's not a throne of rejection, but a throne of acceptance. It's not a throne of control, but of freedom. The Lord's throne rules with righteous judgment and justice for all. His throne glistens with trust and never tarnishes for lack of integrity or from soiled character. It is simply, and ever so, an accessible a throne of grace to receive His mercy. With humility and consistency bow to Christ in reverent fear and worship. It's out of your praise and adoration from a hurting heart that He hears and answers prayer. Your time of need is His time to lead.

"Out of his fullness we have all received grace in place of grace already given" (John 1:16).

Related Readings: Psalm 45:6; 47:8; Hebrews 12:2; 2 John 1:3; Revelation 1:4

PRECIOUS SAINTS

Precious in the sight of the LORD is the death of his saints.
Psalm 116:15, KJV

———————◄•►———————

Precious saints are special, because they are precious in the sight of the Lord. More specifically, He sees the death of saints as precious reward in His sight. Their faithful living leaves a residue of righteousness in the wake of their relationships. Their countenance reflects Christ as they speak His truth and exhibit His grace. Precious memories remain for those who are precious to Jesus. They leave behind a legacy of having loved well.

Precious saints provide a picture of Jesus. They allow us to look into the life of our Lord by their godly example. Their sensitive spirit rejoices when we rejoice, and weeps when we weep. They do not cast stones of judgment; rather, they are a rock of reassurance and encouragement. They are on the lookout for ways to serve and draw attention to their Savior Jesus, not themselves. The inner beauty of their character is beautiful to behold. Precious saints finish well, so their death is a celebration of their faithfulness to God. Thus, live wise, precious to your Lord.

"Rather let it be the hidden person of the heart, with the incorruptible beauty of a gentle and quiet spirit, which is very precious in the sight of God" (1 Peter 3:4, NKJV).

Related Readings: Ecclesiastes 4:2; Isaiah 6:1; 1 Peter 1:19; 2:3-5; 2 Peter 1:4

GOOD GOERS

He went to him and bandaged his wounds, pouring on oil and wine. Then he put the man on his own donkey, took him to an inn and took care of him. Luke 10:34, NIV 84

What does it mean to be a good goer? It involves giving time and resources as we roll up our sleeves and do whatever it takes to meet the need in front of us. Our head assesses the situation, diagnosing the need; then our heart engages our calendar and our checkbook. Good goers understand the correlation between serving and greatness.

Good goers initiate service to others in the name of Jesus. They don't wait for the needy to come to them—instead they are quick to show up and serve. It may mean giving an anonymous gift to relieve pressure from a friend's huge medical bills. It could be keeping the lawn of a neighbor who travels a lot, or paying a mechanic to repair the car of a single mom. Being a good goer for you could involve opening your home to a prodigal who is trying to find his or her way, but who desperately needs an environment of love, hope, and acceptance. Good goers have the uncanny ability to look around them and, like radar, lock onto to those who need a helping hand.

"Whoever wants to become great among you must be your servant" (Mark 10:43b).

Related Readings: Proverbs 11:24; Ephesians 6:7; 1 Thessalonians 1:9; 1 Peter 4:11

GENESIS OF WISDOM

The fear of the LORD is the beginning of wisdom; and all who follow his precepts have good understanding. To him belongs eternal praise. Psalm 111:10

———◦◦◦———

The fear of the Lord is foundational to the attaining of almighty God's wisdom. It is out of holy reverence that heaven opens its doors of understanding. The creation will never begin to understand the Creator until there is a coming together of minds over who is superior and who is the author of salvation.

Once there is capitulation to Christ, surrender to your Savior, you are in position to receive His good gifts, chiefly wisdom. Your holy heavenly Father rewards respect and awe with wisdom from above. However, the cavalier take Christ for granted and lose sound judgment. But, the fear of the Lord is your foundation for wise living. It is in these humble beginnings that wisdom originates. Wisdom places faith in Christ out front and humbly deflects attention away from self. Therefore, use wisdom to gain understanding, obey God, and lead people into a growing relationship with Christ. To Him alone belongs eternal praise for His gift of wisdom!

"It is because of him that you are in Christ Jesus, who has become for us wisdom from God— that is, our righteousness, holiness and redemption" (1 Corinthians 1:30).

Related Readings: Job 28:28; Psalm 25:21-14; Proverbs 1:7; 9:10; Acts 9:31

ENHANCING GOD'S PRESENCE

For where two or three gather in my name, there am I with them. Matthew 18:20

The power of God's presence is enhanced in the presence of His people. It may be a small group of two or three—or large corporate worship at camp or church—where His presence becomes preeminent. The Lord is always with His children, but it becomes more pronounced in authentic community where His bountiful blessings are celebrated.

It is not good for men or women to remain alone in unaccountable autonomy without encouragement, comfort, counsel, and correction. Unwise are those who seek financial freedom but leave out a fraternity of other God-fearing friends. Life is richer when other people's perspectives intersect our own in intimate dialogue. Jesus pronounces His truth, displays His love, and extends His comfort through those who convene in Christ's name.

As an immigrant from heaven, you gain eternal energy from your family in the faith who pray with you and for you. Reserve a mountain home, a country cottage, or a beach house today and invite two or three faith-hearted friends to communion with you over Christ. Laugh, love, pray, and enjoy His enhanced presence.

"So when you are assembled and I am with you in spirit, and the power of our Lord Jesus is present" (1 Corinthians 5:4).

Related Readings: 2 Chronicles 34:27; Acts 10:33; 1 Thessalonians 3:9-13; Revelation 7:15

NEVER GIVE UP

Know also that wisdom is like honey for you: If you find it, there is a future hope for you, and your hope will not be cut off. Proverbs 24:14

Hope from heaven is a dependable handle to hang on to through the ups and downs of life. Like a skilled mountain climber we hook our rope of trust to the face of the solid rock, so we have secure support. It does not mean we are absent of fear, but it does mean in the middle of our fears we can have faith in Holy God to handle the inclement conditions.

The wisdom of the Lord is not elusive but available to all who humble their hearts and take the time to invite His influence. Truth is sweet to the soul, and it will nourish your heart like spiritual nectar. Belief is a worker bee on behalf of God that takes the pollen of providence and produces the sustenance of salvation. You may have tried religion and found it lacking, but do not give up on God. Make sure you follow Him by faith—do not ask Him to follow you. Hope in the Lord adds fuel to your fire of faith. Don't give up. Finish well by giving all you have for Christ!

"I have fought the good fight, I have finished the race, I have kept the faith" (2 Timothy 4:7).

Related Readings: Psalm 119:116; Isaiah 57:10; 1 Thessalonians 1:3; 1 John 3:3

SECURITY REJECTS FEAR

He will have no fear of bad news; his heart is steadfast, trusting in the LORD. His heart is secure, he will have no fear; in the end he will look in triumph on his foes.
Psalm 112:7-8, NIV84

A secure servant of Jesus has nothing to prove, for he rests in the pronounced peace of the Lord. His or her love for God is deep and wide, and their confidence in Christ is unshaken and uncompromising. Security's only fear is distrust in almighty God; therefore it maintains a holy heart, a meditative mind, and a courageous countenance.

Fear tries to seduce security into thinking that its Savior Jesus is undependable and detached, but God's promises ring true of His faithfulness and intimate concern. This world is always pregnant with bad news, so do not make it your focus or you will be driven by worry, fear, and insecurity. Trust rests secure—it jettisons fear. Security is found nestled between the strong shoulders of God.

"Let the beloved of the LORD rest secure in him, for he shields him all day long, and the one the LORD loves rests between his shoulders" (Deuteronomy 33:12).

Related Readings: 2 Samuel 22:33; Proverbs 14:16; 26; Hebrews 6:19; 2 Peter 3:17

HOLY SPIRIT AWARENESS

"**D**id you receive the Holy Spirit when you believed?" They answered, "No, we have not even heard that there is a Holy Spirit." Acts 19:2

In some Christian circles God the Father and His Son Jesus Christ get all the attention, while the Holy Spirit—like an unruly stepchild—is ignored. Some followers of Jesus—out of ignorance or fear—fail to acknowledge and engage the Holy Spirit's work in their life. They are stunted spiritually because they miss the Spirit's revelation of wisdom.

The Trinity (God the Father, God the Son, God the Holy Spirit), all play significant roles in growing believers into the likeness of Christ through godly wisdom. He is gracious to give us wisdom through grace from God the Father, through relationship with God the Son, and through revelation from God the Spirit.

The Holy Spirit's work is not meant to be overly mystical or weird but practical and real. He provides comfort when you hurt, conviction when you stray, and direction when you are unsure. Therefore, daily enter into the fullness of the Spirit by confessing, repenting, and receiving the Spirit's fullness—be aware of what God has already given you by faith. Obey His leading.

"For ye have not received the spirit of bondage again to fear; but ye have received the Spirit of adoption, whereby we cry, Abba, Father" (Romans 8:15, NKJV).

Related Readings: Zechariah 4:6; 2 Corinthians 1:22; 5:5; Ephesians 1:13-14; 1 John 5:6-8

APRIL 12

SPIRIT-LED LEADERSHIP

For as many as are led by the Spirit of God, these are sons of
God. Romans 8:14, NKJV

Spirit-led leadership is not intimidated by the fear of man; rather,
it is motivated by the fear of God. Unfounded fear drives the flesh
to make misinformed, even disastrous decisions. But the Holy
Spirit shows unselfish seekers direction: As a son or daughter
they cry out, "Abba (Father) Father," in utter dependence on
their heavenly Father.

They recognize that almighty God has adopted them into His
forever family of hope, love, and holiness. Institutions give a
certificate of adoption to loving parents on earth, but the Holy
Spirit seals the Lord's adopted now and forevermore with His
grace and care. Gratitude gushes from the heart of God's children
to affectionately cry out, "Abba, Abba!" Do not apologize for
your unique leadership style or for the unconventional way the
Spirit leads your life. Go with His revelation—even if it leads
to revolution—for many times His ways are radical. Be a Spirit-
led leader who trusts boldly, who loves wholly, and who serves
assertively.

"Woe to the foolish prophets who follow their own spirit and
have seen nothing!" (Ezekiel 13:3)

Related Readings: 1 Kings 3:5-12; Psalms 119:129-136;
Luke 4:1; Acts 9:17

APRIL 13

RADICAL PRAYERS

You have heard that it was said, "Love your neighbor and hate your enemy." But I tell you, love your enemies and pray for those who persecute you, that you may be children of your Father in heaven. Matthew 5:43-45a

---

Mature prayers show no respect of persons; they even include those who don't—according to human standards—deserve prayer. But the Lord requires righteous prayers to have no bias toward those who have been acting badly. The flesh does not default to prayer for those who bring harm, but the Spirit does. Radical prayers include enemies.

Anybody can pray easy prayers, however hard prayers change the person who perseveres in offering them. What we pray about is what we care about. Whom we pray for is whom we feel for. It is often a severe struggle to pray for someone who inflicts emotional, relational, and physical pain, but this is the Lord's path to grow us. Those outside of Christ do not have a context for character, but those who know better do.

So, by faith, move from mediocre petitions to radical prayer and love: Apply both to your enemies. Your Christlike example attracts others who want to become children of God.

"Jesus said, 'Father, forgive them, for they do not know what they are doing'" (Luke 23:34a).

Related Readings: Luke 6:36; Acts 7:54-56; 1 Peter 1:15-16; 3:9

INTERNAL COMBUSTION

After they prayed, the place where they were meeting was shaken. And they were all filled with the Holy Spirit and spoke the word of God boldly. Acts 4:31

The Holy Spirit inflames the heart of Christ followers who submit to Him in faith-filled prayer. He is looking for those devoted disciples who depend on the Spirit's filling power for internal fortitude to proceed by faith. It is in this holy place of prayer that the Holy Spirit does deep soul work. Prayer ignites the Spirit's power like gasoline in an engine.

Is your faith tired and your spiritual muscles weak with atrophy? If so, gather with some committed Christians, or get on your knees by yourself, and ask your heavenly Father to fill you to overflowing with His Spirit. It's the Spirit's fullness that energizes individual believers and causes a team of Christians to resonate in unified direction. The Holy Spirit aligns humble hearts around heaven's purposes that produce sanctified results.

Moreover, the Spirit ignites God's Word. So, be bold to lovingly share Scripture. Lean into the Spirit's promptings to lead you when and how to come out for Christ!

"If you then, though you are evil, know how to give good gifts to your children, how much more will your Father in heaven give the Holy Spirit to those who ask him!" (Luke 11:13)

Related Readings: Acts 28:24-26; Romans 5:5; 9:1; 15:13-16; Jude 1:19-21

SELFISH TAKING

Do nothing out of selfish ambition or vain conceit. Rather, in humility value others above yourselves, not looking to your own interests but each of you to the interests of the others. In your relationships with one another, have the same mindset as Christ Jesus. Philippians 2:3-5

Selfish taking demands its own way—a sense of entitlement behind its behavior. The desire may be to buy something now, or drink something now, or travel somewhere now—with no regard to the relational ramifications. We fall into this reckless relational routine when we have to have what we want—when we want it—regardless.

Fortunately for us there is a more mature approach that is modeled by our Master and Lord Jesus Christ: selfless giving. Christ could have demanded anything He wanted, but He chose to give up His earthly expectations and use His authority to benefit others. Jesus became a servant and served to the point of giving His very life, so that those who believed in Him could have life. Selfish taking takes life, while selfless giving gives life.

"I have been crucified with Christ and I no longer live, but Christ lives in me. The life I now live in the body, I live by faith in the Son of God, who loved me and gave himself for me" (Galatians 2:20).

Related Readings: Proverbs 11:24; Zechariah 7:9; John 13:14; 34; Romans 12:10

MORAL FATIGUE

Whoever sows to please their flesh, from the flesh will reap destruction; whoever sows to please the Spirit, from the Spirit will reap eternal life. Let us not become weary in doing good, for at the proper time we will reap a harvest if we do not give up. Galatians 6:8-9

All Christians are subject to moral fatigue—tiring under the burden of doing what's right. The culture does not always commend moral efforts. On the contrary it may be the decent people who are marginalized or made fun of because of their faith. Even family can contribute to one's weariness by not appreciating and ignoring another loved one's integrity. So, how do Christians remain faithful when their moral fortitude begins to fade?

Like a fatigued farmer who engages the elements and continues to sow seed in prepared soil in spite of the harsh conditions, so committed Christians stay true to sowing to please the Spirit, regardless of rejection and the temptation to quit. Each follower of Jesus will enjoy heaven's great harvest or will be embarrassed and judged for lacking a fruitful life. So, we sow to please the Spirit—even when is seems unproductive—for here is faith's test.

"But he knows the way that I take; when he has tested me, I will come forth as gold" (Job 23:10).

Related Readings: Job 4:8; Psalm 126:5; Proverbs 11:18; Hosea 8:7; 10:12; 2 Corinthians 9:6; James 3:18

OUTGIVE GOD

Give away your life; you'll find life given back, but not
merely given back—given back with bonus and blessing.
Giving, not getting, is the way. Generosity begets generosity.
Luke 6:38, The Message

It is impossible to outgive the Lord, because He augments any
gift given in Jesus' name with His almighty influence. He can
take a penny and make it a dime. He can take a dime and make
it a dollar. He can take a dollar and make it a hundred dollars.
He can take a hundred dollars and make it a thousand. Eternally
motivated gifts grow exponentially.

He can take one life surrendered to Jesus and influence a family.
He can take a family under the Lordship of Christ and influence
a church, a ministry, and a community. He can take a Christ-
centered community and influence a state. He can take a state
that stands for God's standards and revive a nation. Indeed, He
has taken a nation founded on His principles and influenced the
world. One submitted life is leverage in the Lord's hands.

"The generous will themselves be blessed, for they share their
food with the poor" (Proverbs 22:9).

Related Readings: Psalm 146:7; Matthew 14:17-21;
2 Corinthians 8:2; Hebrews 6:10

GOVERNMENT DEBT CRISIS

The LORD will open to you His good treasure, the heavens, to give the rain to your land in its season, and to bless all the work of your hand. You shall lend to many nations, but you shall not borrow. Deuteronomy 28:12, NKJV

A government debt crisis becomes a crisis for those it governs—everyone is affected. Institutions, individuals and businesses are not immune, and, sadly, some have even contributed to the crisis with their careless management of money. An avalanche of debt causes emotions to run rampant: Fear, anger, self-preservation, hoarding, and helplessness escort those indebted to debt. It's like treading water in the middle of a vast ocean.

The Lord looks at national debt as unwise, even wrong. He says it's OK for nations to lend, but not to borrow, because—as with households—we become enslaved to those we owe. Sadly, He even says there are curses associated in growing a government that has to grovel to other governments for money. A nation's values are at stake when a foreign influence has financial control. Liberty is mortgaged away for new money. Thus, avoid personal debt and model well fiscal responsibility at work, church, and home. Raise the standards for what's expected of those who manage taxpayer money. Hold them accountable. Financial freedom frees nations and its citizens.

"The borrower is slave to the lender" (Proverbs 22:7b).

Related Readings: 2 Kings 4:1-7; Proverbs 3:27-28; 6:1-5; Romans 13:8; James 4:13-15

RESOLUTION BRINGS RELIEF

Therefore, if you are offering your gift at the altar and there remember that your brother has something against you, leave your gift there in front of the altar. First go and be reconciled to your brother; then come and offer your gift. Matthew 5:24

Resolution brings relief to all parties, for it puts an end to the problem or dispute. Without resolution there is a "disconnect" and turmoil that lead to distrust. People feel heavyhearted and unable to move forward completely focused because of unresolved conflict hovering over their life. Christians can be the culprits, because they tend to smile when, in fact, their faith is frowning.

It is easier to talk about someone than to talk with him or her, so the object of scorn is left unaware of their fault, thinking everything is OK. But the way of Christ requires courage of conversation, so behaviors can be corrected and relationships made whole. You cannot focus on God in faith if there is a relational fissure within your family, work associates, or friends. Resolution takes time to revisit, clarify, forgive, and reconcile. Therefore, go; humble yourself and gain freedom through relational reconciliation. Your humility and willingness to be honest is healing. Trust the Lord to bless your sincere confession.

"Therefore confess your sins to each other and pray for each other so that you may be healed" (James 5:16).

Related Readings: Luke 12:58; John 17:11; 2 Corinthians 5:18-20; Colossians 1:20

NURTURED BY NATURE

Your love, LORD, reaches to the heavens, your faithfulness to the skies. Your righteousness is like the highest mountains, your justice like the great deep. You, LORD, preserve both people and animals. Psalm 36:5-6

The Lord's creation is able to comfort the soul. The blazing hot sun is a reminder of the security that glows from His faithfulness. The light of God's love cuts into the innermost crevices of the heart and offers a warm embrace. Christ's boundless love bounces off of creation's canopy and reflects back onto the beauty of His children. His nature nurtures.

Like a rock, His righteousness scales the highest mountains and stands triumphant, bearing the flag of truth. A gaze over the rugged, cloud-covered pinnacles pronounces the Lord's power in silent and worshipful majesty. It's hard for the mind to conceive such sovereign supremacy—for it puts man's pride in a place of awe—reserved only for humble praise. A life encumbered by the noisy concrete jungle created by man misses out on the reassuring voice of Christ waiting to communicate in the countryside. Pace yourself by receiving God's grace from His grandeur.

"Let the sea resound, and everything in it, the world, and all who live in it. Let the rivers clap their hands, let the mountains sing together for joy; let them sing before the LORD" (Psalm 98:7¬9a).

Related Readings: Isaiah 49:13; Jeremiah 33:22; Luke 6:12; Acts 17:24-25

PRAYER IS PLANNING

Many are the plans in a person's heart, but it is the LORD's purpose that prevails. Proverbs 19:21

Prayer taps into the purpose of God. The human heart can conceive and birth ideas, but what is the Lord's best direction to follow? This is the beauty of being lead by the Spirit and not driven by the flesh. It is in communion with Christ that Christians can be clear on next steps in their service for God. Prayer positions an individual and a group before God in utter dependence on Him for understanding and carrying out His plan. It's when we rush ahead in bold but blind determination that we miss out on engaging an eternal agenda in the process. Yes, the Lord can and does work through our immature maneuvers, but why not wait on Him in prayer and save ourselves time?

So, slow down so you can speed up later—confident of a plan consecrated to Christ. Stay diligent in a process of prayer and discern along the way what is good versus what is best. Ask Jesus to renew your mind so your thinking is based on His abundance. Prayer is planning that produces eternal outcomes.

"'All this,' David said, 'I have in writing as a result of the LORD's hand on me, and he enabled me to understand all the details of the plan'" (1 Chronicles 28:19).

Related Readings: Psalm 40:5; Proverbs 16:1-9; Romans 1:13; 2 Corinthians 1:17

PRAYER BRINGS CLARITY

Let the morning bring me word of your unfailing love, for I have put my trust in you. Show me the way I should go, for to you I entrust my life. Psalm 143:8

Are you confused about what God has next for you in life, work, and relationships? Do you feel trapped in your aloneness—unsure if anyone really cares or not? It is in these moments of doubt and uncertainty that Jesus deeply desires to commune with you and care for your soul. A lack of clarity is a calling card for Christ to show up and show you the way.

The human mind needs help to understand the ways of God. Without the Holy Spirit's illumination we default to untruthful thinking—wrong assumptions that lead to confusing conclusions. For example, someone may not feel loved— it is in the absence of love that fear and distrust set up shop. One who struggles in thinking they don't deserve to be loved is wise to bow in prayer and receive their heavenly Father's loving embrace. Prayer is first, last, and along the way the process of aligning with almighty God's agenda. He already has the plan laid out for His children. Our part is to patiently wait and listen for Christ's clarity—He is not the author of confusion.

"For God is not the author of confusion but of peace, as in all the churches of the saints" (1 Corinthians 14:33, NKJV).

Related Readings: Ezekiel 11:25; Zechariah 1:9; Acts 10:28; James 3:16

PRAYER IS WORK

Epaphras, who is one of you and a servant of Christ Jesus, sends greetings. He is always wrestling in prayer for you, that you may stand firm in all the will of God, mature and fully assured. Colossians 4:12

Prayer is not a passive undertaking—rather it is an energized exercise of faith. Status quo believers only tip God with prayer, but eager followers of Jesus are compelled by an intense commitment to pray. Spiritual sweat flows from the pores of a soul earnestly engaged with eternity. There is a desperate dependency that devoted Christians display.

Adversity has a way of bringing us to our knees in utter reliance on our Lord. Prodigal children bring parents together in prayer. Death convenes communities and families in prayer. Misunderstandings, mistreatment, and misguided motives move hearts to pray. These aggressive prayers respond to rough circumstances with a need for holy help. And, there is another type of laborious prayer that petitions Christ on behalf of others. Earnestly pray for others, and you will experience the joy of unselfish service and the exhilaration of Christ's replies.

"Devote yourselves to prayer, being watchful and thankful. And pray for us, too, that God may open a door for our message, so that we may proclaim the mystery of Christ" (Colossians 4:2-3).

Related Readings: 1 Kings 18:36-39; Matthew 6:5-6; Acts 3:1; 16:13

UNPROFITABLE PROFIT

For what will it profit a man if he gains the whole world, and loses his own soul? Or what will a man give in exchange for his soul? Mark 8:36-37, NKJV

Profit is good, if it produces the right results; but profit is bad if the results are unwise. The world, the flesh, and the devil offer an exchange that is enticing to the eye but starves the soul. The world offers power in exchange for a compromise in character. The flesh offers self-indulgence in exchange for discipline and service to others. And the devil, through his deception, offers fortune in exchange for neglect of family responsibilities.

Even Christians can get sucked into society's strong solicitations—like standing too close behind a giant box fan—they feel the pull of unfaithfulness. Less their soul be shredded, there must be intentionality toward a heart pure with motives that honor the Lord and a mind wise in its application of truth. Wise people pursue the Lord first and do not chase profits that compete with Christ. God's gains give real life to the soul, not death.

"'Truly I tell you,' Jesus replied, 'no one who has left home or brothers or sisters or mother or father or children or fields for me and the gospel will fail to receive a hundred times as much in this present age.'" (Mark 10:29-30a).

Related Readings: 2 Corinthians 2:17; 2 Timothy 1:2; Titus 1:16; 1 John 2:16

SWEAT AND SUCCESS

God is not unjust; He will not forget your work and the love you have shown Him as you have helped His people and continue to help them. We want each of you to show this same diligence to the very end, in order to make your hope sure.
Hebrews 6:10-11, NIV84

Often there is a direct correlation between hard work and success. It is not a prerequisite to success, but it increases its probability. Yes, you can work hard on the wrong things and fail miserably, or you can labor lazily on the right things and still not get the job done. Or, you may have the privilege of building on someone else's sacrifice, but it still requires your focused intensity and investment of time and thinking. However, for most, perspiration and persistence is the preamble that constitutes success.

If you only talk about what you are going to do, spiritual and smart people will begin to grow suspect. Avoid behavior that is full of busyness but void of progress. Work hard at the things that matter and your work will matter. For example, be punctual for appointments, even early. Your attention to being on time communicates respect and value to the other parties. Hard work begins with a focused and responsible attitude.

"All hard work brings a profit, but mere talk leads only to poverty" (Proverbs 14:23).

Related Readings: Ezra 5:8; Luke 5:5; 1 Corinthians 15:10; 1 Thessalonians 5:12

PRAYER SAVES TIME

So Peter was kept in prison, but the church was earnestly praying to God for him… Peter motioned with his hand for them to be quiet and described how the Lord had brought him out of prison. Acts 12:5, 17a

———————

Prayer is a timesaver. It saves followers of Jesus from unnecessary seasons of anxious worry. It saves an employer from a wrong hire and the valuable investment of time, money, and training.

It saves a dating couple from a naïve emotional engagement without counting the cost of a lifetime commitment to love, respect, and serve each other. Prayer waits for God's best.

The flesh forces issues when prayer is void in the relational process. A person who is self-motivated but not Spirit led exerts a lot of energy yet can waste a lot of time. A prayerless approach to life and work can easily end up focused on the urgent to the neglect of what really matters. Prayer protects you from the clutches of another's crisis.

"I was ashamed to ask the king for soldiers and horsemen to protect us from enemies on the road, because we had told the king, 'The gracious hand of our God is on everyone who looks to him, but his great anger is against all who forsake him.' So we fasted and petitioned our God about this, and he answered our prayer" (Ezra 8:22-23).

Related Readings: 2 Chronicles 32:20; Job 42:8; Luke 21:36; Acts 10:9

CONFIDENT CONFESSION

During the days of Jesus' life on earth, he offered up prayers and petitions with fervent cries and tears to the one who could save him from death, and he was heard because of his reverent submission. Hebrews 5:7

God established His Son Jesus as high priest in heaven and on earth. You can be confident of this because the Almighty gave His solemn oath never to change His mind. Therefore, political incompetence and economic earthquakes cannot shake the security you place in your Savior Jesus. He stands before you as priest with divine ordaining. His priestly order begins and ends with Himself, for only He is eternal. He sits in glory in complete character atoning for you by the merit of His blood sacrifice on the cross.

Therefore, bring your soiled soul to your Savior for confession and cleansing. Christ is your most reliable confidant with whom you can entrust your clouded conscience. Say to Him what you feel, and He will acknowledge your feelings while reminding you of the truth. Indeed, you go confidently to Christ in confession of sin and repentance toward changed behavior. Jesus is your high priest who heals and forgives!

"Therefore, holy brothers, who share in the heavenly calling, fix your thoughts on Jesus, the apostle and high priest whom we confess" (Hebrews 3:1, NIV84).

Related Readings: Psalm 110:4; Proverbs 28:13; Daniel 9:8; Mark 1:5; Romans 4:7

DIVINE APPOINTMENTS

When a Samaritan woman came to draw water, Jesus said to her, "Will you give me a drink?" John 4:7

Christ connects us with people for His unique purposes. It could be an occasion to meet someone for the very first time; it may be a causal acquaintance or a familiar friend. Regardless of the relational connection, it is important to ask the Lord how to bless the one in our presence and be open to receive a blessing from them. Our calendar of appointments can become a prayer list for us to ask for wisdom from God as we seek to serve others over a meal, coffee or tea, or in a meeting.

It's uncanny how we can be in a needy situation and our Savior sends someone who becomes His hands and feet of faith and hope. They provide a kind and encouraging word or an insight that gives us courage and direction to do the right thing. Thank God for His inspiring ambassadors. You never know how the seed of a kind word, a listening ear, a practical idea, or an encouraging prayer will germinate and grow in one seeking soul. Divine appointments are much bigger than your agenda—so, see daily encounters through the lens of eternity.

"Many of the Samaritans from the town believed in Him because of the woman's testimony" (John 4:39a).

Related Readings: Genesis 24:12-14; 1 Corinthians 16:7; 2 Corinthians 1:15; 1 Peter 2:12

DIVINE TEST

When Jesus looked up and saw a great crowd coming toward him, he said to Philip, "Where shall we buy bread for these people to eat?" He asked this only to test him, for he already had in mind what he was going to do. John 6:5-6

———————

Life is full of tests. There are a series of tests through the years of formal education. A test is required to receive a learner's permit—then a driver's license. There are personality tests, vision tests, hearings tests, and blood tests. There are tests of endurance in mountain climbing, mental tests for marathon runners, and tests for alcohol intake. Like it or not, tests measure current progress, and they are an indicator of future direction.

More specifically, the Christian life is a series of divine tests. These are moments along our path of faith when our Heavenly Father wants to reveal to us what's really in our heart. This raw revelation can be rewarding, or it can be a reality check of regression. Either way His tests are meant to motivate us forward in a step of growth in grace and love. When you pass His tests, you can pass on His hope to others being tested.

"The LORD your God is testing you to find out whether you love him with all your heart and with all your soul" (Deuteronomy 13:3b).

Related Readings: 1 Chronicles 29:17; Psalm 26:2; 139:23; Acts 15:18; 1 Thessalonians 2:4

WORK STRUGGLES

To Adam he said, "Because you listened to your wife and ate fruit from the tree about which I commanded you, 'You must not eat from it,' cursed is the ground because of you; through painful toil you will eat food from it all the days of your life."
Genesis 3:17

Work is often work. Painful toil is a consequence of what happened in the beginning—God cursed the ground, because of Adam and Eve's disobedience. Labor became laborious. Instead of paradise in the sinless Garden of Eden, there was blood, sweat, and tears mingled with sin. Work is not meant to be accomplished with ease but, rather, with intense effort.

"So the LORD God banished him from the Garden of Eden to work the ground from which he had been taken" (Genesis 3:23).
Is your work a struggle? Are you in one of the most stressful seasons of your career? If so, God doesn't waste pain; it's in your discomfort He comforts, and in your unease He gives courage. If the Lord has your attention in an environment out of your control, stay true to what you can do and leave the results to Him. In stress seek Jesus.

"So my heart began to despair over all my toilsome labor under the sun" (Ecclesiastes 2:20).

Related Readings: Ecclesiastes 8:15; 2 Corinthians 11:26-31; Revelation 9:19-20

MAY

All Scripture is breathed out by God and profitable for teaching, for reproof, for correction, and for training in righteousness, that the man of God may be competent, equipped for every good work.
2 Timothy 3:16-17

A PRAYERFUL NATION

If my people, who are called by my name, will humble
themselves and pray and seek my face and turn from their
wicked ways, then I will hear from heaven, and I will forgive
their sin and will heal their land. 2 Chronicles 7:14

A nation that prays pays forward a faithful legacy to the next
generation. But a prayerless nation jeopardizes the favor of God
for future families. Indeed, when a people "progress" past prayer
in their psyche, pride has captured their hearts. Only humility can
conquer the enemy of estrangement from almighty God. Yes, a
posture that kneels in submission to the eternal Sovereign, Jesus
Christ, is positioned to hear from heaven and be healed.

Our nation exhibits humility when we recognize a National
Day of Prayer and observe its solemnity in quiet reflection on
the roots of our religion. This day is more than symbolic of a
nation brought to its knees because of its neediness. It is a day
of dependency that sets the stage for the following days of the
year. A group of states that dedicate a day to Christ state that
they need a Savior for their sins. Prayer pronounces its desire for
God. Your life is a light for the Lord, so shine brightly for your
Savior Jesus. Pray He heals our land.

"I confess the sins we Israelites, including myself and my
father's family, have committed against you" (Nehemiah 1:6).

Related Readings: 1 Chronicles 16:11; Psalm 14:1; Isaiah 53:5;
Romans 1:21

UNLEARN TRUTHS

Do not conform to the pattern of this world, but be transformed by the renewing of your mind. Then you will be able to test and approve what God's will is—his good, pleasing and perfect will. Romans 12:2

———————

God calls His children to think anew—not like they did in the past with old prejudices and skewed perspectives—but with renewed thoughts captured by Christ. Like medical science that discovers new remedies for old illnesses, the Christian mind grows under God's influence. We love the Lord with our mind when we humbly unlearn untruths.

The mature follower of Christ learns to unlearn beliefs that are untrue. For example, the Bible does not teach: "God helps those who help themselves." Yet, because we hear it repeated multiple times without rebuttal, it begins to blend into our belief system. God helps those who die to themselves and who come alive by faith in Jesus Christ. Yes, the Lord wants us to work hard, but not as a substitute for our utter dependence on Him.

"We remember before our God and Father your work produced by faith, your labor prompted by love, and your endurance inspired by hope in our Lord Jesus Christ" (1 Thessalonians 1:3).

Related Readings: : Job 6:24; Psalm 119:15; 2 Corinthians 10:5; 2 Timothy 2:25-26

OPEN-MINDED

Then he opened their minds so they could understand the
Scriptures. Luke 24:45

————•••••————

Open-mindedness to God comes from God. Just as the Lord
inspired the writing of the Scriptures in the past, so He opens the
mind to understanding the Scriptures in the present. The Bible
says, "All scripture is given by inspiration of God…" (2 Timothy
3:16a). The longer you walk with Jesus, the more dearly you
love Him and more clearly you understand His Word. It is in a
close encounter with Christ that He applies truth to thinking that
leads to life transformation.

Therefore, make it a holy habit to daily huddle around Holy
Scripture in prayer and meditation. As a result, His Word becomes
a lamp to your feet and a light to your path (Psalm 119:105). Keep
a Bible at your desk so you can draw inspiration before you go
into an engaging meeting. Scripture is a solace for your soul, but
you need the Spirit to guide you into understanding and personal
application. Read the Bible for the purpose of conforming your
character to Christ's. Insight for others is helpful, but the first
step is your individual life change. Above all, ask Christ to open
your mind to the wisdom of His Word.

"The mind governed by the flesh is death, but the mind governed
by the Spirit is life and peace" (Romans 8:6).

Related Readings: Psalm 81:10; Isaiah 37:17; Acts 26:18;
Romans 8:9

TIMELY TRANSITIONS

When Israel came out of Egypt, the house of Jacob from a people of foreign tongue, Judah became God's sanctuary, Israel his dominion. Psalm 114:1-2, NIV84

Timely transitions are necessary for teaching trust in the Lord. Spiritually, they move a life from being shackled with sin to one freed up by faith in Christ. Following Jesus is a transition from distrust to trust—fear to faith—insecurity to security—selfishness to selflessness—hell to heaven—lost to found—isolation to community—getting to giving—scarcity living to abundant living.

We move from the darkness of deception into the light of His love. Obedience to God transitions us from the foreign tongue of faithless living to the Lord's familiar language of faith. So, trust the Lord, whether a transition feels forced or is a conscious choice. In either case, Christ is in control. Do not settle for a comfortable circumstance if God is calling you to what may feel like an uncomfortable opportunity. Grow and go with Jesus during timely transitions.

"You were taught, with regard to your former way of life, to put off your old self, which is being corrupted by its deceitful desires; to be made new in the attitude of your minds; and to put on the new self, created to be like God in true righteousness and holiness" (Ephesians 4:22-24).

Related Readings: Joshua 14:8; 2 Samuel 22:23; Hebrews 13:6

PRIDE'S DOWNFALL

But after Uzziah became powerful, his pride led to his downfall. He was unfaithful to the LORD his God, and entered the temple of the LORD to burn incense on the altar of incense. 2 Chronicles 26:16

Lust for power is as insidious as it sounds. It is a dysfunctional drive that demands blind loyalty with nothing in return. Power hungry leaders are insensitive and shortsighted as they take whatever means necessary to accomplish their egocentric ends. They become entangled in their own web of wanting more control and find themselves trapped in a morass of manipulation.

Power has built-in arrogance that needs to be confronted with honesty, humility, and truth. Moreover, it is unnatural for the spiritually minded to need power. They give it away to avoid greedily getting more. The devil used the promise of power to tempt Christ, however Jesus knew that Satan's temptation was a ploy to appeal to His pride (Matthew 4:8-10). Therefore, use power as an excuse for persistent prayer and honest feedback. Give it away—for then it loses its prideful control and you avoid an embarrassing downfall.

"For all those who exalt themselves will be humbled, and those who humble themselves will be exalted" (Luke 14:11).

Related Readings: Psalm 10:4; Proverbs 8:13; 11:12; Isaiah 2:11-17

TAKE PRIDE

I am talking to you Gentiles. Inasmuch as I am the apostle to the Gentiles, I take pride in my ministry. Romans 11:13

There is a good pride. It is a feeling of accomplishment when a job is well done. It knows God has placed you in a work environment or family that you are proud of, because they honor you, the Lord, and others with their lives. Bad pride brags and takes credit for good work, but good pride is grateful to God for the opportunity to represent Him well at work.

Take pride in your work, because it is a reflection of your relationship with Jesus. If your work is sloppy or incomplete, then you lose the moral high ground to speak to people about God. But, if you arrive early and stay late until the project is complete, then people want to learn why you are motivated to take such pride in doing your job with excellence. Good pride is being content as the person Christ has called you to be. The Lord expects you to take pride in yourself and take pride in being a servant of Jesus. Good pride gives God the glory.

"I have spoken to you with great frankness; I take great pride in you. I am greatly encouraged; in all our troubles my joy knows no bounds" (2 Corinthians 7:4).

Related Readings: 1 Corinthians 4:17; 2 Corinthians 5:12; Ephesians 2:10

SUSTAINABLE LIFESTYLE

Surely God is my help; the Lord is the one who sustains me.
Psalm 54:4

A lifestyle is sustainable when the Lord is the sustainer. Behind every sustainable life is dependence on a Savior: to help in time of need, to provide calm in a crisis, to give perspective when feeling pressure, and to slow someone down who is way too busy. The grace of God gives sustainability to a life paced by prayer and energized by faith in Jesus.

Are you involved in many good initiatives, only to find yourself unable to keep up with your commitments? Is your pace of life without margin—unable to really invest in those who need you the most? Indeed, it is extremely important to take periodic audits of our pace of life and make sure we make room for real relational investments. A life is unsustainable if it is always darting from one good deed to the next with no down time. A sustainable life has almighty God as its architect and belief in Jesus as its builder. He sustains those who regularly seek Him with a pure heart and a teachable mind. He helps the humble and lifts up those who worship Him in Spirit and in truth.

"The LORD sustains the humble but casts the wicked to the ground" (Psalm 147:6).

Related Readings: Job 36:19; Psalm 119:116, 175; 146:9; Isaiah 46:4; 50:4; 59:16

JOINED BY GOD

What therefore God has joined together, let no man separate.
Mark 10:9, NASB

Divorce is not an option for committed followers of Christ—it is omitted from their vocabulary. Yes, human frailty wants an out. It doesn't want to be uncomfortable or inconvenienced, but marital challenges are God's process of purging. Relational reconciliation within the bonds of marriage is a proving ground for all other relationships.

Marriage mandates focused fidelity and faith in God. It is not a relationship of convenience; rather, it's one of conviction. We cannot give up on our spouse, except in the case of adultery. But, even in unfaithfulness, their repentance and our forgiveness can heal the severance of trust and intimacy. Indeed, whatever God does is not to be taken lightly, for the Lord is in the marriage-making business. He joins a man and a woman together as a mirror of our relationship with Him—final and forever. Thus, see your marriage sealed by the Holy Spirit, never to be separated by man; so be hopeful by persevering. You were joined together in marriage by Jesus and for Jesus, not to be destroyed by man's decree of divorce. A lifetime of commitment is Christ's choice.

"'The man who hates and divorces his wife,' says the LORD, the God of Israel, 'does violence to the one he should protect,' says the LORD Almighty. So be on your guard, and do not be unfaithful" (Malachi 2:16).

Related Readings: Malachi 2:10; Matthew 5:31-32;
1 Corinthians 7:11-13

MAY 9

CARING CANDOR

Instead, speaking the truth in love, we will in all things grow
up into him who is the Head, that is, Christ.
Ephesians 4:15, NIV84

———————

Sometimes Christians can be too nice, because there are
unrealistic expectations of total harmony and complete happiness.
However, utopia doesn't happen until we get to heaven. In the
meantime, we are sinners in need of a Savior—we are saints who
struggle to get along from time to time. Healthy relationships
and authentic community flow freely when sharing from the
heart and communicating concerns with candor and care.

But unaddressed and unresolved issues will eventually come
out in sarcastic jabs or be concealed in angry apathy. So make
sure in your family and at work you create safe environments
for everyone to express how they really think and feel. Perhaps
you ask others to vent their frustrations after you have prayed
together. Prayer prepares your heart to give and receive truth
delivered in love. Hearts softened by prayer are sensitive to hear
Spirit-led speech. Become a bold vessel of truth—only after you
have gone boldly to God's throne of grace. Become empty of
yourself before you talk with others about themselves.

"For the ear tests words as the tongue tastes food" (Job 34:3).

Related Readings: Psalm 19:14; 55:21; Proverbs 12:18;
2 Corinthians 6:7

ATTENTIVE TO INSTRUCTION

They read from the Book of the Law of God, making it clear and giving the meaning so that the people understood what was being read. Nehemiah 8:8

The Lord God Almighty instructs individuals from His Word, the Bible. His gift of an instruction manual for living is necessary to know how to live life purposefully. If we wonder what is the wise thing to do, we look into the pages of Scripture and learn from those who made smart and foolish decisions. Yes, people who already experienced what we have not experienced can show us what to do and what not to do. The Bible is full of practical teachings that demand our keen attention.

So we learn, not to impress with our newfound information, but to humbly apply insights for living. We are not just moved by emotion, but we are moved to make Jesus Christ the Lord of our lives. We grow intensely attentive to the Holy Spirit's work the more we grow in understanding of Scripture. Instruction frees us from ignorant assumptions.

"Instruct the wise and they will be wiser still; teach the righteous and they will add to their learning. The fear of the LORD is the beginning of wisdom, and knowledge of the Holy One is understanding" (Proverbs 9:9-10).

"You gave your good Spirit to instruct them" (Nehemiah 9:20a).

Related Readings: Psalm 25:12; 32:8; Daniel 11:33; Romans 15:14; 1 Corinthians 2:12-16

BEST PARENTAL GIFT

However, each one of you also must love his wife as he loves
himself, and the wife must respect her husband.
Ephesians 5:33

Outside of a personal faith in Christ, the best gift a parent can
give his child is a healthy marriage. This secure and stable
environment gives little ones a large amount of peace. A husband
and wife who learn to love and respect one another create a
culture of calm in their family. Why would a child want to
wander from a home where acceptance is assured? A marriage
marked by service to each other motivates children to do the
same.

We have to remind ourselves as a father and mother that we
were first a husband and a wife. Neglect of our marriage
responsibilities puts additional pressure on our roles as dad and
mom. Productive parenting flows from a maturing marriage.
So, effective parents wisely ask, "How am I investing in my
marriage?" "Is it time to get away, before we drift away?"
Parents who collaborate with Christ and one another win their
child's heart.

"As a young man marries a young woman, so will your Builder
marry you; as a bridegroom rejoices over his bride, so will your
God rejoice over you" (Isaiah 62:5).

Related Readings: Proverbs 1:8; Matthew 19:10;
1 Corinthians 7:28; Philippians 4:8-9

PARENTAL PRAYERS

"**I** prayed for this child, and the LORD has granted me what I asked of him. So now I give him to the LORD. For his whole life he will be given over to the LORD." And he worshiped the LORD there. 1 Samuel 1:27-28

A parent's prayers for their child produce the best results: both in the short-term and the long-term. Smart prayers include their salvation, future spouse, and a sensitive heart to the Spirit's leading. Faith-focused prayers penetrate pride, dissolve selfishness, and give wisdom. Satan flees in the face of just prayers. Spiritual battles rage for the family's soul, and wise are the parents who engage in a prayer offensive.

Indeed, when we pray with our spouse, our own hearts are warmed to God, our children, and to each other. There is a mutually compounding benefit when you make prayer an investment priority for your progeny. A child who knows he or she is prayed for by their dad and mom are confident they are cared about. We build our son's or daughter's self-esteem when we petition heaven on their behalf. Prayer produces confidence and wisdom.

"I have not stopped giving thanks for you, remembering you in my prayers. I keep asking that the God of our Lord Jesus Christ, the glorious Father, may give you the Spirit of wisdom and revelation, so that you may know him better" (Ephesians 1:16-17).

Related Readings: Genesis 25:21; 1 Chronicles 5:20; Colossians 4:12; 2 Thessalonians 3:2

A GRANDMOTHER'S GIFT

I am reminded of your sincere faith, which first lived in your grandmother Lois and in your mother Eunice and, I am persuaded, now lives in you also. 2 Timothy 1:5

Every God-fearing grandmother can give the gift of faith to her grandchildren. It is a gift that keeps giving to those in the path of its influence. Like the ripple effect of a stone released onto the surface of calm water, so faith deposited in tender hearts swells to touch other souls. A grandmother's position garners trust for the purpose of giving Christ's love. Her unique role is a righteous responsibility that reaps faith's fruit in her child's children.

So, wise are we as grandparents to keep growing in grace and wisdom. Our seasoned season of life does not guarantee that we qualify as wise mentors; hence, we keep learning so we can have fresh experiences of God's faithfulness. Once we receive from our heavenly Father, grandmothers and grandfathers have the most to give. Our daily walk with Jesus gives us grace to give to others. Thus, we make time for grandchildren. Intentionally pray for ways to walk with your grandchildren in fun and faith. Your gift of love and laughter attracts them to Jesus!

"When Abram was ninety-nine years old, the LORD appeared to him and said, 'I am God Almighty; walk before me faithfully and be blameless'" (Genesis 17:1).

Related Readings: Deuteronomy 5:33; Joshua 14:9; Isaiah 2:5; Zechariah 3:7

A MOTHER'S LOVE

As apostles of Christ we could have been a burden to you, but we were gentle among you, like a mother caring for her little children. 1 Thessalonians 2:6b-7, NIV84

A mother's love reflects the love of the Lord, deep in its capacity and generous in its application. She awakens in the middle of the night to nurse a hungry infant or care for a sick child. Her intuition injects love at points of pain and in situations that require extensive encouragement. A mother's love lingers long in conversation and understands with her sensitive heart. She loves, because Christ's love compels her to love like Him.

Moreover, a mother's love is loyal and longstanding. A child may be in trouble, but Mom is always close by, full of compassion and acceptance. Her love can be blind in its loyalty, but her offspring never doubt where they are welcome. Jesus was rejected by angry, jealous men and abandoned by His closest friends, but His mother was waiting with Him to the bitter end, "Near the cross of Jesus stood his mother…" (John 19:25a). A mother's love reflects the gentle way in which God relates to His children. He calls her and us to love and lead like Jesus.

"God's servant must not be argumentative, but a gentle listener and a teacher who keeps cool, working firmly but patiently with those who refuse to obey" (2 Timothy 2:24, The Message).

Related Readings: Genesis 47:12; Ruth 4:16; John 21:15-17; James 3:17

HUMILITY PRECEDES WISDOM

When pride comes, then comes disgrace, but with humility comes wisdom. Proverbs 11:2

The mind and the heart require humble preparation before they can receive wisdom and process it properly. Otherwise, without the influence of humility, knowledge promotes prideful thinking and hardens the heart. Information can increase intelligence, but it only creates educated fools— unless a heart of humility rejects any attitude of superiority.

Humility hunts down arrogance and, like a skilled trapper, locks it up in a protective cage of prayer and praise to Christ. It's very difficult for pride to reproduce itself in an environment full of faith in God and empty of ego and self—it shrivels up for lack of attention. We are positioned to receive wisdom when humility harnesses our hearts for Him. When we enter into the yoke of Jesus, His gentleness and meekness rub off on us. Resist the temptation to fill your mind with information without immersing your heart in humility. The idol of being awed by intelligence competes with your reverence for God. The Lord grows wisdom in a humble heart and teachable mind—so stay true to both.

"Take my yoke upon you and learn from me, for I am gentle and humble in heart, and you will find rest for your souls" (Matthew 11:29).

Related Readings: Proverbs 2:2-10; 7:4; Ecclesiastes 2:3; Isaiah 10:13; Luke 2:40

EXCHANGED LIFE

You were taught, with regard to your former way of life, to put off your old self… and to put on the new self, created to be like God. Ephesians 4:21b, 24

There is a great exchange that takes place when a person places their faith in Jesus Christ. Their old way of living is replaced with living for the Lord. Their old way of thinking is replaced with thinking on the truth of Jesus. Their old way of speaking is replaced with speech sprinkled with the grace of God. The old has passed, the new has come.

The life of Christ becomes the life of the follower of Christ. No longer are we led down the dead end road of unrighteousness, but we are set free to journey down the less traveled road of righteousness. We give up what we could not keep, our life on earth, in exchange for what we can keep, eternal life in heaven. To a watching world it seems foolish to give up for God, but what we get from God—forgiveness, peace and love—is true life. He wants your troubled heart in exchange for His tender heart.

"Since, then, you have been raised with Christ, set your hearts on things above, where Christ is, seated at the right hand of God. Set your minds on things above, not on earthly things" (Colossians 3:1-2).

Related Readings: John 17:3; Romans 5:12-21; Galatians 2:20; 1 John 5:13; 2 Timothy 1:9-10

ETERNAL REWARDS

He regarded disgrace for the sake of Christ as of greater value than the treasures of Egypt, because he was looking ahead to his reward. Hebrews 11:26

———◆———

Eternal rewards are based on a disciple's effort on earth. A believer who ignores their spiritual opportunities and obligations will miss out on their heavenly Father's affirmation and remuneration. But those sober saints who take seriously their Savior's expectations will enter into the joy of their Master. Christ rewards obedience to Him.

Rewards in heaven are meant to be a godly motivation. Yes, our first response is to serve Jesus out of love and our overflowing gratitude for His goodness and grace. And it is wise to fear the Lord and allow our holy awe of the Almighty to be foundational for our life of faith and works. But there is an end in mind. Jesus wants His children to be compelled in their daily devotion to anticipate His generous gifts. Resist—even reject—rewards from the culture so you are positioned to receive Christ's rewards. Remain faithful to God's call and look forward to His reward.

"Look, I am coming soon! My reward is with me, and I will give to each person according to what they have done" (Revelation 22:12).

Related Readings: Amos 6:1-7; Isaiah 54:2; 2 Peter 1:3; Revelation 2:7-10

DISCIPLINED EXERCISE

I discipline my body like an athlete, training it to do what it should. 1 Corinthians 9:27a, NLT

―――――•◆•―――――

For the most part, Jesus walked everywhere He went; He had built-in exercise in His daily routine. Indeed, the comforts of modern society are actually in conflict with creating an exercise regimen. Discretionary time is filled with less important activities to the detriment of keeping the body in condition to be a blessing and not a burden.

For example, when someone stays up late to watch television, they typically sleep later the next day. If morning is the best time to walk, run, lift weights, or engage in aerobics, then the probability of exercise is much lower. A disciplined life understands the need to calendar activities that compliment one another. Disciplined exercise plans ahead.

There are those who turn exercise into an idol and miss the point of good health as an offering to Jesus Christ. It is not for vainglory that we get into shape; rather, it is for the glory of God. So, point people to Jesus as you prepare His earthly temple for a life of love and worship. Yes, exercise for eternal purposes.

"No discipline seems pleasant at the time, but painful. Later on, however, it produces a harvest of righteousness and peace for those who have been trained by it" (Hebrews 12:11).

Related Readings: Daniel 1:5; Proverbs 5:23; 1 Timothy 4:8; Titus 1:8

MODEL THE WAY

You became imitators of us and of the Lord, for you welcomed the message in the midst of severe suffering with the joy given by the Holy Spirit. 1 Thessalonians 1:6

Parents are in a unique position to model the way for living to their children. The role of father and mother carries a humbling responsibility to be a parent worth following. Whether parents like it or not, they are the Lord's authority over their little ones. It's imperative they take seriously their obligation to steward well their parental roles. What a privilege to present Christ to our progeny in our speech, actions, and attitude. Indeed, our words carry weight when our actions align with almighty God's expectations.

The Lord looks for parents to depend on Him for wisdom and direction—it plants the same seeds of dependence on God in the heart of a child at home. A parent regularly prays for Christ's provision; thus, the son or daughter desires to do the same. God will give you the grace to model for your children a life of love and forgiveness. Pray with them and for them to walk in the truth while trusting in the Lord. Do not underestimate the power of your influence. You are God's representative of righteousness to their tender hearts. Be a compelling example for Christ.

"Listen, my sons, to a father's instruction; pay attention and gain understanding" (Proverbs 4:1).

Related Readings: Isaiah 38:19; Jeremiah 32:18; Malachi 4:6; Luke 2:27

DISTANT GOD

O God, do not remain silent; do not turn a deaf ear, do not stand aloof, O God. Psalm 83:1

Sometimes the Lord seems a million miles away; prayers go unanswered, loneliness assaults the heart and fear grips the mind. His arm is not shortened; He is able to save. However, at times His tender touch cannot be felt with absent faith. Indeed, faith can become AWOL (missing) for any sincere child of God. It's when the feelings of abandonment absorb the soul that a soul must stay abandoned to its Savior Jesus. Has a temporary tempest in your trust caused you to tread lightly into the Lord's presence? Are you scared?

Almighty God is the one who causes whirling winds to cease and hurricane gales to go silent. What we cannot control, He can. What we cannot understand, He does. When we cannot trust, He gives us the faith, hope, and peace in Christ to carry on. Perhaps you ask effective prayer warriors to intercede on your behalf for intimacy with the Almighty. Do not be embarrassed that the Lord feels absent; instead, ask His children to come alongside you for support and encouragement. Enjoy His presence while you are in their presence.

"I have told you these things, so that in me you may have peace. In this world you will have trouble. But take heart! I have overcome the world" (John 16:33).

Related Readings: Deuteronomy 31:6-8; Psalm 63:1; 139:7-10; Romans 8:37-39

STAY PUT

Remain in me, as I also remain in you. No branch can bear
fruit by itself; it must remain in the vine. Neither can you bear
fruit unless you remain in me. John 15:4

What does it mean to remain in Jesus? Remain is to stay
behind with Jesus and not run ahead of Him. Unbridled zeal
can get sideways with what the Spirit wants to accomplish.
But, a believer bridled by the Holy Spirit has been with Jesus
in focused abiding. His presence is pregnant with possibilities
within an unhurried heart.

Our heavenly Father desires for us to be present in His presence.
In humility, we stand in awe with the One who gave His all.
When we stay put at the feet of our Savior Jesus, we position
ourselves to listen and learn from our Lord. We remain in Him,
so we can maintain our Master's grace and glory. Remaining in
Christ leads you to remain true to the Lord. There is a righteous
resolve that flows from faithful abiding. You remain in His love
and love flows from your life. You remain in His peace, and
peace punctuates your presence. You remain in Christ, and you
become like Christ. So, stay put with your Savior!

"If you keep my commands, you will remain in my love, just
as I have kept my Father's commands and remain in his love"
(John 15:10).

Related Readings: Psalm 38:15; 1 John 2:27; 1 John 3:9;
Revelation 2:13

POOR CHOICES

Is it not to share your food with the hungry and to provide the poor wanderer with shelter—when you see the naked, to clothe him, and not to turn away from your own flesh and blood?
Isaiah 58:7, NIV84

———————◆◆◆———————

Some of the least are overlooked because some smell, some are sick, and some are surly. It may be unpleasant to uncover and understand the needs of those in severe poverty, but believers in Jesus are called to care for the poor in His name. Love looks for ways to eradicate poverty, not just expedience that provides temporary relief. Chronic hunger and health problems need healthy, long-term solutions. Perhaps you partner with people with a common passion to care for the poor. Be the best steward by seeking prayerful collaboration with ministries already embedded in the community. Care for the poor at the point of their most basic needs.

So, begin to pray for the underprivileged, the uneducated, the under-resourced, and the unredeemed. Be careful how you pray, as the Lord may use you to become an answer to your own prayers. Pray God opens doors for you and your family to serve the poor and needy. Love unconditionally those cast out by the culture. Share Jesus and they will know you are His disciples by your lovingkindness.

"By this everyone will know that you are my disciples, if you love one another" (John 13:35).

Related Readings: Proverbs 29:7; Mark 10:21; John 12:6; 1 Corinthians 13:3; James 2:5

HARVEST OF HAPPINESS

When the LORD brought back the captives to Zion, we were like men who dreamed. Our mouths were filled with laughter, our tongues with songs of joy. Psalm 126:1-2a, NIV84

———————◄●●►————————

Happiness is found in our heavenly Father. It comes from seeing the big picture of where He has brought us to where He is taking us. If happiness were contingent on cash and comfort, then the modern world would be one laughing lot. However, without heaven as the end goal, contemporary conveniences actually work against authentic happiness. Stuff without our Savior becomes seductive and controlling for its own cause.

But joy fills our heart when we think of the Lord's deliverance from our captivity in Christless living into a life of significance. Happiness is the result of giving, not getting; of serving, not being served; and from leading people into a growing relationship with Jesus Christ. There is a harvest of happiness waiting as you sow the seeds of selfless service, unconditional love, immediate forgiveness, generous giving, abundant gratitude, and persistent prayer on behalf of your Savior Jesus. Righteous living reaps a grace-filled harvest of happiness.

"Sow for yourselves righteousness, reap the fruit of unfailing love, and break up your unplowed ground; for it is time to seek the LORD, until He comes and showers righteousness on you" (Hosea 10:12, NIV84).

Related Readings: Proverbs 15:30; Ecclesiastes 11:9; 1 Thessalonians 1:6; 2 John 1:4

NOT LOSE HEART

For the one who sows to his own flesh shall from the flesh reap corruption, but the one who sows to the Spirit shall from the Spirit reap eternal life. And let us not lose heart in doing good, for in due time we shall reap if we do not grow weary.
Galatians 6:8-9, NASB

We lose heart when we linger too long in our own strength instead of the Lord's. The heart cannot handle a ministry or work that features the flesh juxtaposed to a life submitted to and scripted by the Holy Spirit. Living in the flesh flushes out faith and replaces it with fatigue, frustration, and fear. Spirit-filled living on the other hand, harnesses the resources of heaven as it taps into the treasure troves of God's mercy and grace. Prayer is the Lord's potent prescription for not losing heart. Petitioning God allows us to process faulty thinking, replacing it with insights from the Almighty, and to persevere.

You grow strong and lose your weariness when your prayers to God propel you forward in mercy. You lose heart when you stop giving away your heart. Yes, it is a risk to love well, but you gain God's "well done" and receive a heart of grace and gratitude. You gain a full heart by emptying your heart.

"At all times they ought to pray and not to lose heart" (Luke 18:1b, NASB).

Related Readings: Matthew 5:16; 1 Timothy 2:10; 5:10; Hebrews 10:24; 1 Peter 2:12

BE PRESENT

When he was at the table with them, he took bread, gave thanks, broke it and began to give it to them. Then their eyes were opened and they recognized him, and he disappeared from his sight. They asked each other, "Were not our hearts burning within us while he talked with us on the road and opened the Scriptures to us?" Luke 24:30-32

As we walk with Jesus day in and day out, it's easy to take Him for granted. He travels with His children, but are we always aware that He is there? We can always find Him in the pages of Scripture, where our Lord Jesus shows Himself in all His glory. The written Word of God ignites our faith, and the Spirit illumines our mind and heart to see Christ.

It is scary to think the Lord may be speaking in the now, but our preoccupation with the past or future can cause us to miss His heart. Indeed, God speaks in the present what He wants us to know now. He is with His children even when we are unaware. To behold His glory requires living in the moment with Him by faith. So, learn to practice His presence in the middle of traffic or in the pressure of a deadline. Listen to the Lord before you speak for the Lord.

"I was filled with delight day after day, rejoicing always in his presence" (Proverbs 8:30b).

Related Readings: Psalm 31:20; 51:11; Hosea 6:2; 1 John 3:19

HEART SICK

Have compassion on me, LORD, for I am weak. Heal me, LORD, for my bones are in agony. I am sick at heart. How long, O LORD, until you restore me? Return, O LORD, and rescue me. Save me because of your unfailing love.
Psalm 6:2-4, NLT

The human heart is fragile and can easily fracture under the weight of disappointment and fear. Questions lurk in the background waiting to assault someone's confidence: Am I good enough? Am I attractive enough? Am I smart enough? Am I wealthy enough? Am I secure enough? Am I mature enough? Outside of Christ there is never enough.

We struggle with these insecurities when we suffer rejection from those we thought accepted us. Our trust is tortured when we experience severe relational letdown. After all we ask, "Wasn't this the one I was supposed to marry?" Or "Why do we have to sell our dream home after all these years of hard work?" Heart sickness depletes our energy. Let go of the pain of rejection and forgive the one who turned his back on you. Turn your eyes upon Jesus and look to His healing hand. Your sick heart needs the reassuring support from your sympathizing Savior. Hope heals.

"And hope does not put us to shame, because God's love has been poured out into our hearts through the Holy Spirit, who has been given to us" (Romans 5:5).

Related Readings: Lamentations 5:17; Psalm 31:24; 62:10; Acts 2:26; Ephesians 1:18

GREAT MERCY

For His merciful kindness is great toward us: and the truth of
the Lord endureth forever. Praise ye the Lord.
Psalm 117:2, KJV

The mercy of the Lord reaches out to the vilest sinner. The breadth
of His grace has no boundaries; therefore, we are compelled to
erupt in gratitude to God. His mercy encompasses the basest evil
and is grander than the greatest offense. The Lord's mercy fails
not; daily, like freshly baked bread, it is warm and appetizing to
all who partake.

Mercy is twice blessed; it blesses him that gives and him that
takes (Shakespeare). God's mercy is foundational for all our
comfort, and His truth is fundamental for all our hope. It is our
mandate from God to be merciful to mankind—it makes us more
like Jesus. In Christ Jesus, God has shown us great merciful
kindness. He made us alive in Christ.

So, enjoy the benefits of mercy: forgiveness, kindness,
benevolence, acceptance, healing, peace of mind, and
reconciliation. Mercy is your friend who does not seek to make
enemies. Be merciful as your heavenly Father is merciful, and
you will experience mercy. By God's grace righteous actions
can be reciprocated, so be merciful for Christ's sake.

"Be merciful, just as your Father is merciful" (Luke 6:36).

Related Readings: Deuteronomy 4:31; Daniel 9:9; Matthew
5:7; Hebrews 2:17; Jude 1:22

TODAY'S GIFT

This is the day the LORD has made; let us rejoice and be glad in it. Psalm 118:24, NIV84

Everyday is a new gift from God, created by Him and for Him. The dawning of each day displays the light and love of the Lord's creation. Christians celebrate Sunday, the first day of the week, as a reminder of the Almighty's achievements, namely the resurrection of Christ. However, the workweek does not need to be wasted on worldly agendas alone.

Seize today as a trust from almighty God. Steward it with a sense of divine destiny. Perhaps you pray over a blank sheet of paper (or computer screen), and then list by faith how you believe the Lord wants you to focus your time. Follow through with the difficult assignments first, execute some easy ones, and then trust God and others with the tasks out of your immediate control. Today has enough time for you to accomplish His agenda.

Today is the only day you have to live, learn, and come alive. Seize the day for your Savior Jesus and watch Him do a wonderful work of grace. Progress comes in God's timing, in His way. A day dedicated to Christ has more possibilities than a thousand days unrecognized as a gift from heaven. Unwrap God's gift of today and worship the giver.

"Teach us to number our days, that we may gain a heart of wisdom" (Psalm 90:12).

Related Readings: Genesis 24:12; Deuteronomy 11:13; Proverbs 22:19; 1 Timothy 3:16

WISE COMPANION

Walk with the wise and become wise, for a companion of fools suffers harm. Proverbs 13:20

What does it mean to have quality of life? Good health? Harmony at home? A happy heart? Financial security? Freedom of speech and worship? A fulfilling career? Grateful and content children? A meaningful marriage? A life of significance? Peace with God? These elements, and more, make up a life worth living—a quality life.

The quality of our life is determined by the quality of our relationships. Those we spend time with are those we emulate. If we spend time with those wise in their finances, and if we pay attention, we can become wise in our finances. If we are intentional in our faith, we will worship with those of great faith. Our life is a reflection of our relationships.

Be careful not to excuse bad behavior because you are trying to relate to questionable company. Draw a line far away from eroding your character's credibility. You can influence others for good, without being bad. In some situations, what you don't do defines you more than what you do. Use your integrity to model faithfulness not foolishness. Stand for what's right, when others won't.

"Do not be misled: 'Bad company corrupts good character'" (1 Corinthians 15:33).

Related Readings: Psalm 56:13; 2 Corinthians 6:14; Philippians 2:1-4; 1 John 1:7

MAY 30

LOVE HER

Under three things the earth trembles, under four it cannot bear
up… an unloved woman who is married.
Proverbs 30:21, 23a, NIV84

———◆———

What does a woman long for from her husband? Simply love.
A husband's love is like a fresh breath from heaven for a wife
who feels vulnerable and at times, fearful. His love is a rock of
refuge after she reels from a relational conflict at work, church,
or from another family member. The love of her husband goes
a long way in satisfying that deep desire of a woman to love
and be loved. Husbands, a gracious woman is not to be taken
advantage of or to be taken for granted. Instead, thank God for
a wife who wants to please the Lord and serve her family.

When was the last time you loved your bride in a way that
she wanted you to love her, in a way that only you can love
her? By God's grace, love her by protecting her. Love her by
trusting her. Love her by giving her encouragement and hope.
And always love her through the good times and the bad times.
Love her with your words, love her with your time, and love her
with gifts and kind words. A wife loved well by her husband is
beautiful to behold—she is a trophy of God's grace.

"His banner over me is love" (Song of Solomon 2:4b,
NIV84).

Related Readings: Ecclesiastes 9:9; Hosea 3:1; 1 Corinthians
13; Ephesians 5:25-26

RESPECT HIM

The wife must respect her husband. Ephesians 5:33b

————◆◆◆◆————

Respect for a husband is like love for a wife. It is a catalyst for his confidence and encouragement to fulfill his role as provider and leader. Most men question their ability to be everything they need to be for their family. But, insecurities become insignificant in a home where a husband feels respect. A wife's support energizes her man like jet fuel to a booster rocket. Husbands need the respect and support of their wives. Of course it works both ways—the wife needs to feel the respect and support of her husband.

Nonetheless, respect is huge for a man. A God-fearing husband knows the Lord has placed him in a position of leadership. It is overwhelming sometimes to feel squeezed from the pressures of life. The last thing a husband needs to feel is distance or distrust from his wife. Her spousal support may be the only thing that is preventing him from giving up. So, trust him to lead—even when it means he fails. God will pick him up and grow him up. Your respect cultivates the heart of your husband to love you well. By God's grace, give him great respect.

"Give to everyone what you owe them: If you owe taxes, pay taxes; if revenue, then revenue; if respect, then respect; if honor, then honor" (Romans 13:7).

Related Readings: Deuteronomy 1:15; Proverbs 31:23; Luke 11:43; 1 Timothy 3:2-4

JUNE

A gentle answer turns away wrath,
but a harsh word stirs up anger.

Proverbs 15:1

CULTURE OF FAITH

"Choose for yourselves this day whom you will serve... But as for me and my household, we will serve the LORD."
Joshua 24:15

Is there enough evidence in your home for you to be convicted of following Jesus Christ? This is a choice that God gives us, a choice to center our home around faith or a facade. What happens behind the doors of your home? Is your home an incubator for faith? Indeed, your ministry begins at home. When your faith works at home, you have the credibility to export it to other environments. It is your laboratory for living.

This does not mean you are without problems, conflicts, and challenges at home. On the contrary, it is when your faith sustains you through family difficulties that it becomes a compelling reason for others to follow Christ. As the spiritual leader of your home you may ask, "How am I to lead?" Perhaps you read a chapter in Proverbs over dinner. Pray with your spouse. Abstain from media screens one night a week for 30 minutes in order to discuss God's Word or act out a Bible story in a play; then pray for one another. Teach your children to pray for the sick, the lost, and the hurting. Model for them the joy of giving and serving. Seek daily to facilitate faith in your home. Pray like Jesus...

"Give us each day our daily bread" (Luke 11:3).

Related Readings: Genesis 18:19; 2 Kings 23:24; John 4:53; Acts 18:18

BLAMELESS BEHAVIOR

Blessed are they whose ways are blameless, who walk according to the law of the LORD. Psalm 119:1, NIV98

Christians aspire to a higher standard of behavior, as outlined in Holy Scripture. There is an eternal expectation woven into their earthly activities. It is not a cold and dry decision to a lifeless existence; on the contrary, it is an adventurous commitment to Christ's life transforming their lives from the inside out. Blameless does not mean we are always perfect, but it does mean heaven does not blush because of our behavior.

It means in our struggles people see us cling to Christ our Savior. It is a pattern of living that is quick to confess sin and, by God's grace, produces fruit that remains. Blameless behavior is accountable to clear and conservative boundaries around its blind spots of pride and self-destructive proclivities. There is a heightened awareness of the Almighty's attributes of holiness and love. It is a relentless resolve to righteousness that leads to reward on earth and in heaven. Above all, blameless behavior begins and ends with walking according to the law of the Lord.

"I have been blameless before him and have kept myself from sin" (2 Samuel 22:24).

Related Readings: Job 1:8; Psalm 37:18; Proverbs 2:7; 28:6; Ephesians 1:4; Revelation 14:5

JUNE 3

DISTRESS CALL

I call on the LORD in my distress, and he answers me.
Psalm 120:1

Some people die a thousand deaths of distress, allowing it to highjack their hope. It may be the material distress of overwhelming financial pressures. It may be physical distress of a body that is accelerating down a path of pain and disease. Relational distress can be traumatic and dramatic—couples can feel confined to a cycle of confusion and cynicism. The rough edge of a cruel tongue can sting and sabotage your quiet confidence.

So what are the next steps when you or someone you love is drowning in distress? Some people want to discuss their distress and accept help willingly. Others struggle to preserve their independence and behave, at least outwardly, as if nothing is wrong. Distress can define you as having a humble dependency on God, or it can drive you into a shell of self-pity. It is a facilitation of faith that provides the best benefits. His Holy Spirit assures you that He cares. He is attentive to every detail of your distress, so rest in His reassurance and let your soul be secure. Yes, use distress to enjoy your dependency on God.

"David was greatly distressed because the men were talking of stoning him; each one was bitter in spirit because of his sons and daughters. But David found strength in the LORD his God" (1 Samuel 30:6).

Related Readings: 2 Samuel 22:7; 2 Chronicles 15:4; Psalm 4:1; Mark 14:33; 2 Corinthians 2:4

162

BUILT BY GOD

Unless the LORD builds the house, its builders labor in vain.
Psalm 127:1a, NIV98

The Lord does not build shabby structures. What He touches becomes a testimony to His greatness. Relationships built on Jesus Christ flourish because He becomes the reference point for love. An organization or a home with the values of Jesus woven throughout create a cultural fabric of excellence. A life structured by its Savior is able to withstand the trials, tribulations and successes of society.

Is the Almighty the architect of your endeavors? If not, it is a vain business model. Without the Lord's blessing you will lose your way and, eventually, the will to continue. Sometimes working harder only drives you further from heaven's help. This is especially true during difficult days. So take an extended time to fast and pray for the Lord's leading. Make sure your efforts are united under God to execute excellent outcomes. Adversity exposes inefficiencies, like light reveals termite-infested damage to the dark places in a house. So, replace confusion with a clear mission. Build on the foundation of faith in God, and pray for the Lord's plan to be preeminent.

"The rain came down, the streams rose, and the winds blew and beat against that house; yet it did not fall, because it had its foundation on the rock" (Matthew 7:25).

Related Readings: Amos 9:6; Haggai 1:8; Luke 6:46-49; Ephesians 2:21

CUT FREE

But the LORD is righteous; he has cut me free from the cords
of the wicked. Psalm 129:4

———————◆◆◆———————

Christ cuts us free from the cords of wicked oppressors. It may
seem like the wicked have won at times, but this is the testing
of our trust. The obstinate may be an tool of God's discipline to
break our pride and smooth the edges of our ego. Then we can
see those who oppose righteous ways as an instrument of the
Lord to instruct us in how to live by faith.

You may have a family member whose faith is a facade. If
so, serve them with authentic and unselfish living. Pray their
pretentious life will lose its appeal, and they will be cut free
from a caricature of Christian living. We have been cut free by
Christ, freed to serve Him and others. Does a secret sin hold
you back from enjoying all that Jesus has to give you? If so,
seek out His forgiveness and healing. Submerge yourself in the
security and accountability of other Christ followers. You can
be unencumbered by earthly weights that hold you down like a
helium balloon released from its ties to the ground. Go to God,
receive His freeing grace!

"But now that you have been set free from sin and have become
slaves of God, the benefit you reap leads to holiness, and the
result is eternal life" (Romans 6:22).

Related Readings: Acts 13:39; Romans 6:7-20; Hebrews 9:15;
Revelation 1:5

CLEAN SLATE

If you, O LORD, keep a record of sins, O Lord, who could stand? But with you there is forgiveness; therefore you are feared. Psalm 130:3-4, NIV84

———————

With our Savior Jesus there is a clean slate when we bring our sin to the cross. God placed our sin on His Son for our salvation. Sinfully exposed, we are at the mercy of almighty God. His holiness helps us better understand our helplessness outside of heaven. However, our King Jesus extends a full pardon to all who believe. Forgiveness is at the forefront of our heavenly Father's thinking. The power of pardon is permanent with God, and He is ready to forgive in an instant.

So go to God with guilt, and leave lust and lies with Him. Invite the grace of God to govern your actions and attitudes. Freed-up people free others to enjoy the fruits of forgiveness. Since Christ has given you a clean slate, you can extend a clean slate to those who have slighted you. Wipe clean the slate of sin with the grace of God that has been given to you, and watch Him, by faith, paint a beautiful canvas of forgiveness and love. You can start over with someone, because your Savior Jesus believes in second chances.

"Bear with each other and forgive whatever grievances you may have against one another. Forgive as the Lord forgave you" (Colossians 3:13, NIV84).

Related Readings: 1 Corinthians 13:5; Hebrews 10:22; 2 Timothy 1:9

STILLED AND QUIETED

But I have stilled and quieted my soul; like a weaned child
with its mother, like a weaned child is my soul within me.
Psalm 131:2, NIV84

———————◆◆◆———————

The raging waves of the world's worries crash against the shore of
our soul. At work it may be missed deadlines, or mismanagement
of money. At home it may be miscommunication, or a monster
of a child. At school it may be the misconduct of others, or the
misfortune of feeling alone. Life is loud, and sometimes its
deafening tones drown out our trust in God. Only in silence can
our soul be resuscitated by our Savior Jesus. He works wonders
when we wait before Him. We are clamorous without Christ, but
by grace our soul is subdued and soothed.

Calm and contentment come forth by faith, when we are stilled
and quieted before Christ like a weaned child. Therefore, by
God's grace remain childlike in your faith and character. Keep
your heart humble and honest under heaven's hope. Like a little
one looks to her mother for comfort and security, look to your
Savior Jesus for His quiet confidence and strength. A heart kept
by Christ, lives for Christ. Yes, settle your soul in stillness and
solitude with Jesus.

"As a mother comforts her child, so will I comfort you; and you
will be comforted over Jerusalem" (Isaiah 66:13).

Related Readings: Job 6:24; Psalm 23:2; Isaiah 30:15;
Mark 6:31; 1 Thessalonians 4:11

HARDSHIPS ENDURED

No LORD, remember David and all the hardships he endured.
Psalm 132:1, NIV84

Hardships are meant to point us to heaven. It is our hope in heaven that helps us through turbulent times. Yes, it can try our trust in the Lord, but He is our one constant support. The foundation of circumstances may shift under our feet from economic earthquakes, but these temporal tremors need not distract our focus on the eternal. Christ does not change. His desire is to change us into becoming more like Him. Jesus is our dependable refuge.

In our pain it is OK to plead with God for relief, and to remember the sufferings of His Son Jesus on our behalf. It's by the merit of Christ's afflictions and death that we are able to approach the Lord for healing and hope. Moreover, see hardships as heaven's hammer to chip away pride, ego, false beliefs, and bad behavior. We are all a work in progress in need of the Lord's loving conviction. You can endure a downturn in financial fortune because your security is in your Savior, not your net worth. You will endure this bruising of your reputation because, like Jesus, you are a person of "no reputation" (Philippians 2:7, KJV).

"But he was wounded for our transgressions, he was bruised for our iniquities: the chastisement of our peace was upon him; and with his stripes we are healed" (Isaiah 53:5, KJV).

Related Readings: Psalm 69:7-10; Proverbs 18:14;
1 Corinthians 10:13; Revelation 2:3

JUNE 9

GOD IS GREAT

But may all who seek you rejoice and be glad in you; may those who long for your saving help always say, "The Lord is great!" Psalm 40:16

God is great. He is greater than the human mind can conceive. Great is His faithfulness, for His mercies are new every morning. Great is His love, for it crosses all cultures and languages to communicate hope and forgiveness. Great is His salvation, for it frees adolescents from the shadow of sin's influence and rescues adults from the snares of evil's deception.

God is great in the beauty of His holiness. His awe invites reverence and respect that can only bow in the presence of greatness. The grandeur of His glory grips a humble heart and fills it with His grace. God's greatness goes before those who trust and seek Him. It is in the shadow of His greatness that we feel His presence and are able to persevere.

Our great God infuses our faith with greatness. Greatness is gained when influenced by greatness. Indeed, Jesus described greatness as being a servant to all. The greatest one who ever lived, modeled greatness by His humble service. So, seek out those who serve and learn from them—then serve your great God. Yes, the Lord is great!

"The greatest among you will be your servant" (Matthew 23:11).

Related Readings: Job 36:26; Psalm 48:1; 95:3; 1 John 5:9; Revelation 11:17

LIVE IN UNITY

How good and pleasant it is when brothers live together in unity… For there the Lord bestows his blessing, even life forevermore. Psalm 133:1, 3b, NIV84

———◆———

It is good and pleasant to live in unity. It is bad and unpleasant to live in disunity. Unity is Christ-centered. Disunity is man-centered. Unity talks with others. Disunity talks about others. Unity is productive. Disunity is destructive. Unity prays to God. Disunity plays with God. Unity is the place where God's blessings are bestowed. We are in a position to be blessed by the Lord when we are unified around His will.

Envy and agendas are set aside for the greater good of the whole. Fear is marginalized because the focus is on faith in our heavenly Father, not the methods of men. The Holy Spirit is the mediator of diverse perspectives and opinions. There is oneness in Christ when He is the object of our unity. Harmony invites heaven's blessing. Unity around Christ causes the world to wake up and watch, wanting what you have. It unleashes the opportunity for the Lord to grow you into an influencer for Him.

"He made known to us the mystery of his will according to his good pleasure, which he purposed in Christ, to be put into effect when the times reach their fulfillment—to bring unity to all things in heaven and on earth under Christ" (Ephesians 1:9-10).

Related Readings: 2 Chronicles 30:12; 1 Corinthians 12:12; Ephesians 4:3, 13; Colossians 3:14

BE COURAGEOUS

Be on your guard; stand firm in the faith; be courageous; be
strong. 1 Corinthians 16:13

———————

Courage is an asset Christ dispenses to His disciples. It is the
ability to stand for what's right in the face of what's wrong.
Courage comes in various forms and functions. It may be a
phone call from a trusted friend who listens and affirms your
character. A single verse from the Bible may ring true to your
spirit and ratchet up your faith. The chorus from a praise song
to Jesus can become a capsule of courage that, when ingested in
worship, soothes your soul. It may be a prayer, a smile, a kind
word, a check, or a sermon that bolsters belief.

Alertness to courage dismisses dullness to sin and replaces
it with energy for eternal matters. Courage from Christ gives
confidence in the face of conflict. It provides a quiet assurance
that almighty God is in control and He will carry out His purpose
in His time. The Lord gives sufficient courage to stand firm in
the faith and remain faithful to Him. You receive courage so you
can give courage. Be courageous in Christ and infect others.
Courage creates courage.

"I eagerly expect and hope that I will in no way be ashamed, but
will have sufficient courage so that now as always Christ will
be exalted in my body, whether by life or by death" (Philippians
1:20).

Related Readings: Joshua 10:25; 2 Samuel 7:27; Mark 6:50;
Acts 27:22-25

THE LORD'S SERVANT

Praise the LORD, all you servants of the LORD. Psalm 134:1a

———◦◦◦◦———

Servants of the Lord have one goal, and that is to serve at the pleasure of their master Jesus Christ. It is an honor to represent the vision, mission, and values of heaven. Servants of God are quick to praise Him. They show respect by blessing His name and loathe the thought of disrespect in cursing His name. Followers of Jesus think and speak well of Him. He is the object of their affection, the adored One of their worship.

Servants of the Lord bless the One from whom all blessings flow. They speak well of their Master. Wise servants understand that the purpose of serving God is not just accomplishing the work but representing Him in their work. Therefore, toil in trust and do not give up for Christ's sake. You are a servant of the Most High, so hold your head high and your heart low. He keeps His covenant of love for those who long for Him. Jesus came to seek and to save the lost, so your best service leads others to understand the way to be saved. May others see you in this same way...

"These men are servants of the Most High God, who are telling you the way to be saved" (Acts 16:17b).

Related Readings: Nehemiah 1:11; Psalm 85:8; Isaiah 56:6; Acts 4:29; Revelation 22:6

POOR AND NEEDY

But as for me, I am poor and needy; may the Lord think of me.
You are my help and my deliverer; you are my God, do not
delay. Psalm 40:17

Mature and growing disciples of Jesus understand their utter
dependence on Him. A man or woman of high position must
come low before the Lord to learn of Him. Money cannot buy
the blessing of God. It's only in going before Him in brokenness
that spiritual riches can be received. A needy soul needs a Savior
to see her through troubled times.

We don't wait and go to God after we have it all together.
Instead, we enter into His presence poor in our ability to change
circumstances and people. We long for the Lord's help sooner
than later, because we understand He has the right answers. The
world's solutions prove sterile and ineffective compared to the
wisdom from intimacy with Jesus. Thus, cease from striving
in your own strength and surrender to the Spirit's resources.
Relational discord, health issues, or problems at work are
opportunities for God's grace to grace your attitude and actions.
Spiritual riches await the poor in spirit.

"You're blessed when you're at the end of your rope. With less
of you there is more of God and His rule" (Matthew 5:3, The
Message).

Related Readings: Psalm 109:22; 1 Corinthians 1:18-30;
2 Corinthians 1:12

PROTECT CHILDREN

If anyone causes one of these little ones—those who believe in me—to stumble, it would be better for them if a large millstone were hung around their neck and they were thrown into the sea. Mark 9:42

Parents and other adults in authority are morally responsible to protect children. If grown people neglect or excuse away their righteous role, it is an offense that Jesus does not take lightly. This faithless infraction brings out an intense consequence that is worse than being drowned in the depths of the sea. Indeed, watchfulness over little ones is huge to God. Protection is a prerequisite for being a responsible parent. It is implied in the role of any adult with influence over children. You are Christ's representative who guards God's kids. As they see Jesus in your life, lead them to receive Jesus into their lives.

Children are a gift from almighty God in need of care by affectionate adults. Their hearts are tender for truth and their minds are malleable and ready to be molded by men and women with moral authority. Pray over your circle of influence: children, grandchildren, nieces, nephews, neighbors, a classmate of your child, a foster child, or an orphan. Become the answer to your prayers and protect a little one with your loving presence. Love protects.

"It [love] always protects, always trusts, always hopes, always perseveres" (1 Corinthians 13:7).

Related Readings: 1 Samuel 1:24-28; 3:13-14; Judges 13:5-7; Acts 2:39; 1 Timothy 3:12

JUNE 15

COURAGEOUS FATHERS

LORD Almighty, God of Israel, you have revealed this to your servant, saying, "I will build a house for you." So your servant has found courage to pray this prayer to you. 2 Samuel 7:27

Courageous fathers fight for their family. They have a righteous resolve to do whatever is necessary to take them out of direct fire from the enemy's arrows of discouragement. Precious children are emotionally, physically, and spiritually vulnerable without their daddy's protection. A father's courage applied to a child's fears provides peace. Wise is the dad who doesn't dismiss danger but protects his family.

Faithful fathers are called by Christ to intercede with bold prayers for their wives and children. They receive love from their heavenly Father, so they in turn can love well in their home. Courage from Christ causes loving fathers to spend unhurried time listening to the hurts, dreams, and concerns of their children. Courage creates courage for children. As a courageous father you bring heaven's hope to your home. It takes courage to symbolically label the entrance to your house with "Love God" and the exit with "Love People." It takes courage to stand on behalf of your family against a secular and cynical culture and proclaim your 100% allegiance to almighty God. Your courage is a gift of security for your child.

"Be on your guard; stand firm in the faith; be courageous; be strong" (1 Corinthians 16:13).

Related Readings: Deuteronomy 31:6-7; Joshua 10:25; Acts 27:22-25; Philippians 1:20

POISONOUS WORDS

They make their tongues as sharp as a serpent's; the poison of
vipers is on their lips. Psalm 140:3

———————◆◆◆◆—————

Poisonous words come from a proud heart. When mankind first
fell into sin, Satan, the old serpent, infected us with the venom
of injurious words. We have to watch what we say, or we may
regret what we say. In their anger people tend to say what their
parents said in their anger. It is a vicious cycle of hurt that only
Christ can break.

Instead of lashing out with language that stings or even slanders,
there needs to be a cooling down time for calm and clear thinking.
Frustration tends to feed judgmental behavior. When our throat
is dry and our blood pressure is up is not the best time to speak,
because poisonous words pronounce judgments driven by anger
and emotion. Moreover, pleasant words work out the hurt and
replace it with hope. Words like "I love you," "I believe in you,"
"How can I help?" "How can I pray for you?" bring out the best
in those in need of soul nourishment. Emotions venture back out
in vulnerability within a safe environment of encouragement.
Offer pleasant words that feed hungry hearts often. Poisonous
words kill; pleasant words heal.

"Pleasant words are a honeycomb, sweet to the soul and healing
to the bones" (Proverbs 16:24, NIV84).

Related Readings: Proverbs 12:25; 15:4; Zechariah 1:13;
Acts 20:2; 1 Peter 5:12

GOD KNOWS

O LORD, you have searched me and you know me.
Psalm 139:1, NIV84

God knows everything about us. He knows our dreams, fears, and failures. He knows our noble thoughts and our foolish ones. He knows, but He knows with an eye toward eternity. His motive for the use of this exhaustive information is intimacy with His creation. Indeed, His infinite knowledge is an invitation to know Him. He understands our nature and character way beyond our comprehension. He searches the soul for our sake, not His, for He already knows. We do much better when we sense our Savior is watching.

So, our first step in accountability is to daily ask the Almighty to search our heart and diagnose its condition. Through prayer, fasting and godly counsel, invite the Holy Spirit to align your expectations with an eternal agenda. You trust in the Lord even when you are unable to completely comprehend His understanding because He is God. In time He will reveal just what you need to know. You know that God knows, and that's all you have to know.

"God, who knows the heart, showed that he accepted them by giving the Holy Spirit to them, just as He did to us" (Acts 15:8).

Related Readings: 1 Samuel 2:3; Psalms 44:21; 1 Corinthians 2:11; Philippians 4:10-13

RIGHTEOUS REBUKE

Let a righteous man strike me—it is a kindness; let him rebuke
me—it is oil on my head. My head will not refuse it.
Psalm 141:5a, NIV84

A righteous rebuke wins the respect of the teachable and trusting.
It is seen as an act of love and concern. We all need people
in our lives who challenge us with truth. Bold messengers
motivated by kindness and correction make us more effective
leaders, spouses, parents, friends, and followers of Jesus.
The unrighteous smile upon us with cruel flattery, while the
righteous do not rest until words of admonition are offered.

We invite instruction from those with integrity because we trust
their intentions. Fools resent reproof, but the wise profit from
its sometimes stinging sensation. A righteous rebuke is sweet
to the soul, like pleasant perfume it refreshes and renews. It is
a loving act. Immature gossips talk about others, but mature
friends only talk directly to others. Like a child who respects
the flames of a fireplace by backing away, so wise and humble
is the child of God who steps back from the blistering force of
sin. A rebuke followed by earnest repentance leads to lasting
sweet fellowship with Jesus and trusted friends. You are wise
to have friends who tell you what you need to hear.

"It is better to heed the rebuke of a wise person than to listen to
the song of fools" (Ecclesiastes 7:5).

Related Readings: 2 Samuel 12:1-14; Psalm 39:11;
Proverbs 17:10; Mark 16:14

GRATEFUL PRAISE

Let everything that has breath praise the LORD. Praise the
LORD. Psalm 150:6

"Praise the Lord" is not just a celebration of gratitude to God
and reverent worship of our King; it is also a command. Jesus
directs us to worship our heavenly Father in "spirit and in truth"
(John 4:23-24). The pinnacle of praise found in this last Psalm is
an exhortation to praise Him in His sanctuary. It is with music,
instruments, dancing, spiritual songs, and hymns that we praise
Him. You praise Him for His glory, but in the process you receive
the benefit of His blessings. His security, comfort, courage, and
peace feed your soul.

The church's chorus of praise to Christ rises high above to the
courts of heaven. In reverence and thanksgiving we praise Him
for His mighty acts: His creation for its beauty and majesty, His
redemption for its forgiveness and freedom, and His holiness
for its purity and power. Praise to the Lord reveals the Lord.
Make it your holy agenda to worship your Savior and Lord
Jesus Christ with a grateful heart, and His work of grace will
transform you into His likeness. Grateful praise brings glory to
God and genuine joy to His children. Praise Him and so will
other needy souls.

"Stand every morning to thank and praise the LORD, and
likewise at evening" (1 Chronicles 23:30, NASB).

Related Readings: Deuteronomy 32:3; Ezra 3:10-11;
Psalm 40:3; 103:1-2

COMPLAINT TO CHRIST

I pour out my complaint before him; before him I tell my trouble. Psalm 142:2, NIV84

A heavy heart needs an outlet to express fears and frustrations. If this option is absent, there is a loss of perspective and an extended stay in pain. It may be the weight of leadership sapping your joy and testing your trust. The death of a loved one may have sent you into a downward spiral of loneliness and loathing. Maybe you feel unappreciated and ignored to the point of painful rejection. Troubles need a trusted and safe outlet. It is in these moments of madness that we need a safe place to share our souls.

We have permission to complain to God, but not about God. Christ patiently hears our protests like a caring and just judge. It is better to vent your frustrations to your heavenly Father than for your soul to stew in bitterness. Complaints to Christ are your opportunity to come clean in your heart and to harness heaven's hope. He listens, He loves, He understands, He consoles, He encourages, and He gives grace. Pour out your heart to Him. He will fill your heart with His Spirit's comfort.

"He went a little farther and fell on His face, and prayed, saying, 'O My Father, if it is possible, let this cup pass from Me; nevertheless, not as I will, but as You will'" (Matthew 26:39, NKJV).

Related Readings: Job 7:13; 23:2; Jeremiah 12:1; Habakkuk 1:12; Mark 15:34

EVERYDAY RELATIONSHIP

I am the good shepherd; I know My sheep and My sheep know Me—just as the Father knows Me and I know the Father—and I lay down My life for the sheep. John 10:14-15

Jesus desires an everyday relationship with those He has given eternal life. Like a sensitive shepherd individually cares for his sheep, so Christ cares for His flock of followers. A wise sheep herder daily looks to keep the sheep from harm and leads them into green pastures. Similarly, the Lord watches out each day for the interests of His children, whom He protects and for whom He provides.

If we wander away from the influence of our great shepherd Jesus, we risk exposure to evil elements. However, as we remain in the shadow of His long supportive staff, we benefit from His benevolence and His capacity for good. Each day we have the opportunity to engage eternal resources for His Kingdom purposes. So, pray that every day with Jesus is sweeter than the day before. Daily you have the opportunity to rest in the Lord or get worked up. He longs to walk with you and talk with you. Listen intently to the one voice that is guaranteed to lead you to life.

"Blessed are those who listen to me, watching daily at my doors, waiting at my doorway" (Proverbs 8:34).

Related Readings: Job 37:5; Psalm 95:7; Luke 9:23; Hebrews 3:13

ACTIVITY VERSUS RESULTS

A wise man who built his house on the rock… A foolish man who built his house on sand. Matthew 7:24b, 26b

---

Activity can become competition for the best results, because sincere but inappropriate actions can lead to the wrong outcomes. It is not important to be busy in a lot of things but to be focused on a few essentials for success. On the surface, a busy life can look like good things are being accomplished, but below the genuine intention is the sandy foundation of unacceptable results. More measured and less frantic activity is needed when gauging right results.

For example, at work be on guard against reams of information that lack interpretation and analysis. Too much data can become a deterrent to making a decision and moving forward. Also, look out for those who are blindly busy but going nowhere fast. The busiest people may be the most unproductive people, because there is no time for evaluation and improvement. Diligence that partners with the right strategy and execution leverages the most effective results. Actions aligned with the best overall plan produce long-term sustainability; so build on the rock of right results.

"Every way of a man is right in his own eyes, But the LORD weighs the hearts. To do righteousness and justice is more acceptable to the LORD than sacrifice" (Proverbs 21:2-3, NKJV).

Related Readings: Job 32:1; Proverbs 12:15; Acts 15:38; 1 Corinthians 3:6; 4:6

GOD MEMORIES

I remember the days of long ago; I mediate on all your works and consider what your hands have done. Psalm 143:5

God memories help us to remember what is really important in life. The expressions of the Lord's wonderful work come from a variety of expressions. For example, we may have seen His hand at work during our conversion experience while attending church or an old-fashioned revival meeting. Or, maybe His answer to prayer arrested our hearts during a contemplative conversation with Christ along a quiet creek bed. Perhaps it was an answered prayer for a special person for a season.

Our meditation on the Almighty's activities activates our heart with faith and hope. It is when we ruminate on His righteous acts that we tend to feel secure and certain. When our own work leaves us to wander, we can still wonder at the works of His hands. He can work through our works in spite of our works. A mind always on the move needs the maintenance of God's memories to meditate and muse on His encouraging acts. Use God memories to galvanize your faith and make you more like your memory maker, Jesus.

"So I will always remind you of these things, even though you know them and are firmly established in the truth you now have. I think it is right to refresh your memory" (2 Peter 1:12-13a).

Related Readings: Psalm 42:4; Ecclesiastes 12:1; Isaiah 46:9; Ephesians 2:12

DELAYED UNDERSTANDING

Jesus replied, "You do not realize now what I am doing, but later you will understand." John 13:7

———◆◆◆———

God's will is not always understood in the moment, but in retrospect it becomes clear. This is the design of the faith walk: Remain faithful today, even though understanding may not come until tomorrow. Delays in the comprehension of circumstances seem like a divine detour, but it is a fruitful path for the Lord to show Himself trustworthy and wise.

Be comforted, for Christ is doing a deeper work—even if on the surface it seems shallow, insignificant, and unnecessary. The details of how He takes time to prepare us for His next assignment may seem redundant, but counterintuitive actions are not learned in one lesson. The idea that greatness comes from being a servant to all takes time to transform a heart. Jesus does not allow us to move on until humility truly moves in. His love is not delayed, only your ability to totally comprehend His grander plan in the larger landscape of life. God's delays are designed to accelerate your love for and trust in Jesus.

"Yes, LORD, walking in the way of your laws, we wait for you; your name and renown are the desire of our hearts" (Isaiah 26:8).

Related Readings: Lamentations 3:24-26; Micah 7:7; 1 Corinthians 1:7; 1 John 5:20

SOULFUL REST

"This is what the Lord says: 'Stand at the crossroads and look; ask for the ancient paths, ask where the good way is, and walk in it, and you will find rest for your souls.' But you said, 'We will not walk in it.'" Jeremiah 6:16

The soul longs for rest in the Lord's love and security. When a body's activity and emotional capacity runs ahead of its soul, distress begins to define a disciple. Rest for the inner life is required for the outward life to leave behind an eternal impression on those it encounters. Indeed, God speaks inwardly with truth and trust to listening hearts.

We each confront crossroads in our everyday lives that invite a secular frame of mind or a scriptural mindset. The new way may seem nice, but behind its modern mask is confusion, clutter, and contempt for Christ. The old way may seem stale and sedate, but when applied prayerfully it is refreshing, rejuvenating, and relationally healthy. Soul rest comes with regular doses of doing nothing and routine acts of doing something. Just as a body's muscles stretch and grow with exercise and inactivity, so a soul's spiritual stamina stretches and grows with strident service and quiet contemplation. Thus, walk in the good way with God in soulful rest.

"Yes, my soul, find rest in God; my hope comes from him" (Psalm 62:5).

Related Readings: Psalm 62:1; 116:7; Matthew 11:29; Hebrews 4:1-6

YOUNG AT HEART

To these four young men God gave knowledge and
understanding of all kinds of literature and learning.
Daniel 1:17a

There is a tension between being young at heart and mature in
mind. It is a good tension that need not be dismissed, because
youth has its advantages: energy, excitement, and unbridled
expectations. The fleeting satisfaction of a young adult longs
for more very quickly. They dream of a time one day soon when
their contribution to culture makes its significant mark with
everlasting consequences. I remember this idealism. Even now
my heart vacillates between youthful exuberance and middle
age prudence. I long for a young heart, a total trust in the Lord,
and an optimism anchored in Scripture.

Moreover, you remain young at heart by being with young
hearts. You go where they go: coffee shops, rock climbing,
museums, and mission trips. You listen to what they listen to:
artists, entertainers, politicians, and preachers. You read what
they read: blogs, books, and websites. Embrace youth where
they live, and you will earn the right to influence how they
live. Your transparency about your own troubles and struggles
garners their respect and makes you approachable. So, the secret
to being young at heart is being with the young at heart.

"Let no one despise your youth, but be an example to the
believers" (1 Timothy 4:12, NKJV).

Related Readings: Numbers 11:28; 1 Samuel 12:2;
Job 33:25; Psalm 71:17; 2 Timothy 2:22

GOD'S VISION

Therefore go and make disciples of all nations.
Matthew 28:19a

———————•◆•———————

Jesus was a visionary leader. He communicated His vision with compelling clarity, and before He ascended back to heaven He commissioned a stunning strategy for its fulfillment. He told His disciples to start as His witnesses in Jerusalem and then progress to Judea, Samaria, and the uttermost parts of the earth (Acts 1:8). We can see from Jesus' example that clearly defined milestones move the mission and vision toward maturity.

Visionary leaders have the innate ability both to keep a finger on the pulse of the present and have faith in the future. They create an immediate urgency balanced with a stabilizing focus on the most important priorities. Visionary leaders do not vacillate but, instead, inspire followers with their consistent calling to the cause. They show the way on a shared journey of faith. In time spent with your team, it's wise to lead them one step closer to owning the vision. Whatever your vision, stay true to its original intent. In the short term it may sputter and stall, but remain faithful and watch it flourish within the flaming fires of faith. Worship the God of the vision, not the vision.

"In the last days, God says, I will pour out my Spirit on all people. Your sons and daughters will prophesy, your young men will see visions, your old men will dream dreams" (Acts 2:17).

Related Readings: Genesis 46:2; Daniel 2:28; Acts 16:10; Revelation 1:9

SPIRITUAL RICHES

I pray that out of His glorious riches he may strengthen you
with power through his Spirit in your inner being.
Ephesians 3:16

An individual, family, company, government, church, or ministry
can spend more than they can afford. Their lack of means to pay
can be overcome by their ability to generate income. In earthly
economies it is common to overspend and under-budget, but in
God's economy there is unlimited access to the spiritual riches
of our Savior Jesus Christ. A Christian's spiritual riches are
never depleted or overdrawn in their heavenly bank account.

God gives grace upon grace to His children so they can give
grace to the deserving and undeserving. He heaps humility
in great portions upon His people so they can in turn walk in
humility with one another. The Lord sends a flood of faith so the
faithful can infuse faith into the faithless. Indeed, His storehouse
of salvation is ready save to the uttermost. Perhaps you start with
a prayer for the Lord to remind you of your spiritual wealth.
Your spiritual riches are available to be spent now, not stored up
for later. Therefore, be strengthened inwardly by God's glorious
riches. Like a spiritual philanthropist, prayerfully spend His
riches on the spiritually impoverished.

"To them God has chosen to make known among the Gentiles
the glorious riches of this mystery, which is Christ in you, the
hope of glory" (Colossians 1:27).

Related Readings: Luke 16:11; Romans 2:4; 9:23;
Ephesians 1:7; Philippians 4:19

SMELL OF SUCCESS

Cursed is the ground because of you; through painful toil you
will eat of it all the days of your life… By the sweat of your
brow you will eat your food until you return to the ground.
Genesis 3:17b, 19a, NIV84

The smell of sweat can be the fruit of success. There is a
correlation between energy exerted and outcome produced.
God gave Adam the command to work hard. It is laborious and
painful, but there is reward in results. Some days I struggle with
this because I enjoy the accomplishments of hard work but not
the painful process.

However, I am learning that sweat is a blessing from a curse.
It is cleansing for the body, soul, and spirit. Sweat cleanses the
body from impurities. Spiritual perspiration purifies the mind
of pride and conceit. Emotions may travail in hurt and pain,
but they are replaced by the birth of forgiveness. Fulfillment
and significance in life does not come from ease and avoiding
exertion but through engaging with people and problems while
depending on the Lord. Hard work with a heart for the Lord
leads to good results.

"Simon answered, 'Master, we've worked hard all night and
haven't caught anything. But because you say so, I will let down
the nets'" (Luke 5:5).

Related Readings: 2 Chronicles 32:5; John 4:38; Acts 20:35;
Romans 16:6, 12

CONFIDENCE IN LEADERSHIP

Have confidence in your leaders and submit to their authority, because they keep watch over you as those who must give an account. Do this so that their work will be a joy, not a burden, for that would be of no benefit to you. Hebrews 13:17

Confidence in leadership is necessary for credibility in leadership. When confidence is lost, credibility is not far behind, exiting out the door of lost influence. A leader at home, work, church, or government is expected to meet basic requirements to gain the trust of followers. A leader's role requests confidence from others, but their consistent character accompanied by right results maintains the status of a trusted role model.

Are you a leader worth following? Do your wife and children have confidence in your decision-making process? Do they see a spiritual leader who follows the Lord well? If so, you have the benefit of being someone whom others hold in high esteem because you can be trusted. Submissive followers are the natural outcome for a leader who is accountable. So, seek to be a loving leader who garners confidence gladly from those you serve. Be confident in Christ.

"Keep watch over yourselves and all the flock of which the Holy Spirit has made you overseers. Be shepherds of the church of God, which he bought with his own blood" (Acts 20:28).

Related Readings: Ezekiel 34:10; John 10:11-12; Romans 3:19; 2 Corinthians 3:6

JULY

But seek first the kingdom of God and his righteousness, and all these things will be added to you.

Matthew 6:33

JULY 1

MANAGEMENT COMPLIMENTS
LEADERSHIP

And he [Jesus] directed the people to sit down on the grass. Taking the five loaves and the two fish and looking up to heaven, he gave thanks and broke the loaves. Then he gave them to the disciples, and the disciples gave them to the people. Matthew 14:19, NIV84

———————◆◆◆————————

Jesus was a leader worth following, but He was also a manager who managed well. He understood the importance of an orderly process, and He implemented it effectively. Management is the method for executing the mission. Leadership ensures the enterprise is on the right strategic path. However, without good management leadership will languish, unable to move critical initiatives forward toward their milestones.

Wise managers clearly define who, what, when, and where. There is an attention to detail that supports the overall objectives of the team. Managers diagnose problems and then bring solutions to bear that remove obstacles and reclaim progress. Managers implement methods that support the success of the organization. Managers oversee productive processes. Like the Lord in His creation, they bring order and discipline to the enterprise. Stay faithful to manage well, and you will be in a position to be entrusted with much more.

"You have been faithful in handling this small amount, so now I will give you many more responsibilities" (Matthew 25:21, NLT).

Related Readings: Genesis 39:2-6; Nehemiah 2:11-20; Luke 12:42; 16:1-8

PERSONAL PEACE

But now in Christ Jesus you who once were far away have been brought near by the blood of Christ. For he himself is our peace. Ephesians 2:13-14a

———————◆◆◆———————

Jesus Christ is a personal Savior who brings a personal peace. One of the advantages of knowing Jesus is knowing His peace: a peace that passes all understanding. A person outside of the Lord is exposed to the unsettling elements of evil that eliminate any thought of peace. Indeed, personal peace is a by-product of personally engaging God.

Are you at peace in your life in general and your work in particular? If not, submit to the Prince of Peace (Jesus) and allow Him to shepherd you through your valley of trepidation. You may not know what the future holds, but you know who holds the future. Because Christ is peace, do not overlook His inventory that already resides in your heart by faith. Personal peace is a product of being with the one who is peace. Your Prince of Peace awaits; allow Him to escort you into His calming courts of peace.

"You know the message God sent to the people of Israel, announcing the good news of peace through Jesus Christ, who is Lord of all" (Acts 10:36).

Related Readings: 2 Chronicles 20:30; Isaiah 9:6; Romans 15:13, 33; 1 Corinthians 14:33

CHOOSE TO SERVE

But made himself nothing, taking the very nature of a servant, being made in human likeness. Philippians 2:7, NIV84

Jesus voluntarily became a servant for the sake of others. He made Himself nothing so others could be something. He served out of humility and obedience to God. Jesus was first motivated to serve His Master in heaven, which lead to His service of mankind on earth. Some days I don't feel like being a servant. I grow weary and afraid, but by God's grace I make myself nothing for the greater something. It is our labor of love the Lord loves. He blesses service that is not concerned with receiving the credit.

Jesus was a suffering servant who was obedient to death. Service like Jesus' requires Him working in you, and serving through you. His children are His creation for His good works. Maybe you are to serve overseas for a season, or you are to serve your family by taking a less stressful job. Are you to relocate your parents in your home, or close by, to care for and honor them during their last days? Service like Jesus' is not always easy and leads to death of self. Choose to serve, even when you don't have to serve.

"For we are God's handiwork, created in Christ Jesus to do good works, which God prepared in advance for us to do" (Ephesians 2:10).

Related Readings: Joshua 22:5; Judges 2:7; Psalm 22:30; Luke 4:8; Acts 20:19

JULY 4

FREE TO PRAY

So Moses and Aaron went to Pharaoh and said to him, "This is what the LORD, the God of the Hebrews, says: 'How long will you refuse to humble yourself before me? Let my people go, so that they may worship me.'" Exodus 10:3

———❖———

Will we stand by in silence as public figures who humbly pray to our Lord and Savior Jesus Christ are mocked by some? Or will we join them in prayer in our homes, at work, in a restaurant, at sporting events and during civic gatherings? Shyness is the excuse of those who are scared. Humble prayer births in us a holy boldness that expresses itself in joyful praise of Jesus. Yes, some will scorn us, but better to be known as courageous for Christ.

The soul of a nation with a prayerful persona is sensitive to sin. Bad behavior is not ignored or excused. Fiscal stewardship, integrity, and relational purity are the norm, not the exception. A country with a conscience invites the blessing of almighty God. Begin by gathering your family together in confession and repentance to Christ. Healing comes to a homeland that sees righteousness as the remedy for its ills. Contrite prayer begins with the Lord's people in His house of worship. We are to humble ourselves and seek almighty God's face and forgiveness.

"For some days I mourned and fasted and prayed before the God of heaven" (Nehemiah 1:4b).

Related Readings: Exodus 15:26; Nehemiah 1:4-11; Psalm 106:6; Luke 24:47

LOYALTY CREATES LOYALTY

At that time Abimelek and Phicol the commander of his forces said to Abraham, "God is with you in everything you do. Now swear to me here before God that you will not deal falsely with me or my children or my descendants. Show to me and the country where you now reside as a foreigner the same kindness I have shown to you." Abraham said, "I swear it."
Genesis 21:22-24

In a society of self-preservation, loyalty is lacking. The old-fashioned sentiment that we will stick together through trying times loses its luster with the disloyal. However, for those who value the giving and receiving of loyalty—you are a friend for a lifetime. There is relational honor, because prized is the belief that God has ordered this divine engagement.

We value loyalty because the Lord values loyalty. Our relationship with Jesus doesn't become expedient when externals become threatening. In situations when we need Him the most is not the time to flee from His presence out of fear. Indeed, fearful circumstances are the times we ratchet up our righteous fear of God. He desires and deserves our loyalty.

"Be strong and courageous. Do not be afraid or terrified because of them, for the LORD your God goes with you; he will never leave you nor forsake you" (Deuteronomy 31:6).

Related Readings: Joshua 1:5; Judges 8:33-35; 2 Timothy 1:5-7; 1:14-16

LIFTS THE FALLEN

The LORD upholds all those who fall and lifts up all who are bowed down. Psalm 145:14

It is hard to get up when you have fallen, especially if there is extreme fatigue and fear. Relationally you may have fallen in your marriage because of unfaithfulness. Financially you may have fallen because of the deceit of debt. Morally you may have fallen because of a series of unwise decisions. Spiritually you may have fallen because the cares of this world choked out your confidence in Christ.

Fallen people are vulnerable to giving up, but in reality they are some of the best candidates for God's grace. You may have been pushed down by the proud and dominant. This is man's method of control, but the Lord is always there to lift and uphold you. What God lifts up He supports, sustains, and restores for His purposes. Indeed, He lifts us up, so we can be His instruments of encouragement to lift up others. The fallen need faith their Heavenly Father loves them. He loves for He is love. The old hymn declares, "Love lifted me, love lifted me, when nothing else could help, love lifted me." Let the Lord's love lift you up.

"He lifted me out of the slimy pit, out of the mud and mire; he set my feet on a rock and gave me a firm place to stand" (Psalm 40:2).

Related Readings: Psalm 3:3; 113:7; Luke 1:52; James 4:10; 1 Peter 5:6

FRIENDSHIP WITH JESUS

You are my friends if you do what I command. John 15:14

Jesus is a friend to His followers. He is Lord, but He is a friend. He is Savior, but He is a friend. He is the Son of God, but He is a friend. He is sinless and holy, but He is a friend. He is friend to sinners and a friend to those He saves. Jesus is a friend to His followers, but it's a friendship based on obedience. Compliance to Christ creates companionship.

If I do not obey Christ's commands, He does not call me friend. It is out of our actions that friendship with Jesus is validated. Obedience to Jesus inspires intimacy with Jesus. It is imperative we obey Jesus so we can really get to know Jesus. His friendship is free for all who follow hard with a heart hungry to obey. Friendship flourishes with faithful fidelity. Furthermore, as you grow in your friendship with Christ, you better understand His heart, and your prayers align more with His will. Friendship with Jesus facilitates friendship with people. True friends flock to be with fellow friends of Jesus. Evangelism of the lost and edification of the saved flow freely when Jesus is your best friend.

"When Jesus saw their faith, he said, 'Friend, your sins are forgiven'" (Luke 5:20).

Related Readings: 2 Chronicles 20:7; Job 29:4; Jeremiah 17:17; James 2:23; 4:4

GIFT OF GRACE

For it is by grace you have been saved, through faith—and this is not from yourselves, it is the gift of God—not by works, so that no one can boast. Ephesians 2:8-9

Grace is the guarantor of being in the good graces of almighty God. It is a gift that only the Lord can bestow, because He is the only one qualified to give something totally unmerited. A gift is not a gift if it can be earned or deserved, so His grace is inexplicable in human terms. The world demands results for reward, but God gives His very best with no expectation of the receiver earning His gift of grace. Grace guarantees that God's glory is preeminent.

Thus, through belief in Christ Jesus as the Son of God, we experience the riches of His grace. His grace is glorious, because it gets us to heaven. His grace is matchless, because it covers a multitude of sins. His grace is eternal, because it lifts us from the wretchedness of this world and places us in heavenly places. He gives us grace to get over a grudge, to extend mercy, to get through an illness, to persevere at work, to serve at home, and to rest.

"Out of his fullness we have all received grace in place of grace already given. For the law was given through Moses; grace and truth came through Jesus Christ" (John 1:16-17).

Related Readings: Proverbs 22:11; Luke 2:40; Acts 20:32; 2 Corinthians 8:6-9

GIFT OF THE SPIRIT

If you love me, keep my commands. And I will ask the Father, and he will give you another advocate to help you and be with you forever—the Spirit of truth. John 14:15-17a

---

Obeying the commands of Christ is tied to enjoying the comfort of the Holy Spirit. Comfort is made manifest from the gift of the Spirit in a fertile heart of faith. Conversion to Christ embeds His eternal Spirit in the heart of His disciple. A benefit of belief in Jesus is the gift of discernment from His Spirit. Unpacked at salvation and propagated in prayer, the Holy Spirit is the eyes and ears of heaven for all who walk faithfully with Jesus on earth.

It is not uncommon for some Christ followers to misunderstand or ignore this guarantor of the Godhead. Perhaps fear of a few corrupt charlatans keeps some Christians distant from the dynamic affects of the Spirit's work in and through them. Indeed, the Holy Spirit seals new believers at salvation and secures their faith journey through the schemes of Satan. This gift from our heavenly Father is meant to lead us into Christlike character. The Holy Spirit hunkers down in a humble heart and extends grace. He gives you wise guidance.

"But when he, the Spirit of truth, comes, he will guide you into all the truth" (John 16:13a).

Related Readings: Isaiah 63:14; Luke 12:10; John 3:34; Galatians 5:22-23

SPIRITUAL GIFTS

Now about the gifts of the Spirit, brothers and sisters, I do not want you to be uninformed. 1 Corinthians 12:1

Spiritual gifts are given by God and for God. These divine manifestations are diverse in their application, but they all originate from the same Spirit. Hence, heavenly ordained abilities give God all the credit for their accomplishments for good on earth. Gifts of the Spirit generate an eternal energy that is able to administer grace and love to lonely hearts and confused minds. Understanding spiritual gifts gives confidence to Christ followers.

Godly gifts are not for the personal benefit of a man, only in service to mankind. The aim of spiritual gifts is to build up the body of Christ—to be the eyes, ears, and mouth of Jesus to the spiritually blind, to those tone-deaf to truth and to the morally mute. Today's disciples of Jesus can do greater works. Why? Because they are equipped with spiritual resources. No longer are we bound up in sin; rather, we are freed up by God's gifts.

Therefore, prayerfully use your Holy Spirit-inspired gift not for show, but for service. Employ your gift and your work will not feel painstakingly laborious but almost effortless. Spiritual gifts are evidence of your salvation in Jesus.

"Since you are eager for gifts of the Spirit, try to excel in those that build up the church" (1 Corinthians 14:12b).

Related Readings: Ecclesiastes 3:13; Proverbs 2:6; Luke 11:13; 1 Corinthians 14:1

GIFT OF CHILDREN

Leah conceived again and bore Jacob a sixth son. Then Leah
said, "God has presented me with a precious gift."
Genesis 30:19-20a

At times children can feel more like a burden than a blessing,
but they are still a precious gift from God. A mom wipes away
moist food from a messy little face only to find a sweet smile—a
precious gift from God. A dad takes his daughter on a date, and
enjoys her funny stories and laughs out loud—this is a precious
gift from God. Babies are brought into this world because God
Almighty is the genesis and the genius behind life.

What the Lord conceives in the womb of a woman is inconceivable
to the mind of man. The gift of a daughter or a son is a mystery
reserved for the collective knowledge of God the Father, God
the Son, and God the Spirit. A child is not a mistake that brings
their parents inconvenience; instead, he or she is a gift from God
who brings joy. Grateful parents delight in and celebrate the gift
of their children. A child is a precious gift from God who needs
your prayers, care, and wisdom.

"She never left the temple but worshiped night and day, fasting
and praying. Coming up to them at that very moment, she gave
thanks to God and spoke about the child" (Luke 2:37-38a).

Related Readings: Proverbs 3:1-4; 1 Samuel 2:18; 3:19;
Luke 1:13; Colossians 3:20

SPIRITUAL STABILITY

The one who doubts is like a wave of the sea, blown and
tossed by the wind… Such a person is double-minded and
unstable in all they do. James 1:6b, 8b

Spiritual stability comes from thinking properly about the
things of God. His ways are like the secure moorings of a ship
that is docked safe and secure in its harbor. And His Spirit is
like the wind that propels the billowy sail of a boat in need of
movement in the right direction. However, doubt can creep in
like a selfish bandit and steal away thoughts of security. It is
at this testing point of trust that a calm child of God relies on
Christ's character.

Jesus is all-knowing, all-powerful, and ever-present. He
is a rock of stability, a fortress of protection, and a cleft of
comfort. The Lord's love is everlasting, His peace reaches
beyond comprehension, and His wisdom is generous in its
doses. Regardless of a disciple's storm— sickness, loneliness,
sadness, debt, or rejection—there is a hopeful option. Pride is
like a hard grape that requires circumstances to crush the fruit,
so it can become fine wine. Thus, trust that what He says is true
and where He says to go is good. Jesus gives spiritual stability
when doubt assaults your faith.

"In all your ways submit to him, and he will make your paths
straight" (Proverbs 3:6).

Related Readings: Psalm 107:30; 131:2; Isaiah 7:4;
1 Corinthians 1:9; 2 Peter 3:16

UNDERSTANDING GROWS TRUST

My purpose is that they may be encouraged in heart and
united in love, so that they may have the full riches of
complete understanding, in order that they may know the
mystery of God, namely, Christ. Colossians 2:2, NIV84

———————

We tend to trust those who understand us. Understanding is a
bridge to belief and intimacy. This is one reason it is wise to
first seek understanding of the Lord's ways. When we seek to
understand our Savior we see the path of His providence more
clearly and we trust. Understanding scouts ahead of God's will
looking for opportunities to follow Him.

One facilitator to gaining understanding is fear of the Lord. This
is foundational for faith, salvation, and growing in grace. An
education in eternal consequences requires humility, attention,
and application. We seek to understand the Lord and thoroughly
trust Him so we can better understand others. When others feel
understood, they are open to influence. Thus, take the time to
understand, and trust will transfer into a growing relationship
with God and others. Ask God first for understanding, and He
will reveal the truths found in His Son Jesus.

"To God belong wisdom and power; counsel and understanding
are his" (Job 12:13).

Related Readings: Exodus 31:3; 1 Kings 4:29;
1 Corinthians 14:15; Philemon 1:6

A SUSTAINABLE LIFE

The LORD sustains the humble but casts the wicked to the
ground. Psalm 147:6

———◦❖◦———

God sustains the life of the humble. There is a heavenly
determination that is dispatched to Christ's humble servants.
Because the Holy Spirit holds you up, you continue to show
up in less than desirable circumstances. Christ is counter to our
culture, for He lifts up the lowly and meek and casts down the
proud and exalted. So, the humble remain faithful, knowing
they will receive the Almighty's affirmation and recognition in
His good timing.

We serve unseen for our Saviors' sake and not to be seen for
our sake. It is our reverence of Holy God, humbleness in our
own eyes, and gentleness toward our fellow man that sustains
a life blessed by the Lord. Our Savior supports us when we
apply humility over a promotion at work, projecting an image
of control, or having to win arguments with antagonists. It's
choosing the low place that places us in a position to be used by
God. Your humble heart is supported by God's sustaining power
for His purposes. He sustains your unpretentious Christian faith
by His unwavering grace.

"The LORD sends poverty and wealth; He humbles and he
exalts" (1 Samuel 2:7).

Related Readings: Nehemiah 9:21; Psalm 3:5; 41:3; 55:22;
Proverbs 18:14

CLOSE TO CHRIST

He has raised up for His people a horn, the praise of all his saints, of Israel, the people close to his heart. Praise the LORD.
Psalm 148:14, NIV84

Children of God can draw close to His heart. This is a benefit of becoming a believer in Jesus Christ. He came low to earth so you could go to the Most High in heaven. You are chosen by Christ to draw near to His heart. The closer you get to Christ, the more confident you become of His character. It is in nearness that you know who you believe, and you are persuaded that He will keep you secure in His grace.

His Spirit fills you with His abundant presence and provision. Up close and personal you hear His heartbeat of love and forgiveness. You fear Him because you love and respect Him. Closeness to Christ calms your soul and ignites your faith, so draw near to know Him. Sit next to the fire of His love to warm your heart and melt your fears. Prayer and praise places you in the proximity of Christ. When you feel distant from God, determine to praise Him even more. Praise Him for His grace, mercy, and love. Praise is a remedy for feeling remote from God.

"Let us draw near to God with a sincere heart and with the full assurance that faith brings" (Hebrews 10:22a).

Related Readings: Exodus 3:5; Psalm 34:18; John 1:18; Ephesians 3:17; Colossians 1:19

GOD'S GAME PLAN

"For I know the plans I have for you," declares the LORD, "plans to prosper you and not to harm you, plans to give you hope and a future." Jeremiah 29:11

Wise followers of Jesus want what God wants for their family, faith, and friends. We want His plan for which relationships to invest in. We ask Him who needs our attention, our prayers, and our encouragement. It may be a struggling college student, a single parent on the brink of giving up, or a friend emotionally and physically crippled by illness. God's plan involves service to others.

Perhaps He is leading you to step into a new job opportunity. It may be a completely new career arena that requires new relationships and a new application of your current skills and past experiences. Are you willing to fully trust Christ with your job?

The Lord Jesus brings you healing, not harm. His plans for you include fulfilling work, real rest, significant friendships, forgiving family members, laughter, weeping, and trusting Him. You gain perspective on His plan through humble prayer, understanding and applying biblical truths, and collaborating with other Christ followers. Ask God to guide you in His game plan for this season. He will, but He wants you first.

"They gave themselves first of all to the Lord, and then by the will of God also to us" (2 Corinthians 8:5).

Related Readings: Deuteronomy 28:11: Job 36:11; Psalm 4:6; 37:11; Luke 16:1-15

UNCERTAINTY OF WEALTH

Command those who are rich in this present world not to be arrogant nor to put their hope in wealth, which is so uncertain, but to put their hope in God, who richly provides.
1 Timothy 6:17a

———————

If there is one thing that is certain, it is the uncertainty of wealth. Riches can fluctuate up and down like a terrifying rollercoaster ride. My financial net worth can evaporate overnight or incrementally deteriorate over time. Hope in wealth is a recipe for sleepless nights and emotional fatigue. Why would I place my hope in money that migrates all over the map of life? Hope in money leads to false security and creates discontentment.

Yes, it is embarrassing to lose anything, especially money, but it can be replaced. Financial purging peels back our true intent, and exposes the object of our affections. Do we love money, or do we love God, because we can't love both. Fortunately, hope in heaven is the most certain. Christ is our reliable compass during a cash crisis. Jesus' utmost desire is for you to toil for true riches: loving God and people. Money comes and goes, but Jesus remains faithful. Hope in Christ, not cash, brings contentment and the enjoyment of true wealth—this is for certain.

"Cast but a glance at riches, and they are gone, for they will surely sprout wings and fly off to the sky like an eagle" (Proverbs 23:5).

Related Readings: Job 13:15; Psalm 42:5; Matthew 10:42; John 17:8

ONE THING

*I'm asking God for one thing, only one thing: To live with him
in his house my whole life long. I'll contemplate his beauty;
I'll study at his feet. Psalm 27:4, The Message*

———◀•▶———

There are rival voices in the mind of a Christian that compete
for the ear of God. It may be a voice of concern over a wayward
son or daughter. Another voice cries out for healing of a diseased
body. A sincere voice asks to know God's will and direction for
living. All of these voices vie for the Lord's attention and are
close to His heart. But there is one request that collates all of
these needs—to enter into the presence of Jesus in prayer.

We need the personalized presence of Christ like a hiker
reaching a mountain summit needs oxygen. It is in this place
of praise that we see the beauty of His holiness and we study
at His feet. The doors to His house of worship are always open
to our hungry hearts and inquisitive minds. We enter into His
courts because He is the One Thing we need. What you focus
on is what you become. Ask the Lord for one thing: to live
closely with Him.

"But one thing I do: Forgetting what is behind and straining
toward what is ahead, I press on toward the goal to win the
prize for which God has called me" (Philippians 3:13b-14a).

Related Readings: Psalm 62:11; Mark 10:21; Galatians 3:2;
1 Peter 3:8

GLAD IN GOD

Let Israel rejoice in the their Maker; let the people of Zion be glad in their King. Psalm 149:2

You can be glad in God. Your circumstances may be in a sad state, but your Savior can bring a smile to your face. Salvation in Jesus is a joy, delight, and privilege. Fear may have caused you to forget the free gift of eternal life extended to you by God's grace, but gladness is its ambassador. I can't help but be grateful when I think of the situations the Lord, by His grace, has led me through.

The divorce of parents, feeling abandoned, working three jobs simultaneously, marriage conflict, cancer treatment, career upheaval, challenging children, and financial disappointments were all sad situations, but my Savior saw me through. You may find yourself in a sad state of affairs, but be glad because your Lord Jesus is still in control. The goodness of God is your gauge for being glad. Your joy-filled heart will make music and sing praises to Christ your King. You may discover yourself dancing with the stars under the canopy of heaven. Sing the new song written on your heart by the Holy Spirit, and you will be glad in God.

"Worship the LORD with gladness; come before him with joyful songs" (Psalm 100:2).

Related Readings: Psalm 69:32; Ecclesiastes 9:7; Isaiah 25:9; Acts 11:23

REAL NET WORTH

So that they may have the full riches of complete understanding, in order that they may know the mystery of God, namely, Christ. Colossians 2:2b

---

Our financial net worth need not define who we are; if it does, we become fickle, fearful, and faithless—enslaved to economic security. Our worth is not wrapped around Wall Street or Main Street but the Streets of Gold. For followers of Jesus, what He believes about us defines us. My worth is defined by the wonder of His grace, His unconditional love, and His gift of eternal life.

Money does not make the man, man makes the money; but, most importantly, our master Jesus Christ marks us. The fingerprints of God are forever embedded on our body, soul, and spirit. He bought us, so He owns us through the blood of His Son Jesus. Our born again birth certificate reads Christian. We are highly valued in heaven.

Therefore, define your net worth by the things Jesus deems valuable. You are rich indeed. Count your many blessings, not your coins, and you will become content. You are of high net worth if "Christ in you" is your hope of glory. Your real net worth is His eternal riches.

"For you know the grace of our Lord Jesus Christ, that though he was rich, yet for your sake he became poor, so that you through his poverty might become rich" (2 Corinthians 8:9).

Related Readings: Ephesians 1:11-14; Hebrews 10:19; 11:26; 1 Timothy 4:8

GIFT OF SLEEP

In vain you rise early and stay up late, toiling for food to eat—for he grants sleep to those he loves. Psalm 127:2

———————◆———————

God gives the gift of sleep to His saints. It is a gift easily taken for granted, because it is an every day occurrence. Our Creator bestows even the air we breathe, so it is important to acknowledge and thank the Lord as the Giver of all good things. Sleep can be elusive when it is in competition with an ill-timed illness, erratic circumstances, or a guilty conscience.

What contributes to a restful night, unencumbered by external forces or internal issues? Peace of mind that comes with resting in the security of Christ secures significant sleep. Trust in Him trumps any tension at work or conflict at home. A head falls quickly on a peaceful pillow, and eyes shut quietly in a soul stilled by Jesus. Trust turns off a racing mind and reminds it that God works out worries throughout a silent, dark night. The Savior of your soul gives peace to your mind, rest to your body, and security to your soul. So, receive Jesus' gift of sweet sleep.

"In peace I will lie down and sleep, for you alone, LORD, make me dwell in safety" (Psalm 4:8).

Related Readings: Psalm 3:5; Isaiah 29:10; John 11:12; Acts 12:6; 2 Corinthians 6:5

START YOUNG

For you have been my hope, O Sovereign Lord, my confidence since my youth… Since my youth, O God, you have taught me, and to this day I declare your marvelous deeds.
Psalm 71:5, 17, NIV84

———◦◦◦———

Start young learning the ways of the Lord. This is your wisest and best investment. Youthful learning is leveraged for the Lord. Start young so you do not have to wade through the muck and mire of disobedient living. There is no need to stray and go your own way, for you may end up back at the point where you originally drifted from God. Stay the course with Christ while you are young, and this will catapult you into obedient adulthood. Youthful dependence on God results in an adult who depends on God.

Even as those older in the faith falter in fear, your heavenly Father frees youthful hearts to attempt big things for Him. Courage and conviction fertilize well a young heart hungry for God. The Holy Spirit is calling faithful young people to further His Kingdom. Listen to the heart of your heavenly Father and do what He says. Yahweh is calling His youth to something much bigger than themselves. Challenge youth to break out of their boxes of unbelief and change the world.

"Let no man despise thy youth; but be thou an example of the believers" (1 Timothy 4:12, KJV).

Related Readings: Numbers 11:28; Job 13:26; Psalm 25:7; 2 Timothy 2:22

GOD OR MONEY

No servant can serve two masters. Either he will hate the one and love the other, or he will be devoted to the one and despise the other. You cannot serve both God and Money.
Luke 16:13, NIV84

———————

There is a servitude that accompanies the love of God or money, for we serve what we love. In the case of Christ and cash, we cannot serve both at the same time. The service of one cancels out the service of the other. We cannot love Him and stuff at the same time. If we are not careful our actions build an altar to the almighty dollar, and we ignore almighty God, unless things go wrong; then we long for the Lord, our first love. Holy God is jealous over love affairs outside of Himself, especially when money becomes our mistress.

Jesus says love of money replaces love for Him, so how do we know if we are unfaithful? To spend excessive amounts of time worrying about money is a sure bet it has captured our love. To scheme about more, or be consumed with running out makes us a likely candidate as a lover of money. However, there is a remedy for our love affair with stuff: Give it away. Be generous and find fulfillment in Christ.

"For the love of money is a root of all kinds of evil" (1 Timothy 6:10a).

Related Readings: Proverbs 23:5; Romans 13:8; Acts 5:8; 8:20; Hebrews 13:5

PAY DEBT DOWN

The rich rule over the poor, and the borrower is servant to the lender. Proverbs 22:7, NIV84

A nation, business, or home built on debt is owned and controlled by outside forces. There is no freedom or liberty to be found in leverage, only obligations and payment plans. Debt is unemotional and uncaring when it decides to call your loan, or make new demands you are unable to fulfill. Debt is deceptive in its ability to draw us into its pleasures in exchange for our time, energy, and focus.

Borrowing is subtle, because it can easily become a shortcut that only satisfies our immediate gratification with long-term ramifications. I have missed God's best because I got in a hurry, and thought I had to make things happen. Ease of credit can lead us to grow impatient with prayer and make purchases prematurely. The blessing, however, comes from waiting on God's prayerful provision. Turn to Christ instead of credit, and watch Him create opportunities you never conceived. Waiting to pay in cash is an exercise in faith and a refraining of the flesh. A smaller home and older car with peace and contentment is much better than more with regret and restless nights. Debt-free living liberates your life and increases your generous giving. Pay down debt so you are free to love and serve others.

"LORD, I wait for you; you will answer, Lord my God" (Psalm 38:15).

Related Readings: Isaiah 30:18; 64:4; Micah 7:7; Hebrews 11:8-12

FALSELY ACCUSED

The high priest stood up and said to Him, "Do You not answer? What is it that these men are testifying against You?" But Jesus kept silent. Matthew 26:62-63a, NASB

It is hard and hurtful when you are falsely accused. Someone may cast doubt on your character or typecast your motives in an inaccurate way. People who falsely accuse represent a variety of motivations. It may fuel a feeling of superiority and power; the desire to control may be all consuming; or they may be on a crusade to clean house. Their worldview is the worse case scenario, and you may be the target of their attacks. False accusers issue criticism not compliments, problems not solutions, directives not collaboration, and blame not responsibility.

If you are the object of false accusations, it is imperative you not lower yourself to use similar innuendo and insinuation. Pray for your accuser, and serve and love them for Christ's sake. Value the relationship, though you do not feel valued. In prayer and forgiveness you release the feelings of anger and defensiveness. Unjust charges will happen when you follow hard after your Jesus, so die to your need to be right and trust God to work out His will—His way—in His time.

"Blessed are you when people insult you and persecute you, and falsely say all kinds of evil against you because of Me" (Matthew 5:11, NASB).

Related Readings: Numbers 35:24-28; Deuteronomy 19:15; Matthew 27:12

SUFFERING TEACHES OBEDIENCE

Son though he was, he learned obedience from what he suffered and, once made perfect, he became the source of eternal salvation for all who obey him. Hebrews 5:8-9

Very few Christians invite suffering or like suffering, but it is during this somber season that sincere saints learn how to obey almighty God. Sorrow seeks to torment a soul's trust in its Savior Jesus. Self wants the attention when afflicted, but it's the glory of God that deserves the recognition. Obedience to Christ is the central concern.

Yes, with fervency we cry and weep to the One who saved us—the One who will save us—the One who can save us from our momentary affliction. But the Lord's school of suffering is meant to shape us into sharp students of His Word and instant applicants of His principles for living. We only graduate once we transition into His glorious presence. Jesus, as the privileged Son of God, learned obedience from what He suffered. Suffering is a prerequisite to being made perfect in compliance to Christ. Thus, let His light shine through your disease, discomfort, or emotional upheaval. Go to Jesus and learn of Him how to receive His love and obey His commands.

"But rejoice inasmuch as you participate in the sufferings of Christ, so that you may be overjoyed when his glory is revealed" (1 Peter 4:13).

Related Readings: James 5:10-11; 1 Peter 4:1-19; 5:1-10; Revelation 2:10

SICK UNTO DEATH

For indeed he was sick almost unto death; but God had mercy on him, and not only on him but on me also, lest I should have sorrow upon sorrow. Philippians 2:27, NKJV

Friends and family who suffer from chronic illness are candidates for God's grace and our loving attention. It is extremely difficult to see a loved one languish through cancer, Alzheimer's or dementia. Once they smiled with joy; now they ache in pain. Once their body was hefty and healthy; now they are hollow and disfigured. The person we once knew seems to no longer exist.

They may be physically alive, but emotionally and mentally they are detached. However, it is in their weak condition you honor them by providing strength. If they lived a self-serving life, you still serve them as a testimony to your siblings, spouse, and children and in obedience to Christ's command. Service to the sick is an opportunity to be like Jesus, so by God's grace represent Him well. Sickness is the Lord's pause to ponder what's really important in life. Enjoy any time of interruption to love loved ones and friends who are sick unto death.

"I was sick and you looked after me" (Matthew 25:36b).

Related Readings: Exodus 23:25; Psalm 41:3; Luke 5:15-17; James 5:14-15

LIFE GIVING PEACE

A heart at peace gives life to the body, but envy rots the bones.
Proverbs 14:30

———◄●●►———

Peace produces life for a life surrendered to God. But, it is in conflict with Christ that a life's internal harmony is replaced with unrest. However, the fruit of peace is life: life-giving energy in relationships, life-giving words at work, life-giving attitudes at home, and life-giving community with other Jesus followers. Spiritual peace gives physical life.

If peace is such an essential ingredient for life, why can it be so elusive and difficult to maintain? Guilt has a way of grinding away at the goodness of God that lies dormant in a heart unaffected by discipleship. Conversion to Christ does not guarantee His peace will have preeminence, but it does position us for easy access to His grace. Like an orphan adopted by loving parents— acceptance of our heavenly Father's love creates peaceful security. Use His peace as a shield against Satan's schemes of discouragement and disappointment. You don't have to look far for life-giving peace; it is already yours in God's Son Jesus.

"I have told you these things, so that in me you may have peace. In this world you will have trouble. But take heart! I have overcome the world" (John 16:33).

Related Readings: Psalm 119:165; Isaiah 54:10;
2 Corinthians 13:11; Ephesians 6:23

SOLICIT PRAYERS

Pray for us. We are sure that we have a clear conscience and desire to live honorably in every way. I particularly urge you to pray so that I may be restored to you soon. Hebrews 13:18-19

The need for prayer is not just a private matter, but it's also one that requires public awareness. Prayer is personal, and it invites the engagement of other Christ followers. Personal needs aren't meant for concealment like a castaway on a deserted island. Instead, during uncertain circumstances, communities of believers rally together in intercession on behalf of their brothers and sisters. Prayer is a platform to say: "I care."

We are not to wait on others to ask how they can pray for us (though asking is a good habit for caring Christians); rather, we are to request prayer. Yes, it sounds selfish but it's not. It is the opportunity to allow another to be blessed as they approach heaven on behalf of your healing. Our pride is put in its proper place when we humble ourselves to ask for prayer. What need in your life needs to be known, so other Christ followers can come around you with powerful solicitations to Jesus? God knows, but His children also need to know now.

"Pray that the LORD your God will tell us where we should go and what we should do" (Jeremiah 42:3).

Related Readings: Job 42:9-10; Psalm 122:6; Acts 20:36; Romans 15:30

SENSITIVE SPOUSE

While Pilate was sitting on the judge's seat, his wife sent him this message: "Don't have anything to do with that innocent man, for I have suffered a great deal today in a dream because of Him." Matthew 27:19

Smart is the spouse who is sensitive to his or her spouse. God placed your husband or wife in your life to speak His thoughts through them. This doesn't mean every word from a marriage partner is perfect advice, but it does mean we are wise if we listen to their admonishments. Suggestions from your spouse are not to be slighted but taken seriously.

Rarely have I suffered harm by taking my wife's advice, but many times have I travailed for not trusting her instincts. Does your spouse know about the financial decision you are considering? Even if they are not interested, you honor them by asking for their input and keeping them informed of the facts. A sensitive spouse takes the time to communicate. Thank the Lord for a spouse who cares enough to speak up when they are concerned. Listen to them and love them through the process with prayer and collaboration. Christ gave you a sensitive spouse so you can learn to be sensitive to them and to Him

"The way of fools seems right to them, but the wise listen to advice" (Proverbs 12:15).

Related Readings: Exodus 18:19; Proverbs 19:20; Jeremiah 38:15; Acts 27:11

HELP HOLD STEADY

When Moses' hands grew tired, they took a stone and put it under him and he sat on it. Aaron and Hur held his hands up—one on one side, one on the other—so that his hands remained steady till sunset. Exodus 17:12

It is necessary we hold steady for our Savior during hard times, but we can't do it by ourselves. We need an Aaron and a Hur to hold up our hands of faith to heaven. Spiritual battle is too bruising to go at it alone. Physical and emotional fatigue set in if we are isolated. But, even a community of three can lift us to the Lord for strength and encouragement.

I have to often ask myself, "Whom am I submitting to for encouragement and accountability?" "Am I sitting on the rock of Jesus, and am I supported by His servants?" We hold steady when we are focused on the Lord and engaged in the prayerful presence of His people. No need to panic, but persevere in prayer, and trust God's control for things out of your control. Hold steady by holding up open hands to heaven, and He will fill you with faith. Encourage others to remain true to the Lord with all their hearts.

"When he arrived and saw what the grace of God had done, he was glad and encouraged them all to remain true to the Lord with all their hearts" (Acts 11:23).

Related Readings: Job 16:5; Psalm 10:17; Acts 15:32; Colossians 4:8

AUGUST

Keep this Book of the Law always on your lips; meditate on it day
and night, so that you may be careful to do everything written in
it. Then you will be prosperous and successful.

Joshua 1:8

AUGUST 1

WISDOM SEEKS GOD

The LORD looks down from heaven on humankind to see if
there are any who are wise, who seek after God.
Psalm 14:2, NRSV

———————————

There could be a large life-changing decision looming. It may
relate to the timing in childbearing, the opportunity for a move
and a new job, the sale of a business, a spiritual commitment,
graduate school, or treatment options related to a health issue.
The Lord looks down from heaven for wise ones who will seek
Him for the best answers. He doesn't look down with disdain
but with determined love, compassion, and insight.

The Lord seeks those who seek Him. He gazes all over the globe
in one grand glance ready to grant grace and truth to trusting
souls. He looks for the once zealous Christ follower and entreats
him or her to come back to the basics of belief. He watches for
the wise who hail from humble circumstances or the learned
who want to lean into the Lord. He looks to unleash His love,
dispense discernment, and convert sinners to saints. You are
wise to seek the Wisest One— Jesus—first in simple salvation
and second as a faithful follower.

"But if from there you seek the LORD your God, you will find
him if you seek him with all your heart and with all your soul"
(Deuteronomy 4:29).

Related Readings: Psalm 33:13; 138:6; Proverbs 18:15;
Acts 17:27; Romans 3:11

SOUL NOURISHMENT

My soul thirsts for God, for the living God. When can I go and
meet with God? Psalm 42:2

Spirit-filled Christians crave Christ—there is an insatiable desire
for intimacy with their Savior. Activity and busyness (even for
God) can taste like sawdust to the soul, but sitting at the feet of
Jesus revives the spirit and satisfies the deepest longings to be
known and loved by the Lord. Like water hydrates the body,
only heaven hydrates the heart.

Our innermost being hungers and thirsts for spiritual food, but
do we take the time to shop at God's grocery store? Are we
hunting for healthy soul food, or are we snacking at the world's
table with a diet that is detrimental to the eternal? Our master
Jesus has a menu made up of spiritual nutrients that nourish the
soul. His filling food is accessed by faith. Wake up and worship
the Lord—mid-morning, snack on Scripture—listen to the
Lord at lunch—mid-afternoon, meditate on your blessings—at
dinner discuss His faithfulness—and thank Him as you retire
in the evening. A soul nourished by God meets with God and is
eternally satisfied.

"Then Jesus declared, 'I am the bread of life. Whoever comes
to me will never go hungry, and whoever believes in me will
never be thirsty'" (John 6:35).

Related Readings: 2 Chronicles 15:12; Isaiah 61:10;
Mark 12:30; Luke 1:46

AUGUST 3

BOLD BAPTISM

All authority in heaven and on earth has been given to me.
Therefore go and make disciples of all nations, baptizing them
in the name of the Father and of the Son and of the Holy Spirit.
Matthew 28:18b-19

Baptism is a bold declaration of a personal belief in Jesus
Christ. It is an outward expression of an inward conversion.
Baptism is symbolic of an individual Christian (normally a
new believer) burying their old way of life and coming alive
in Christ. Jesus commands baptism for His children. He
knows the accountability, the encouragement, and the love that
accompanies this act of obedience.

Who is a candidate for baptism? If you have placed your faith
in Jesus Christ as your Lord and Savior, your next step is to
follow the example of Jesus and be baptized. He modeled the
way of humble submission when as the Son of God He insisted
on being baptized by another. Baptism identifies you with God's
forever family of faith. Baptism is not to be taken lightly; your
Lord Jesus took it very seriously. So, seek out a trusted church
and publicly picture your death to self and new life in Christ.

"Buried with Him through baptism into death in order that, just
as Christ was raised from the dead through the glory of the
Father, we too may live a new life" (Romans 6:4).

Related Readings: Matt. 3:13-17; Acts 2:38; Colossians 2:11-
13; Galatians 3:26-28

LEADERS OF INTEGRITY

But select capable men from all the people—men who fear God, trustworthy men who hate dishonest gain—and appoint them as officials over thousands, hundreds, fifties and tens.
Exodus 18:21

Leaders of integrity are a rare breed within a group of citizens whose utmost concern is, "What is in it for me?" A selfish society does not always select leaders for their integrity but for their ability to manipulate a quick fix for chronic problems. It is this shortsightedness that can set back a generation because of their leader's greed and corruption.

However, men and women of integrity understand the big picture of principled leadership, and they value fear of God, trustworthiness, and honest transactions. A leader of integrity looks out over the long term and discovers what is best for the culture, its citizens, churches, and families. There is a resolve to do the right things, with the right people, for the right reasons. Leaders of integrity integrate uprightness with their quiet influence.

"Then the LORD said to Satan, 'Have you considered my servant Job? There is no one on earth like him; he is blameless and upright, a man who fears God and shuns evil. And he still maintains his integrity, though you incited me against him to ruin him without any reason'" (Job 2:3).

Related Readings: 1 Kings 9:3-5; Psalm 25:21; 78:72; Mark 12:14; 2 Corinthians 1:12

LOVE AND HONOR

Be devoted to one another in love. Honor one another above yourselves. Romans 12:10

What does it mean to be devoted in love and to honor another above oneself? It is much more than being selfless; it is gladly preferring to put another's needs ahead of one's own. Because you hold the relationship in such high esteem, you want them to feel the power of being preferred over your agenda or expectations. In marriage devoted love matters most.

Husbands who look to love by engaging their wives' emotions grow in patience and understanding. The insensitive coldly dismiss and dishonor a loved one's concerns, but a true lover looks for ways to work things out for their spouse's benefit. A wife honors her husband when she seeks to know his work world and empathize with his challenges. Only you, with love and honor, can uniquely meet certain God-given needs in your spouse. Therefore, make it your goal to grow your relationships in love, honor, and glad service for God. A sense of superiority has no room in relationships—love esteems others above self.

"Do nothing out of selfish ambition or vain conceit. Rather, in humility value others above yourselves, not looking to your own interests but each of you to the interests of the others" (Philippians 2:3-4).

Related Readings: Proverbs 21:21; Isaiah 43:4; 1 Peter 2:17; 2 Peter 1:17

AUGUST 6

PROMISE OF HEAVEN

And if I go and prepare a place for you, I will come back and take you to be with me that you also may be where I am.
John 14:3

———•◦•◦•———

Jesus extends the promise of heaven to all who come to Him by faith. Eternal life with Him is reason enough to receive the gift of God's grace in His Son. Jesus prepares a place in heaven for those who have prepared for heaven. He preparations are intentional for people who are intentional in their faith preparation. Heaven is prepared for the prepared.

Are you prepared for heaven? Are you standing on the promises of your Savior Jesus? His promises are profound: forgiveness of sin, eternal life with Him, grace to live life, sweet fellowship with the Holy Spirit, answered prayer, the Spirit's leading in God's will, peace, joy, patience, self-control, and love from the Spirit's fullness. Paradise with Jesus is the promise He makes to all those who come to Him in repentance and faith. Christ was punished for doing right so that our wrongs could be made right by His death. Our hearts need not be troubled, because the Lord has already gone to the trouble of paving the way for heaven. His Father's house is furnished for all His faithful followers.

"Truly I tell you, today you will be with me [Jesus] in paradise" (Luke 23:43).

Related Readings: Matthew 4:17; 16:17; Philippians 3:14, 20; 1 Thessalonians 1:10

AUGUST 7

PROMISE OF HELL

The rich man also died and was buried. In Hades, where he was in torment, he looked up and saw Abraham far away, with Lazarus by his side. Luke 16:22b-23

The promise of hell is not fun to talk about, but is a somber reality relayed by our Savior Jesus. He is our Savior because He saves us from our sins and from eternal damnation in hell. Hell brings separation—Jesus brings reconciliation. Hell brings torment—Jesus brings peace. Hell brings darkness—Jesus brings light. Hell hurts—Heaven heals. Our same loving Lord who promises heaven also promises hell.

Indeed, heaven is sweeter because of the sour taste eternal separation from God leaves on the lips of our soul. We begin our experience of hell on earth when we choose our own way, in contrast to Christ's way. Separation on earth from God is a precursor to separation from the Almighty in eternity. It is a fearful place of loneliness that lacks love and security. Better to be known as a God-fearing man or woman than to experience the wrath of God. The power of man looks powerless in the presence of the One who has the power to cast the unsaved into hell. Sinners in the hands of a holy God desperately need His grace.

"Therefore, there is now no condemnation for those who are in Christ Jesus" (Romans 8:1).

Related Readings: Matthew 23:33; Mark 9:43-47; James 3:6; 2 Peter 2:4

BENEFITS OF REPENTANCE

If you had responded to my rebuke, I would have poured out
my heart to you and made my thoughts known to you.
Proverbs 1:23, NIV84

There are benefits that belong to real repentance. When you and
I respond to correction in humility and teachability, we are in a
position to be blessed by wisdom. Another's rebuke causes our
pride to bristle, but defensiveness is not where wisdom resides.
Wisdom is attracted to the man or woman who comes clean with
their sins and shortcomings. It is when our spouse or supervisor
uncovers inconsistencies in our words and actions, that we are
wise to listen and learn. Even when someone rebukes us with
raw emotion, we are to receive it and repent of our wrong.

Moreover, pray for messengers with mixed motives, and the
Almighty will give them the necessary attitude adjustment. Your
part is to repent and trust Him with the rest. Indeed, God reveals
His heart to those responsive to rebuke. Instruction is an ally
that grows your understanding of, and intimacy with, almighty
God. So, seek out the mature of faith and give them permission
to encounter any erroneous actions in your life.

"God has granted repentance that leads to life" (Acts 11:18b).

Related Readings: Job 36:10-12; Jeremiah 15:19; Luke 13:3-5;
Revelation 3:19

AUGUST 9

ATTENTION TO DETAILS

Then the angel said to him, "Put on your clothes and sandals."
And Peter did so. "Wrap your cloak around you and follow
me," the angel told him. Acts 12:8

Almighty God is in the details, because He knows the details
define a clear path for His will. Like Peter, His angel has to
sometimes shake us out of the slumber of our sleepy selves.
We can nap in our pitiful prison of fear and forget God is still at
work. He wants us to welcome His sudden shake-up so we can
see Christ's course for our lives more clearly. Perhaps the Holy
Spirit is sifting us so we will see the details of what He is doing.
When Christ crashes into our circumstances, it is certainly wise
to wake up and wonder what He is doing.

Pay attention to His work around you, and listen to the Lord's
leading. The smile of an infant may be just the small sign you
need to show He is pleased with you. God's got the details
covered, so seek Him first for His discernment and He will
lead you through every important step along the way. However,
don't drown in the details, but stay moving empowered by Him
for the results.

"Paul greeted them and reported in detail what God had done
among the Gentiles through his ministry" (Acts 21:19).

Related Readings: 1 Chronicles 28:19; Matthew 6:25-34;
Hebrews 9:5

EMOTIONAL INVESTMENTS

That is why a man leaves his father and mother and is united to his wife, and they become one flesh. Genesis 2:24

———◆◆◆———

Growing relationships require regular investments of emotional energy. Because humans have the capacity for emotional engagement, there is a level of feeling and understanding that machines or animals can never attain. God's creation—created in His image—is able to engage in intimate encounters. Emotions are meant to move people toward the eternal. Marriage especially demands growing emotional intelligence to thrive, not merely survive. The Lord has created an emotional vacuum within a husband a wife that only their spouse can fill.

It is folly to seek to meet this very real need with work or children, for false substitutes only stunt emotional maturity in marriage. "One flesh" means to forge an alliance and an allegiance among our mind, will, and emotions. First, by faith, become one with Christ and second, with love, patience, and understanding, become one with each other. Emotional investments today pay the dividends of oneness tomorrow. Your oneness in marriage illustrates your faith in Christ.

"We ought always to thank God for you, brothers and sisters, and rightly so, because your faith is growing more and more, and the love you have for one another is increasing" (2 Thessalonians 1:3).

Related Readings: Galatians 5:13; Hebrews 12:3, 15; 1 Peter 2:2; 2 Peter 3:18

MARRIAGE COVENANT

Who has left the partner of her youth and ignored the covenant she made before God. Proverbs 2:17

Marriage is a covenant before God, not to be messed with by man. It is not a secular ceremony, but a Christ-centered commitment "until death do us part." However, there are tempters, both men and women, who try to take away the trust between a husband and a wife. Their life is unhappy, so they scheme for artificial satisfaction at the expense of someone else's marriage. Sin is not passive but active, so be on prayerful alert not to listen to its allure. Pay attention and do not place yourself in compromising circumstances.

Marriage is a sacred obligation; God is not only a witness but the one who instituted the ordinance, so stay true to Him and your true love. How do you maintain this high standard of honor? By God's grace you romance each other like the days when you were dating. You only share your heart and affections with your true love, the bride of your youth. Lastly, celebrate and uphold marriage as a solemn covenant before the Lord, family, friends, and each other.

"Marriage should be honored by all, and the marriage bed kept pure" (Hebrews 13:4a).

Related Readings: Numbers 5:12-22; Malachi 2:14-16; Matthew 5:27-32

CREATION GIVES LIFE

You give life to everything, and the multitudes of heaven worship you. Nehemiah 9:6b

———◆———

God's creation gives life to life. The conception of a baby gives life to the infant and his family. The canopy of Christ's heaven gives light and life to all living things, especially to those who look to the Lord in reverent worship. The sky captures the eastern sun on an arc-like invisible track, and moves it each day to its resting place in the west. The hope of another sunrise and sunset stream into a cold, fearful heart and warm it with peace and faith.

The sea is an incubator for life: mammals and sea urchins all drink from their watery world the life-giving nutrients needed to survive in their predator infested world. It's when ocean creatures languish on the seashore that they lose life, some slowly, some immediately. In the same way, the Holy Spirit is our sea of strength in the Lord. It's when we wash up on the shore of disobedience that our soul smoothers in a sandy grave. The Lord's stature and trustworthiness grow larger than life when we experience His life-giving creation. The Spirit energizes us as we enjoy His creation.

"Praise the LORD from the earth, you great sea creatures and all ocean depths, lightning and hail, snow and clouds, stormy winds that do His bidding" (Psalm 148:7-8).

Related Readings: Psalm 133:3; Isaiah 42:10; Romans 8:19-22; Hebrews 4:13

THE LORD'S FAVOR

"**I**f now I [Moses] have found favor in your sight, O Lord, I pray, let the Lord go with us." Exodus 34:9, NRSV

The Lord's favor precedes those who follow hard after Him. It is a surrendered life of faith and obedience that is able to enjoy supernatural strength from the Holy Spirit. Favor from above is not bought or manipulated on earth; rather it is an act of grace that God gives to those He can trust. The Lord's favor is found on those faithful to His Word. Are you enjoying the favor of your heavenly Father in your family and work? Are you grateful to God for the opportunities and people He has placed in your life? His favor is not to be taken for granted or forgotten.

In fact, unacknowledged favor from the Lord loses the Almighty's acknowledgement. His favor flourishes where faith is the focus. Handle well His blessing on the little things in your life, and you become a candidate for favor in situations with a larger scope of influence. Thus, with a humble and contrite spirit, obey His Word, and be extremely grateful for the Lord's favor. Yes, stay "blessable," so you can be a blessing to others.

"'The Lord has done this for me,' she said. 'In these days he has shown His favor and taken away my disgrace among the people'" (Luke 1:25).

Related Readings: Genesis 28:10-22; Psalm 90:17; Proverbs 8:35; 11:1; 12; 18:22

PAY BACK

Beloved, do not avenge yourselves, but rather give place to wrath; for it is written, "Vengeance is Mine, I will repay," says the Lord. Romans 12:19, NKJV

People are not capable of properly paying back those who have hurt or offended them. Payback is not in the glossary of followers of Jesus, because He has already paid the debt for another's offense. Christians are not determined to get even with evil intent; rather they offer grace and forgiveness. Payback is God's pay grade—His justice can be trusted.

Vengeance is the Lord's because His perspective is perfect. He sees the heart, weighs motives, and dishes out discipline as He sees fit. Because He owns the process of payback, we are wise not to intervene in His plan. If we take matters into our own hands, we may jeopardize the recognition of divine justice needed to draw someone to Christ. In the end, it's all about all of us being accountable to the Almighty. Justice points to Jesus.

"I will carry out great vengeance on them and punish them in my wrath. Then they will know that I am the LORD, when I take vengeance on them" (Ezekiel 25:17).

Related Readings: Isaiah 35:8; 61:2; Micah 5:15; Nahum 1:2; Hebrews 10:30

GRATITUDE AND CONTENTMENT

I know what it is to be in need, and I know what it is to have plenty. I have learned the secret of being content in any and every situation, whether well fed or hungry, whether living in plenty or in want. Philippians 4:12

Gratitude and contentment go together like turkey and dressing. They feed each other, and both are fostered by faith. When I remember how God has so richly blessed me, I am overwhelmed by His generosity. For example, for His salvation in His Son Jesus, I am eternally grateful. His gift of grace: I am grateful for its freedom. His forgiveness: I am grateful for guilt-free living. His love: I am grateful for the ability to love and be loved.

Your peace and stability is the fruit of contentment, which grows out of the ground of gratitude. Seed this soil in prayer, and you will see abundance abound. You are able to accommodate in adversity because the Almighty has gone before you. You are able to bridle wants in prosperity, because gratitude to God and contentment in Christ governs your generosity. Thank God often, and trust Him to cultivate your contentment.

"The fear of the LORD leads to life; then one rests content, untouched by trouble" (Proverbs 19:23).

Related Readings: Job 1:21; Colossians 2:6-7; 2 Corinthians 6:4-10; Ephesians 4:20-24

UNEXPECTED GOOD NEWS

"Jesus, remember me when you come into your kingdom."
Jesus answered him, "Truly I tell you, today you will be with
me in paradise." Luke 23:42-43

Unexpected good news can take a sincere soul off guard as
much as bad news can. But, it is in the pleasantness of the
Lord's comforting words that gratitude and joy are released.
Emotion erupts in praise and thanksgiving when a "no" was
expected, but a "yes" was lovingly communicated. Humility
asks the Lord for His forgiving presence and love. Grateful
and wise disciples request the Lord to remember them now and
forever.

Sometimes we strive in uncertainty, ever wondering what's
next. We tentatively to get our hopes up, because in the past we
have seen hopeful expectations dashed into discouragement.
So, in some situations we find ourselves somewhat skeptical of
positive outcomes. Guilt and disappointment jar the foundations
of faith with profound persistence. But the Lord does not want
to leave His children in suspense—He clarifies. He remembers
you, so you can remember Him and remember others with
unexpected good news. Faith expects the unexpected.

"You who bring good news to Zion, go up on a high mountain.
You who bring good news to Jerusalem, lift up your voice with
a shout, lift it up, do not be afraid; say to the towns of Judah,
'Here is your God'" (Isaiah 40:9).

Related Readings: 2 Kings 7:9; Proverbs 15:30; Mark 1:1;
1 Thessalonians 3:6

DEMOLISH STRONGHOLDS

We demolish arguments and every pretension that sets itself up against the knowledge of God, and we take captive every thought to make it obedient to Christ. 2 Corinthians 10:5

Strongholds are Satan's attempt to strangle spiritual life out of the saints of God. The enemy is not slack in his attacks, indeed he is always on the prowl to pronounce judgment and dispense shame. Some of his strategic strongholds are pride, addiction, and self-absorption. He sucks in a susceptible heart and a wandering mind with alluring sin. The devil builds a faithless fortress and launches missiles of doubt with false ideologies.

How do strongholds take hold and grow in our lives? Ironically, a strength can become a stronghold. Healthy confidence drifts into arrogance. The gift of discernment grows into a judgmental attitude. The discipline to work out regularly and eat right becomes an obsession that consumes every minute of our discretionary time. The goal to get ahead financially grows into greed and a sense of superiority. A strength can be a stronghold. Divine strongholds defeat Satan's. Trust in the Lord tears down demonic strongholds and erects His faithful fortress over them.

"The LORD is good, a stronghold in the day of trouble; and He knows those who trust in Him" (Nahum 1:7, NKJV).

Related Readings: Psalm 9:9; 27:1; 37:39; Lamentations 2:2-5

CONFESS AND RENOUNCE

Whoever conceals their sins does not prosper, but the one who confesses and renounces them finds mercy. Proverbs 28:13

Sin that man covers, Christ will uncover. Sin that man uncovers, Christ will cover. He covers it with His love. Shame seeks to hide unseemly behavior from heaven, but a loving Savior brings grace to feelings of disgrace. It is better to quickly reveal to God what He already knows. Admission is healing. Sin that is concealed compounds its cruel consequences, but immediate confession and renouncement lessens its unholy effect. Like sodium contributes to rising blood pressure, so sin contributes to a sick and sad heart.

However, the remedy of walking in humility brings down the demon of disillusioned living and replaces it with peaceful wisdom. A clear conscience has clarity regarding the ways of God. Sin ignored is a silent killer of relational intimacy, but sin laid bare finds mercy. The degree of our indiscretions determine the depth of pain, so far better to come clean with Christ than to live a lie in silent suffering. So, bow in humble confession and genuine repentance as His glory and mercy make you whole. Renounce your sins by doing what is right.

"Therefore, Your Majesty, be pleased to accept my advice: Renounce your sins by doing what is right, and your wickedness by being kind to the oppressed" (Daniel 4:27a).

Related Readings: Ezekiel 14:6; Daniel 4:27; Acts 14:15; 2 Corinthians 4:2

RECESSION-PROOF KINGDOM

Our Father in heaven, hallowed be your name, your kingdom come, your will be done on earth as it is in heaven.
Matthew 6:9-10, NIV84

The Kingdom of God is recession proof because the economy of God is based on the character of God. His commerce is not measured by man's GDP (Gross Domestic Product), but by God's Divine Provision. As we pray, "Your kingdom come," our concern with productivity will be surpassed by the acceleration of His kingdom. God gains momentum as man gets his eye off his earthly kingdom and onto the Kingdom of Heaven. Economic decline and distress are opportunities for God's global advancement.

Indeed, Christ's influence is counter cycle to a culture caught up in commerce. Our fiscal slowdown is a prime time for the Lord's Prayer to be answered. It speeds up His kingdom's progress. The gospel of Christ goes forth in prosperous periods, but it is especially appealing during difficult days. Don't waste a recession, it is reason to reach out and represent Jesus well. Use this time of discomfort to bring comfort, and pray for those in pain to be healed. Invite and introduce to Jesus, those who have a fresh interest in heaven's agenda. The Kingdom of God is robust, reassuring, and resourceful during recessionary days. Reach out to the weary for rest.

"Repent, for the kingdom of heaven is at hand" (Matthew 3:2, NASB).

Related Readings: Daniel 7:13-27; Zechariah 9:9; Colossians 1:9-13; Hebrews 10:7-36

FREE TO FORGIVE

So if the Son sets you free, you will be free indeed. John 8:36

———◆◆◆———

Every follower of Jesus Christ is free to forgive, because they have been set free. Freedom to forgive is not an elusive opportunity in which only the super spiritual saints participate. In fact, it is the natural disposition for the normal Christian life. People of faith who don't extend forgiveness to all masquerade their own forgiveness. A lost world watches a disciple of Jesus forgive and wonders how they can experience that same freedom.

Indeed, effective evangelism follows a forgiving lifestyle. It is unconventional and unnatural to not hold a grudge or not to remain bitter toward a person who has violated the moral rights of another—especially one victimized by an unscrupulous authority. But a mature believer lets go of hurt and lets God heal and deal with the offender. Those who have not tasted the forgiveness of God do not know any better—they remain in bondage—but you who are freed by Him, do. Christ's love liberates—His forgiveness sets free—you are free indeed to do the same.

"It is for freedom that Christ has set us free. Stand firm, then, and do not let yourselves be burdened again by a yoke of slavery" (Galatians 5:1).

Related Readings: Genesis 50:17; Matthew 18:35; Mark 11:25; Luke 23:34; Romans 8:2

WARNED BY GOD

By faith Noah, warned by God about events as yet unseen, respected the warning and built an ark to save his household.
Hebrews 11:7a, NRSV

———————

Christ, because of His great compassion—warns His children of unseen events yet to come. His mercy allows those who seek Him by faith to be privy to knowledge the natural man or woman can't perceive. Those insensitive to His intimacy tend to slight the Spirit's promptings, while those sensitive to secret warnings from God prayerfully prepare.

Wise are the children of God who heed their heavenly Father's warnings. Like a child who heeds an earthly father who describes a destructive path ahead, smart and shrewd are the son or daughter who learns from the One who loves them the most. We give our hearts to the Lord to be led by the Lord. Others may ridicule our preparedness, but by faith we persevere in our preparations. We adjust our plans based on a better understanding of God's revelation. Be on the lookout for the Lord's warnings in your life. Astute is the man or woman who responds to the flashing lights on the dashboard of their behavior.

"See to it that you do not refuse him who speaks. If they did not escape when they refused him who warned them on earth, how much less will we, if we turn away from him who warns us from heaven?" (Hebrews 12:25)

Related Readings: Psalm 19:9-14; Proverbs 22:3; Mark 8:15; Acts 2:40; 1 Thessalonians 4:6

AUGUST 22

DISCIPLINED DISCIPLE

Everyone who competes in the games goes into strict training.
1 Corinthians 9:25a

Discipline is a prerequisite for a disciple of Jesus Christ. A wise, disciplined person knows how to stay focused on what's most important, trusting other urgent matters will take care of themselves in the right time. Paul uses the illustration of athletic training to motivate us to discipline. A compelling motivation for the athlete is the reward at the end. The reward at the finish line makes worthwhile the sometimes painful workout process and regimented routine.

This is why we memorize Scripture now for wisdom later. We exercise now for energy later. We rise early now in prayer for peace later. We give generously now for rewards later. Discipline in the now creates benefits for the future. It becomes a habit of life when there are clearly defined goals and steps to achieve them. Discipline provides laser-beam focus through structure and accountability. Disciplined people make discipline infectious. Surround yourself with people of discipline and you will become better disciplined. Maturing disciples create habits of spiritual discipline.

"For God did not give us a spirit of timidity, but a spirit of power, of love and of self-discipline" (2 Timothy 1:7, NIV84).

Related Readings: Deuteronomy 29:6; Proverbs 25:16;
2 Corinthians 5:14

COMPARISON'S CRAZY CYCLE

When Peter saw him, he asked, "Lord, what about him?" Jesus answered, "If I want him to remain alive until I return, what is that to you? You must follow me." John 21:21-22

No one wins when comparison is the criteria for being valued. If people are the plumb line for a sense of success—then there are always those who are smarter, prettier, and richer. An unrealistic appraisal of others feeds a feeling of failure. On the other hand, pride puffs up with a subtle notion of superiority when it looks to others as a standard for living. Jesus smiles and says, "What is that to you?" Comparison is not a win for anyone.

Yes, we can be inspired and instructed by a life that seeks to emulate the Lord, but we are not to idolize any individual. Of course, we are wise to learn from the mistakes of others, but not with a secret delight that believes we look better when the unfortunate look bad. Our discontent is compounded under the demanding nature of comparison. We cannot enjoy what we have for the allure of what we don't have. Comparison kills contentment. It is a crazy cycle!

"We do not dare to classify or compare ourselves with some who commend themselves. When they measure themselves by themselves and compare themselves with themselves, they are not wise" (2 Corinthians 10:12).

Related Readings: Proverbs 8:11; Ecclesiastes 4:5-6; Romans 12:15; James 3:14-16

PUBLIC AFFIRMATION, PRIVATE CORRECTION

The words of the reckless pierce like swords, but the tongue of the wise brings healing. Proverbs 12:18

Men and women alike feel encouraged by public affirmation and respected by private correction. Men especially have needs, facilitated by their egos, that are sensitive to these two scenarios. In fact, a husband who is publicly corrected by his spouse can feel angry and ashamed. Thus, wise is the woman who builds him up and trusts God to keep him humble. Her words of affirmation are an assurance of love, affection, and respect. We all respond much better to words delivered with respect in a relational way.

It's when our heart hurts that we lose perspective and sometimes unknowingly tear down someone dear to us. Healing comes from being known and loved, not from dishonor and shame. So, we are wise to offer love and forgiveness in the form of public affirmation and private correction to those we deeply care about. Love seeks to understand a beloved's needs. It listens to and speaks another's love language. Above all, look to the Lord for eternal encouragement that is able to triumph over earthly disappointments.

"I will set my eyes upon them for good… I will build them up, and not tear them down; I will plant them, and not pluck them up" (Jeremiah 24:6, NRSV).

Related Readings: Isaiah 57:14; Jeremiah 22:13; Acts 20:32; Ephesians 4:16

DEPEND ON GOD

I am the vine you are the branches. If a man remains in me, and I in him, he will bear much fruit; apart from me you can do nothing. John 15:5, NIV84

What does it mean to depend on God, and do I practice dependency daily? It is faith and confidence in Christ, but sometimes it is a struggle to see because dependence is deployed from our soul and spirit. It seems easier to depend on the Lord when disease deteriorates the body than when anger allies with my attitude. Dependence on God means we need Him, and we understand that without Him we are unable to accomplish anything of Kingdom significance.

Reliance on Jesus is the door to faithful and fruitful living. It means we are transformed by the Lord; therefore, we can depend on Him for wisdom and insight. Perhaps He will guide you over the next year to pay down debt, decrease spending, and increase saving and giving. Indeed, we can depend on Him for the fruit of frugality and generosity. Dependence on the Lord deepens your determination. We depend on God because we are desperate and detached without Him. Jesus is our source of strength in good times and our hope in hard times.

"This is what the Lord says: 'Cursed is the one who trusts in man, who draws strength from mere flesh and whose heart turns away from the Lord.'" (Jeremiah 17:5).

Related Readings: 2 Kings 18:22; Psalm 62:7 Romans 9:16; Galatians 3:18

AUGUST 26

PREEMPTIVE PHYSICAL CARE

Please test your servants for ten days: Give us nothing but vegetables to eat and water to drink… At the end of the ten days they looked healthier and better nourished than any of the young men who ate the royal food. Daniel 1:12, 15

There is a physical stewardship for every soul saved by Jesus Christ. In the same sensitive way the spirit of a person is cared for, their body needs proper attention. As age increases with time, it is from a platform of physical care that spiritual opportunities continue. Yes, some are called to physically suffer for Christ's sake, but the Lord does not want His children to ignorantly neglect their health. Bodies need intentional care.

Our body is a finely tuned complexity of cells, tissue, and organs with almighty God as the architect. Divine DNA determines the genes, but individuals write their medical history. This is why prayer and modern medicine are a responsible combination. We educate ourselves in what our bodies need to function best in a fallen world. We look to medical experts and learn from them, and we ask the Lord for the wisest treatment for us. Jesus expects us to love Him with our body and soul!

"For you created my inmost being; you knit me together in my mother's womb. I praise you because I am fearfully and wonderfully made" (Psalm 139:13-14a).

Related Readings: Deuteronomy 8:16; Leviticus 25:7; Galatians 2:20; Ephesians 5:29

AUGUST 27

HEART TENDERIZER

Who comforts us in all our troubles, so that we can comfort those in any trouble with the comfort we ourselves receive from God. 2 Corinthians 1:4

Great trials produce big hearts. But within those who have never been knocked down or have not felt the woes of adversity, hearts are small and insensitive. Indeed, it is on the bed of affliction that human beings find themselves horizontal—looking up to the Lord in heaven. A plague of bad news will pass—leaving behind a righteous residue on all hearts softened by the Spirit.

Where does the core of comfort come from for a Christian? Our consolation comes from Christ, in whom there resides an eternal security that transcends all fiery trials. He wraps us up with His love, and with a fire-resistant blanket of belief. Jesus replaces anxiety with peace and fear with courage. He is a friend who upholds a friend facing great loss and gives His loyal support. A heart grows tender and true under the loving influence of the Lord. Your tenderized heart is trustworthy to Jesus.

"Because your heart was responsive and you humbled yourself before God when you heard what he spoke against this place and its people, and because you humbled yourself before me and tore your robes and wept in my presence, I have heard you, declares the LORD" (2 Chronicles 34:27).

Related Readings: Joshua 22:5; 1 Samuel 10:9; Luke 1:78; Acts 15:8; Hebrews 4:12

250

QUIET COMPASSIONATE CAREGIVER

Then Naomi took the child in her arms and cared for him.
Ruth 4:16

There are heroes of the faith who care for the downtrodden, the dejected, and the diseased. Quietly these saints serve in Jesus' name: foster children, inner city kids, and orphans who need a household of faith. Others unselfishly, nobly, love the handicapped and mentally challenged. Compassion cures the ills of isolation with its consistent love and acceptance. Do you often pray for and support these Christ-like caregivers?

It may be your mother or father caring for their mother or father in the twilight of their years. It could be a church acquaintance at the side of her husband caught in the grip of cancer, or a neighbor's wife withering away from Alzheimer's. Indeed, support those supporting those who suffer. Most of all—rest in the compassionate and caring arms of your heavenly Father. It brings Him great joy to hold you close and whisper in your ear how He's eclipsed your afflictions by His glory and sustains you by His grace and love. His comfort carries you through the most stressful circumstances.

"Even to your old age and gray hairs I am he, I am he who will sustain you. I have made you and I will carry you; I will sustain you and I will rescue you" (Isaiah 46:4).

Related Readings: Deuteronomy 32:10; Hosea 12:13; Acts 7:20; 1 Thessalonians 2:8

ONE WITH GOD

But whoever is united with the Lord is one with him in spirit.
1 Corinthians 6:17

———————

Oneness with God opens the door for intimacy and understanding. It is a place of peace and contentment. At a Christian's conversion there is a recalibration to Christ—alignment with the Almighty is instituted. But the world, the flesh, and the devil try to pull back believers from belief. Thus, wise Jesus followers seek unity around the Lord's agenda. God expects our behavior to bend toward His standards and expectations. Devout saints seek oneness in spirit with the Spirit of God. There is a prayerful and passionate pursuit of living out their holy position in Christ.

Any affection in competition with Christ threatens to seduce a soul into insignificant pursuits. It can be an acute obsession with sports or a chronic sexual exploitation. But, eternal affections become one with God in spirit. We romance a relationship with Jesus so we are not deceived to trust lost lovers. Indeed, prayer powers oneness with the Lord and others. What God joins together in union of spirit draws a lost world to Jesus. Unity in Christ draws others to Christ!

"My prayer is not for them alone. I pray also for those who will believe in me through their message, that all of them may be one, Father, just as you are in me and I am in you" (John 17:20-21a).

Related Readings: Romans 6:19; Ephesians 4:5; Philippians 3:21; Hebrews 2:5, 18

CELEBRATE RECOVERY

"**B**ring the fattened calf and kill it. Let's have a feast and celebrate. For this son of mine was dead and is alive again; he was lost and is found." So they began to celebrate.
Luke 15:23-24

Grateful Christians take the time to celebrate the recovery of loved ones. It may be a son or daughter who returns from the foreign country of selfish ambition and immoral living. Celebration could be an appropriate occasion to honor a friend who is recovering from abuse or addiction. Perhaps a family member is on the road to recovery after a long battle with cancer or another debilitating disease. Recovery calls for celebration!

A call to celebration makes much of God's faithfulness and the wise choices of the one in recovery. We know in our hearts that heaven deserves the credit for our blessings on earth. Thus, we take the time to give glory to God for His gracious healing of our soul, emotions, and our body. Ultimately, Christ causes a transformation of trust in our heart and mind. He loves us back to a place of rejoicing. It's a big deal when a body's healed; it's an even bigger deal when a soul's saved!

"Then Hannah prayed and said: 'My heart rejoices in the LORD; in the LORD my horn is lifted high. My mouth boasts over my enemies, for I delight in your deliverance'" (1 Samuel 2:1).

Related Readings: Deuteronomy 16:15; 2 Samuel 6:21; Psalm 145:7; Romans 12:15

GOD'S WORD

"The word of the Lord endures forever." And this is the word
that was preached to you. 1 Peter 1:25

What does it mean to get a word from the Lord? It means that
God in His infinite wisdom personalizes His principles for
each of His children. The Bible is an individualized love letter
delivered to each disciple of Jesus for his or her unique situation.
A word from the Lord gives hope in the face of discouragement,
wisdom for understanding, and courage to confront injustice.
Scriptures planted in the human heart are seeds of faith for the
soul.

We are blessed when we seek counsel from the wise, but when
we receive direction from almighty God in His Word, we can rest
secure. The Bible is the baseline for our beliefs and behavior. It
is the first and the final say for faith-based living. A day without
scriptural intake for our spirit is like missing three meals for
our body. God's Word nourishes our soul, is a trailblazer for
truth, and leads us into His very best for our life. His Holy Spirit
brings to life the pages of His Word in prayer. Study to know
the truth, and listen to apply the truth. Scripture gives stamina
to your faith.

"Consult God's instruction and the testimony of warning. If
anyone does not speak according to this word, they have no
light of dawn" (Isaiah 8:20).

Related Readings: Genesis 15:1; 1 Samuel 3:1-7; Luke 7:29;
2 Timothy 2:9

SEPTEMBER

Therefore, rid yourselves of all malice and all deceit, hypocrisy, envy, and slander of every kind. Like newborn babies, crave pure spiritual milk, so that by it you may grow up in your salvation, now that you have tasted that the Lord is good.

1 Peter 2:1-3

LACK OF UNDERSTANDING

I am your servant; give me discernment that I may understand
your statutes. Psalm 119:125

Discernment is not always easily understood. Where to live?
Where to go to school? Who to marry? Where to work? Who
to mentor or who to be mentored by? What to purchase? Where
to join a church? What doctor to visit or medicine to take? How
to parent? How to grow a healthy marriage? However, the Lord
wants His children to understand His ways. Answers from the
Almighty are the best, because they align us with His productive
plan.

Thus, we take time to first understand the wisest course of action
so we don't have to redo a wrong result. Listening to the Lord's
voice and understanding His choice brings calm and confidence
to our prayerful posture. It's when we run ahead of Jesus that
we run an unnecessary risk of reacting in the flesh. Indeed, we
learn to wait on understanding, when we remember the past pain
of pushing ahead in ignorance. Lack of discernment causes us
to scratch our heads, but it also guides our hearts in humble
dependence on Jesus. So, seek the Lord first and discernment
second. Walk with Christ, and comprehension will come in His
timing.

"They are shepherds who lack understanding; they all turn to
their own way, they seek their own gain" (Isaiah 56:11).

Related Readings: 1 Chronicles 22:12; Job 12:13;
Ecclesiastes 11:5; 1 Corinthians 2:12

AFFIRMED BY GOD

And I know that this man—whether in the body or apart from the body I do not know, but God knows—was caught up to paradise and heard inexpressible things, things that no one is permitted to tell. I will boast about a man like that, but I will not boast about myself, except about my weaknesses.

2 Corinthians 12:3-5

Can we still be caught up into the paradise of God's heavenly presence? Or, are these eternal encounters only reserved for the exceptionally righteous saints of the past? Trusted testimonies of today and Holy Scripture seem to validate opportunities for anyone graced by God to access the glorious riches of His heart. It is the Lord's discretion whom He allows to hear heavenly tones unable to be translated into man's words.

On occasion the Lord graces His loved ones with special affirmation that creates a most meaningful moment of intimacy. It is an experience of encouragement covered over with fingerprints of faith. This heavenly hug connects eternal reassurance to earthly insecurity. Almighty God's affirmation has no rival in heaven or on earth—His presence brings bold belief and gratitude. It is in this secret place that He reveals the unspeakable.

"Because of that experience, we have even greater confidence in the message proclaimed by the prophets. You must pay close attention to what they wrote" (2 Peter 1:19).

Related Readings: Genesis 32:22-32; Isaiah 6:1-6; 2 Peter 3:16; Revelation 1:9-11

SEPTEMBER 3

A LIFE OF FAITH

By faith Abraham, when called to go to a place he would later receive as his inheritance, obeyed and went, even though he did not know where he was going. Hebrews 11:8

Living a life of faith often means we may not know exactly where we are being led, but we know the One we are following. God protects a trusting heart as He perfects it through His faith-building process. It is a great adventure to align with the Almighty's agenda. Like an experienced and trusted guide, He is always a step ahead on the path of His will. So, we seek to know Him, because He knows where He is going.

Faith living is not always fun, but it is fulfilling. It is not always exciting, but it is engaging. It is not always easy, but it is honorable. It is not always safe, but it is secure. It is not always clear, but it is rewarding. It is not always instantly gratifying, but it is satisfying. Faith living is looking intently into the gracious face of our heavenly Father. Christ's countenance shows He cares. He laughs when we laugh, He weeps when we weep. Faith living lives wisely while waiting. The Lord rewards your faithfulness to His faithfulness.

"And by faith even Sarah, who was past childbearing age, was enabled to bear children because she considered him faithful who had made the promise" (Hebrews 11:11).

Related Readings: Habakkuk 2:4; Acts 3:16; 2 Corinthians 5:7; James 2:17-18

STRENGTH AND PEACE

The LORD gives strength to his people; the LORD blesses his people with peace. Psalm 29:11

God gives strength and peace to those surrendered to Him. The benefits of being a dedicated believer in Jesus Christ include heaven's infinite resources. Sin sucks life from the soul and replaces it with fear, while faith compounds calm and offers energy. Man's methods may manipulate a false sense of security, but God gives eternal security. Strength in the Lord replaces worry with hope—it's what gets us through demanding days. Because God possesses you, He gives you exactly what you need. Your ongoing strength and peace is a by-product of being Christ's.

How can we access Christ's calm and mighty power? What is a wise route to experience the Almighty's assets in an ongoing process? When we daily die to self and come alive to Christ, we position ourselves to be empowered by the Holy Spirit. So, strength and peace come from giving in to God, not giving up on God. As we surrender to our Savior Jesus, we win—indeed it's when we confess our weaknesses that we become strong. Thus, thank Him for His help. And prayerfully look around you for others you can help find strength and peace in God.

"And Saul's son Jonathan went to David at Horesh and helped him find strength in God" (1 Samuel 23:16).

Related Readings: 2 Samuel 22:30; 1 Chronicles 12:18; Luke 7:16; Hebrews 6:10

SEPTEMBER 5

WE, NOT ME

Now you are the body of Christ, and each one of you is a part
of it. 1 Corinthians 12:27

There is a larger context to life than just living for self. A self-
focused life is chronically frustrated and is unable to reach its full
potential. Its demanding demeanor marginalizes wise counsel
and only attracts insecure individuals. However, those who
pray for what's best for the whole become whole. Everyone is
honored in an environment that values individual contributions.
"We, not me" is the vocabulary of those who honor each other.

Every disciple is stronger when they are connected to other
Christ followers. Isolation contributes to spiritual impotence,
but community gives spiritual life. Encouragement and
accountability are exalted in relationships that serve what's best
for the group. A leader who serves the team sees other team
members serve well. A man who serves his family experiences a
family that serves each other. "We overcomes me" with unselfish
service. Thus, by God's grace, put to death the "me monster"
and replace it with love for the Lord and people. "We, not me"
is the motto of mature Jesus followers.

"Each of you should use whatever gift you have received to
serve others, as faithful stewards of God's grace in its various
forms" (1 Peter 4:10).

Related Readings: Romans 12:10-16; 14:13; 15:7;
2 Corinthians 13:11; Galatians 5:13

NEVER LEAVES YOU

Be strong and courageous. Do not be afraid or terrified because of them, for the LORD your God goes with you; He will never leave you nor forsake you. Deuteronomy 31:6

God the Father never lets go of His child—God the Son saves a lost soul once and for all—God the Spirit seals a believer with eternal security. There is a completeness that accompanies faith in Christ. He is stable in the middle of instability. He is a rock in the center of swirling circumstances. He is a light that disturbs the darkest darkness. The Lord does not let go of what's His. Yes, once a child of God, always a child of God!

But we may ask, "What about past indiscretions that brought shame and embarrassment?" "Can't foolish living disqualify me from being a Christian?" Eternal salvation and acceptance are not based on our fickle behavior, but on Christ's unchanging character. We can stray, but He is there. We can doubt, but He is there. We can mess up, but He is there. The Lord is always there to lift us up, give us hope, offer us wisdom, and fully restore us. Have no fear for He is near!

"Keep your lives free from the love of money and be content with what you have, because God has said, 'Never will I leave you; never will I forsake you'" (Hebrews 13:5).

Related Readings: Deuteronomy 31:8; Matthew 28:19-20; John 10:28-30; 1 John 5:11-15

SPIRITUAL LABOR

Therefore, my dear brothers and sisters, stand firm. Let nothing move you. Always give yourselves fully to the work of the Lord, because you know that your labor in the Lord is not in vain. 1 Corinthians 15:58

What is spiritual labor? It is work done with the Lord and for the Lord. It is a new mother rocking her baby, while she prays God's blessing over her little one. It is an employee who in Jesus' name is diligent in his or her duties. They are punctual when others are late; they are eager to work more when others look for ways to work less. Spiritual labor sets high standards of service for the Lord.

Spiritual labor is an executive, a manager, or administrative assistant who will not compromise their character to make more cash. Their word is their bond and their behavior points other people to Christ. We are spiritual laborers when we do our work first and foremost for our heavenly Father. We stand firm in faith-motivated work when we wake up every day grateful to represent Jesus in our jobs. Your spiritual labor in the Lord is not in vain. It brings joy and satisfaction to you, Him, and friends!

"We remember before our God and Father your work produced by faith, your labor prompted by love, and your endurance inspired by hope in our Lord Jesus Christ" (1 Thessalonians 1:3).

Related Readings: 1 Corinthians 3:8; Philippians 1:21-23; 2:15-17; Revelation 14:13

SOURCE OF GRIEF

When Esau was forty years old, he married Judith… They
were a source of grief to Isaac and Rebekah.
Genesis 26:34a, 35

Sometimes a child becomes a source of grief because they choose
to marry someone who does not meet their parent's approval. In
fact, the more the mom and dad express their disapproval, the
more adamant the child becomes in dismissing their parents'
wishes. When relational equity is overdrawn, the opportunity
to influence another vanishes for a season. This time of distress
and disagreement can permanently scar a family. So, someone
has to be mature in the face of immaturity. Even when we are
insulted and rejected by an impetuous young adult with our
same last name, we are obligated by God's grace to rise above
demanding our own way.

Disowning (real or perceived) is not an option for a family full of
love and forgiveness. Yes, rejection is painful—in the same way
the Holy Spirit grieves over our unwise choices, so we grieve
over our foolish child. But, as a parent, pray more and judge
less, lest our love gets lost in the confusing equation of shame
plus blame. Forgiveness is the fuel that reignites a family's love
for one another. Humble yourself first and watch the grace of
God heal wounds!

"Even though he [Esau] sought the blessing with tears, he could
not change what he had done" (Hebrews 12:17b).

Related Readings: 1 Samuel 20:34; Isaiah 63:10;
Romans 9:13; Hebrews 11:20

SPIRIT-FILLED LEADERS LOVE

Brothers and sisters, choose seven men from among you who are known to be full of the Spirit and wisdom. We will turn this responsibility over to them. Acts 6:3

———————◆◆◆———————

Leaders full of the Spirit of God, represent the Lord well in how they serve others. A leader led by the Lord loves well. They look beyond what a person can do for them, and seek to understand what they can do for their colleagues. Love asks what motivates others to feel appreciated. Is it time off, a kind word, an unexpected bonus, or just knowing they are cared about? A Spirit-filled servant of the Lord loves well, being a boss under God's authority.

Furthermore, we may find ourselves in a position of responsibility to choose leaders at our church, in our community, or for civic duties. This process of wisely qualifying a leader cannot become a popularity contest based on charisma, charm, or who communicates the best. We are wise to prayerfully select those who serve for the pleasure of the customers or the constituents. Look for leaders who lovingly look out for others first, who love in the power of the Lord's love.

"If you really keep the royal law found in Scripture, 'Love your neighbor as yourself,' you are doing right. But if you show favoritism, you sin and are convicted by the law as lawbreakers" (James 2:8-9).

Related Readings: Job 32:18; Ezekiel 37:1; Luke 10:21; Acts 11:24

TESTED FAITH

Simon, Simon, Satan has asked to sift all of you as wheat. But I have prayed for you, Simon, that your faith may not fail. And when you have turned back, strengthen your brothers.

Luke 22:31-32

———————————

Satan is always on the prowl to discredit the faith of sincere disciples. He asks the Almighty if he can flush out the mercenaries who see Jesus merely as a means to their own end. The Lord does give the devil permission at times (like with Job) to strain His children with temptation and trials. However, the enemy learns quickly that Jesus increases the intensity of His intercession for those being badgered by Satan's schemes.

A tested faith is an opportunity to grow from inspiration to transformation. We may deny Christ at times, but He does not deny us. We may lose faith, but He remains faithful. In our weakness, He becomes stronger. Stumbling in our faith provides opportunity for faith building. Like a trusted trainer who cares for and instructs a boxer who collapses on a stool in his corner, so Christ soothes your emotional cuts and bruises with His loving grace. He infuses stamina. Out of tests of faith grows your perseverance, so you can strengthen other followers of Jesus.

"Does Job fear God for nothing?" Satan replied… "But now stretch out your hand and strike everything he has, and he will surely curse you to your face" (Job 1:9, 11).

Related Readings: 2 Corinthians 13:5; Hebrews 11:17; James 1:3; Revelation 2:10

HUMILITY, NOT HUBRIS

This is a faithful saying and worthy of all acceptance, that Christ Jesus came into the world to save sinners, of whom I am chief. 1 Timothy 1:15, NKJV

———◆———

Humility is modest and respectful; hubris is proud and arrogant. Humility practices an egoless attitude; hubris exhibits an egocentric persona. Humility has a proper perspective of its capabilities; hubris is overconfident. Humility depends on God and others; hubris thinks it is self-contained. Humility is an aspiring virtue; hubris is a venomous vice.

We cultivate humility in our hearts when we remember how far the Lord has brought us by His grace. We are sinners saved by God's grace, kept by God's grace, and empowered to live the Christian life by God's grace. Our humble living sacrifice to Christ is all of grace or none at all. We need not forget where we came from, lest we lose our fiery faith. Your humility is heaven's leverage in other's lives. Daily dress yourself in the clothes of humility. Consider a hat of submission, a t-shirt of trust, a blouse of belief, a shirt of care, pants of prayer, a dress of dependence, a belt of boldness, socks of service, and shoes of gratitude. Humility erases hubris.

"Yes, all of you be submissive to one another, and be clothed with humility, for 'God resists the proud, but gives grace to the humble'" (1 Peter 5:5b, NKJV).

Related Readings: Exodus 10:3; 2 Kings 22:19; Daniel 5:22; Romans 12:3

AMBUSHED BY GOD

Then the man said, "Your name will no longer be Jacob, but Israel, because you have struggled with God and with humans and have overcome." Genesis 32:28

God does not let go of His children; in fact, there are times when faith exercise feels like a wrestling match. Life can be good and uneventful; then, all of sudden, change ambushes a Christian with a surprise attack. It could be the mental gymnastics of doubting God when a very committed Christian friend seems to be trapped in an unfair circumstance. Or, seemingly from nowhere, the deep depression blues can assault the most ardent of saints. It is not a contentious engagement but one of comprehending Who is really in control.

If we recognize His loving face during these pressure points, we rest in this close proximity to Christ. He energizes our exhausted souls. Change is inevitable as you grow in your intimacy with the Lord. Like the secure sensation of a roaring fire in a fireplace, the closer you get to the heat of the Holy Spirit's heart, the more He will warm you to His ways. When you feel ambushed by God, see it as your "burning bush" (Exodus 3:2) blessing of glory!

"From inside the fish Jonah prayed to the LORD his God. He said: 'In my distress I called to the LORD, and He answered me'" (Jonah 2:1-2a).

Related Readings: Genesis 32:27-29; Mark 1:13; 2 Corinthians 11:16-33

LOVE STRANGERS

He administers justice for the fatherless and the widow, and
loves the stranger, giving him food and clothing. Therefore
love the stranger, for you were strangers in the land of Egypt.
Deuteronomy 10:18-19, NKJV

———— ·••· ————

Strangers can seem strange and distant, but they are still human
beings created in the image of God. They may smell different,
look odd, be eccentric, or speak unclearly, nevertheless their
heart longs for encouragement and acceptance. It is out of a
strange place that a person can find their heavenly Father and
begin their journey of knowing Him. The Holy Spirit daily
directs His disciples to be a conduit for a stranger's salvation.

Therefore, we have an opportunity every day to expose unfamiliar
people to a picture of God's grace. If they know Jesus, our act
of kindness emboldens their belief. If faith living is foreign to
the new acquaintance, our generous gratuity may solicit their
souls to ask why. We love strangers, because we were all once
strangers to Christ's intimate love. Love goes to strange places,
for strange people, so that they no longer may be strangers to
God. Strangers will not remain strangers after your investment
in their lives. Love welcomes guests as new friends.

"I was a father to the needy; I took up the case of the stranger"
(Job 29:16).

Related Readings: Leviticus 25:35; Job 31:32; Psalm 119:19;
Hebrew 11:9

NO SHAME

For I am not ashamed of the gospel, because it is the power of God that brings salvation to everyone who believes: first to the Jew, then to the Gentile. Romans 1:16

Satan sometimes shames seekers when they begin to take God and His Word seriously. The enemy plants seeds of doubt related to intellectual honesty and the fear of being labeled a religious fanatic. The devil wants Jesus believers to be apologetic and embarrassed to live for the Lord, not declaring His teachings as the gospel truth. But, there is no shame in standing up for Christ and His commands. Faith reveals His fame.

Instead, we are to be ashamed of sin and its deplorable outcome, while embracing wise living. Shame enslaves us in our selfish behavior, but we are emancipated by our selfless service to others. Our Savior Jesus does not seek to motivate us out of disgrace; rather He infuses His grace into our inner being for bold initiatives. The good news of salvation in Christ gives us the confidence to love all people. God's power is shameless.

"If anyone is ashamed of me and my words in this adulterous and sinful generation, the Son of Man will be ashamed of them when he comes in his Father's glory with the holy angels" (Mark 8:38).

Related Readings: Genesis 2:25; Psalm 25:3; Isaiah 54:4; Romans 6:21; Philippians 1:20

PARENTING WITHOUT EXASPERATION

Fathers, do not exasperate your children; instead, bring them up in the training and instruction of the Lord. Ephesians 6:4

It can be exasperating to parent with calm consistency and effectiveness. However, one thing is true: Training and instructing a child in the Lord extinguishes exasperation. Godly guidelines give a teachable heart security and a sense of loving protection. A little one's innocence tarnishes into mediocrity when discipline is withheld or ignored. Thus, a wise parent defines clear standards so their expectations bring joy, not sadness. We need boundaries in our behavior as parents so that we can model humility and wisdom for our children.

Indeed, we contribute to a tranquil home culture when we practice, "Do as I say and follow what I do." Parenting with grace and truth flows from our character and conduct. We confess our angry reaction and ask forgiveness from our son or daughter. We keep our commitments, tell the truth, listen well, love liberally, and obey God. Exasperation exists in a leadership vacuum, but when you step up to serve your family, faith flourishes. Loving accountability causes some angst in the beginning but reaps peace in the end.

"We do not want you to become lazy, but to imitate those who through faith and patience inherit what has been promised" (Hebrews 6:12).

Related Readings: Genesis 18:19; Proverbs 22:6;
2 Thessalonians 3:9; Hebrews 13:7

BELIEVING IS SEEING

Jesus said, "You believe because I told you I saw you under the fig tree. You will see greater things than that." John 1:50

Believing sees with eyes of faith. Faith looks into the face of God to face the unknown. What may not be apparent through logic and reason is revealed by looking beyond the material to the spiritual. Belief in God opens up a vista of breathtaking spiritual formations. We see the mountains of His majesty and the fertile valley of His faithfulness. Belief in Jesus allows us to behold the sun of His salvation and the heavens of His hope. Believing sees what God sees.

"I pray that the eyes of your heart may be enlightened in order that you may know the hope to which He has called you" (Ephesians 1:18).

Moreover, believing may allow us to see God do greater things. We believe God for our child's heart to turn back to Him, to heal our friend's body with greater stamina, to open a financial door with His great provision, to get the gospel to thousands with His great power, for a great revival so He changes us, our family, church, city, state, nation, and the world. Faith can facilitate God's greater works. Attempt great things only your great God can accomplish. Believe Him and watch Him work!

"Whoever believes in me will do the works I have been doing, and they will do even greater things than these" (John 14:12).

Related Readings: Job 42:5; Matthew 21:212; Luke 10:17; 2 Corinthians 4:6; Hebrews 11:1

SOURCE OF SATISFACTION

Jesus answered her, "If you knew the gift of God and who it is that asks you for a drink, you would have asked him and he would have given you living water." John 4:10

Every soul longs for satisfaction—a feeling of fulfillment. A dissatisfied soul is discontent and distant from God, but once satisfied, it's content and close to Christ. Dissatisfied emotions look for love in all the wrong places, but once satisfied, receive genuine love from Jesus and His followers. A dissatisfied state of mind is ever learning, but unsatisfied with simple truth. Dissatisfied, we drive ourselves to unhealthy extremes, but we find peace when satisfied with our Savior Jesus.

"My people have committed two sins: They have forsaken me, the spring of living water, and have dug their own cisterns, broken cisterns that cannot hold water" (Jeremiah 2:13).

This dear woman at the well, whom Jesus loved, lacked fulfilling love from her previous husbands. The yearning and thirst in her heart could only be quenched by the living water of her Lord. Has your heart been broken by a lost love? Are you thirsty for someone you can totally trust? Look to your heavenly Father, who loves unconditionally and wholeheartedly. The purified water of God's love, filtered in heaven, is your gift to be received by faith. Christ's love satisfies.

"Whoever believes in me, as Scripture has said, rivers of living water will flow from within them" (John 7:38).

Related Readings: Psalm 78:15-16; Isaiah 41:18; Jeremiah 17:13; Revelation 7:17; 21:6

DETEST DISSENSION

"There are six things the LORD hates, seven that are detestable to him: ... a false witness who pours out lies and a man who stirs up dissension among brothers." Proverbs 6:16, 19, NIV84

———◆———

The Lord loathes liars and those who stir up dissension because they are masters at sowing seeds of doubt, deception, and discord. Dissenters think the worst of others and pose prideful questions like, "Is he or she really fit for the job?" "Do they deal with honest intentions?" or "Can this person really be trusted?" A person who stirs up dissension projects their own insecure feelings on the person they are seeking to discredit or even destroy.

Like Saul, their own anger, hurt, and jealousy drive them to delusionary conclusions. It is sad to see them suffer under their own mental anguish, absent of trust in the Lord. Their perspective becomes man-centered, while faith in Christ is jettisoned as irrelevant. Those who stir up dissension need to be dealt with directly and with a heart of compassion. Conflict with the contentious is meant to grow your character. Hate what the Lord hates, while loving offenders through the process.

"A hot-tempered man stirs up dissension, but a patient man calms a quarrel" (Proverbs 15:18, NIV84).

Related Readings: 1 Samuel 26:1-25; Proverbs 22:10; 26:20; James 3:14-16; 3 John 1:9-10

DISCIPLES ARE MADE

"Come," he replied, "and you will see." So they went and saw where he was staying, and they spent that day with him. It was about four in the afternoon. John 1:39

Disciples are made, not born. God makes them. God makes them for His glory. He makes them so they in turn will make disciples. The Lord makes disciples who serve the needy, feed the poor, and reach out to the rich. Disciples are trained by the Holy Spirit to follow the Spirit's leading. They learn to make much of their master Jesus and make less of themselves.

"He [Jesus] must increase, but I [John] must decrease" (John 3:30, NKJV).

Are you engaged in discipleship training? Are you intentional in your intimacy with Jesus? Start today to be a stronger disciple tomorrow. Aging is meant to mature a heart to become more like Christ. Similar to a good wine aging well, so a disciple's faith grows robust in intentional intimacy with the Lord. Just as these two early disciples (John 1:39) accepted Jesus' invitation to come and see Him, Jesus invites us to come and see. Spend a day seeing your Savior's heart and hearing His voice.

"Strengthening the disciples and encouraging them to remain true to the faith" (Acts 14:22).

Related Readings: Matthew 28:19; John 13:5, 35; Acts 6:7; 19:9; 20:1

MONETIZE YOUR MISSION

The master commended the dishonest manager because he had acted shrewdly. For the people of this world are more shrewd in dealing with their own kind than are the people of the light.
Luke 16:8

Creating an economic structure around passion and purpose can be a prayerful and godly goal. It could be converting informal free advice into a formalized fee for coaching, consulting, or counseling. It may mean engaging a hobby, such as painting, writing, or singing, and moving it into the market as a valued product. God gives gifts and skills to create a living. There are times to give away time and expertise, and there are times to monetize our mission.

Money is not our motivation, but it is a by-product of producing value around what wakes us up in the morning. Why waste our lives just working for a paycheck when we can creatively come up with ways to channel our energies and experiences into an economic endeavor. Christ commends shrewd servants of His who innovate new ways to make friends and influence people. Indeed, we are called to be creative for Christ's sake. Your life is attractive when you live out your mission with passion and productivity. Trust God to give you the wisdom to make a living from living for His call.

"The one who calls you is faithful, and he will do it"
(1 Thessalonians 5:24).

Related Readings: Proverbs 22:29; Ephesians 2:10;
2 Corinthians 5:1; 1 Timothy 6:17-19

HAPPY HEART GIVING

Give generously to them and do so without a grudging heart;
then because of this the LORD your God will bless you in all
your work and in everything you put your hand to.
Deuteronomy 15:10

Happy heart giving is with a grateful, not begrudging heart.
Greed is exiled to the isle of selfishness and generosity takes
command in the country of contentment. A joyful heart never
gets over Jesus' great gift of salvation, abundant life, and eternal
reward. Indeed, a blessed heart cannot help but be a blessing to
those without life necessities. Oh, how delightful to see other's
needs met for Christ's sake! Glad giving gets God's attention.

The Lord wants to bless us more when we have been a blessing
to the less fortunate. Our abundance isn't meant for our
accumulation, aimed at our indulgent and secure façade; rather,
it's to be deployed into rich deeds and aggressive charity. When
our heart is free to give, it is free indeed. Happy heart giving is
as excited about giving one dollar as it is one thousand. Give
generously today and you will most likely give generously in
the future. Once your heavenly Father can trust you with a little,
He will trust you with more. Generosity solicits smiles and
creates happy hearts.

"And now I have seen with joy how willingly your people who
are here have given to you" (1 Chronicles 29:17b).

Related Readings: Nehemiah 9:8; 2 Corinthians 8:5, 9:7;
Philemon 1:7

GENEROUS TOWARD GOD

You, God, are my God, earnestly I seek you; I thirst for you,
my whole being longs for you. Psalm 63:1a

The God of the universe looks for those who would be with Him.
The Lord longs for His children to take time to experience His
tender loving presence. Almighty God is not needy, but wants
His creation to come before Him in humble dependence. He
knows prayer is what's best for those He bought with His Son's
blood. Generosity toward God in daily doses of solitude and
communion are the wisest gift. Our presence gratifies God. Like
an earthly father revels in the joy of being close to his precious
child, so our heavenly Father smiles to be with us.

The grace of God is not garnered with a drive-by life; rather,
when we park our lives in His presence and turn off the engine
of our activity, we activate His perspective in our hearts and
minds. We invest in intimacy with our heavenly Father to fulfill
His agenda in our daily calendar. You may engage Him as you
stroll in your neighborhood, sit by a quiet fire, rest by a bubbling
creek, or as you watch His heavenly handiwork in a brilliant
sunrise or sunset. Most of all, give your all to God.

"For day after day they seek me out; they seem eager to know
my ways" (Isaiah 58:2a).

Related Readings: 1 Chronicles 22:19; 2 Chronicles 14:4;
Acts 10:2; 17:27

CENTER OF ATTENTION

I keep my eyes always on the LORD. With him at my right
hand, I will not be shaken. Psalm 16:8

———————◆◆◆————————

Jesus deserves my undivided attention, yet I struggle with
distractions. My mind is drawn to musing over pressing issues at
work that never seem to go away. My heart engages in emotional
cares for others in crisis that I am unable to control. My eyes
look ahead in worry or behind in regret. It is at these pivotal
points that I desire my eyes to stay fixed on Jesus in prayer, not
on others or myself. Faith makes Christ the center of attention.

The eyes of our souls can be blind to belief or they can open
wide in anticipation of the Almighty's faithfulness. If we close
our spiritual eyes, we extinguish hope and miss our master's
comfort and instruction. It is when we gaze into the eyes of Jesus
that He sees right through us to the heart of the matter. What
matters to the Lord becomes what matters to us. Like reading
glasses, the Bible brings into focus the character of Christ. He is
your rock of refuge and your strength to endure. Keep Christ the
center of your attention and receive His loving attention.

"And let us run with perseverance the race marked out for us,
fixing our eyes on Jesus, the pioneer and perfecter of faith"
(Hebrews 12:1b-2a).

Related Readings: 2 Kings 7:2; Psalm 25:15; 2 Corinthians
8:21; 1 Peter 3:12

DRESSED FOR SUCCESS

Therefore, as God's chosen people, holy and dearly loved,
clothe yourselves with compassion, kindness, humility,
gentleness and patience. Colossians 3:12

There is an inner attire almighty God expects His people to wear. Their inner self is to be adorned with an attitude of compassion, kind words, a humble heart, a gentle demeanor, and patience with people and problems. Each day disciples of Jesus choose to clothe themselves with the character of Christ or remain naked to the world's influences. Chosen people of God gladly put on spiritual apparel, for they want first impressions to point people to Jesus. Your outward demeanor is an indicator of your inward beauty.

Are you as conscientious about clothing your inner self with God's expectations as you are in dressing to impress the world with its latest fashion statement? The Holy Spirit is your faith "fashion police," reminding you of what's really important. Spiritual fads come and go, but character built on Christ is steady and sustainable. Some sincere believers speculate about the second coming of Christ but forget to prepare their hearts and lives in the meantime. Thus, dress for spiritual success, and the Lord will smile down on your attractive life. Adorn your inner beauty with Christ's appealing clothing.

"Rather, it should be that of your inner self, the unfading beauty of a gentle and quiet spirit, which is of great worth in God's sight" (1 Peter 3:4).

Related Readings: Job 40:10; Isaiah 52:1; Matthew 11:29, Luke 6:36; 1 Corinthians 13:4

HOT PURSUIT

Flee the evil desires of youth and pursue righteousness, faith, love and peace, along with those who call on the Lord out of a pure heart. 2 Timothy 2:22

How can we ignore romancing righteousness? How can we chase dreams that leave out the dream-giver? Wise are we to call on Christ out of a pure heart in pursuit of what He cares about: righteousness, faith, love, and peace. This foursome of wisdom plays close to Jesus' heart. He knows the fruit of wise pursuit propels us toward understanding His will. We pursue the Lord, and in the process His Spirit transforms us into godly followers. A life that looks at how Jesus loves begins to love like Jesus loves. Sit at the feet of the Prince of Peace and receive His tranquil trust.

Furthermore, hunt down heaven's agenda to understand what's best for you and your family. Engaging the eternal is as simple as a moment of meditation on Scripture, an hour of worship, Bible study, or a quiet weekend in contemplation. Be intentional with integrity in little things and you will become a person of integrity in big things. Initiate love and you become loving. By faith integrate righteousness, love, and peace from a pure heart and enjoy Christ's affirmation.

"The LORD detests the way of the wicked, but He loves those who pursue righteousness" (Proverbs 15:9).

Related Readings: Proverbs 11:19; 21:21; Romans 9:31-32; 1 Timothy 6:11

HEALING HURT

Therefore confess your sins to each other and pray for each other so that you may be healed. James 5:16a

Hurt cannot be avoided this side of heaven. This is an unfortunate outcome from outside forces; self-absorbed family members, insensitive friends, and self-inflicted wounds. The deepest harm comes from those who should love well but, because of their own unresolved hurt, are emotionally injurious. For example, instead of a spouse meeting a very real need to love and respect their wife or husband, they tear down with cutting words. They may withhold affection, while tempting their marriage partner to find affection elsewhere. Sarcasm scars, rejection injures, anger crushes confidence, and dishonesty destroys trust.

How do we handle deep hurts that have compounded in crazy cycles over many years? Where do we go when the hurt is so unbearable that we stay scared, implode in anger, and grow a root of bitterness? Fortunately, there is a very real hope for healing found in our loving heavenly Father and His caring children. Healing doesn't happen by accident. It begins with an intentional acknowledgment of the need for wholeness by God's grace. Like a deep wound to the flesh, healing takes time, the pain does not go away immediately, the scab is messy, but the scar is a badge of God's grace.

"Gracious words are a honeycomb, sweet to the soul and healing to the bones" (Proverbs 16:24).

Related Readings: Proverbs 12:18; 13:17; Jeremiah 33:6; Acts 10:38; 1 Corinthians 12:28

POOR JESUS

For you know the grace of our Lord Jesus Christ, that though he was rich, yet for your sake he became poor, so that you through his poverty might become rich. 2 Corinthians 8:9

———◆———

Jesus was poor. He owned nothing but had everything He needed. He borrowed boats, donkeys, food, and lodging. He lived on borrowed time—then he died and was buried in a borrowed tomb. The Son of God was born from a virgin womb and buried in a virgin tomb. Christ Jesus voluntarily gave up His riches in glory in exchange for the poverty of mankind on earth. Grace comes at the great expense of Jesus giving up all for all people.

It is the riches of God's grace and forgiveness that are the true riches. Any other riches that compete with Christ's riches are idols of insecurity. Indeed, it is better for us to be poor in the eyes of the world and remain rich in the eyes of our Heavenly Father. It's futile to chase the undependable wealth of the world, when we can rest and revel in the riches of seeking first the kingdom of God. Christ's simple life compels us to live uncomplicated lives for Him.

"Listen, my dear brothers and sisters: Has not God chosen those who are poor in the eyes of the world to be rich in faith and to inherit the kingdom he promised those who love him?" (James 2:5)

Related Readings: Proverbs 28:6, 11; 22:2; Luke 18:22; Revelation 3:17

TOUGH AND TENDER

One thing God has spoken, two things I have heard: "Power belongs to you, God, and with you, Lord, is unfailing love."
Psalm 62:11-12a

The Lord is all-powerful and all-loving. He is tough and tender. Jesus Christ is angry at religious hypocrisy and forgiving toward genuine repentance. He is a strong support in the middle of suffering and provides loving reminders to those who stray from His ways. He is friends with sinners and prays for His enemies. His holy heart lovingly leads with wisdom and mercy. Our image of God influences how we treat others. For example, our children need us to be tough and tender. We love them by explaining the "why" behind "what" we ask them to do. Wise rules enforced with a gracious attitude bring out the best results.

Are you troubled by the tension that God is both tough and tender? If so, use this discomfort to place yourself in an aggressive posture of prayer. Ask the Holy Spirit to lead you in the appropriate way to apply firmness and friendliness in your work relationships. Things and people are normally not as bad or good as they might seem. Your family and friends need to see you tough and tender. By God's grace be humbly bold!

"For the Spirit God gave us does not make us timid, but gives us power, love and self-discipline" (2 Timothy 1:7).

Related Readings: Exodus 15:13; Psalm 36:7; Acts 4:33; 6:8; Ephesians 3:18

283

REJECTING GOD

For God did not call us to be impure, but to live a holy life. Therefore, anyone who rejects this instruction does not reject a human being but God, the very God who gives you his Holy Spirit. 1 Thessalonians 4:7-8

There is a subtle sequence of rejection that takes place in a life that's not surrendered to the Lord. Acknowledgement of obedience is not sufficient without the evidence of follow through. God calls all His children to purity and a productive life around His priorities. Accepting almighty God's instruction releases His influence. A life powered by the Spirit sees the Lord work. Accepting God's game plan unleashes His strength and encouragement. Your acceptance of the Lord's instruction invites His Holy Spirit's comfort, conviction, and control.

Indeed, there are wise rejections. Reject self-righteousness and accept unpretentious piety. Reject pride and accept humility. Reject bitterness and accept forgiveness. Reject egotistical anger and accept just anger. Reject fear and accept faith. Reject sin and accept sinners. Reject holier-than-thou and accept holiness. Reject hurt and accept healing. Reject unbelief and accept belief. Reject Satan and accept Jesus. Reject unwise actions. First accept Christ and then embrace His plan for your life.

"The person without the Spirit does not accept the things that come from the Spirit of God but considers them foolishness, and cannot understand them because they are discerned only through the Spirit" (1 Corinthians 2:14).

Related Readings: Job 22:21-23; Zephaniah 3:2; John 13:20; 1 Peter 2:5

RELATIONAL AUDIT

Then the LORD said to Cain, "Where is your brother Abel?"
"I don't know," he replied. "Am I my brother's keeper?"
Genesis 4:9

There is a relational accountability that comes with becoming a follower of Christ; indeed, no lone soldiers are in the Lord's army. Without regular feedback from others, individual Christians are fair game for the enemy's fiery darts of doubt. Bad habits incubate in a life disengaged from intimate input from a caring community. A life without accountability drifts into irrelevance, but someone fresh from correction grows in emotional intelligence.

Most of us do not enjoy the uncomfortable feeling that accompanies the most loving confrontation. But, we know in our hearts we need the unfiltered observation of those who care deeply about us. Even if unintended harshness hits our heart, we can let go of it by grace and hang on to healthy instruction by faith. Messengers sent by the Lord are His mouthpiece of protection and wisdom. We get better by digesting doses of truth. Life isolated on a relational island implodes for lack of examination. God made you to engage in community to give and receive correction and support. Confront in love and invite other trusted advisors to do the same.

"I myself am convinced, my brothers and sisters, that you yourselves are full of goodness, filled with knowledge and competent to instruct one another" (Romans 15:14).

Related Readings: Romans 12:10, 16; 14:1-13; Galatians 5:13; Philippians 2:5; Colossians 3:13-16

OCTOBER

"For I know the plans I have for you," declares the Lord, "plans to prosper you and not to harm you, plans to give you hope and a future."
Jeremiah 29:11

OCTOBER 1

GOOD CONTROVERSY

"In the Law Moses commanded us to stone such women. Now what do you say?" They were using this question as a trap, in order to have a basis for accusing Him. John 8:5-6

———————◆◆◆◆———————

Christ was controversial. The ultra conservative Pharisees were jealous of the large number of His disciples and His teachings on forgiveness. And the extremely liberal Sadducees were angry with Him for His belief in the resurrection. Today the same is true: The mention of Jesus' name endears Him to some while it enrages others. Jesus embodied both truth and grace. It is a good controversy when the categories of our belief system are challenged and stretched a bit; it causes us to go to God for wisdom.

Likewise, the tension of holding the minority view is no reason to fight back with angry political maneuvering or with fear-based false accusations within the faith family. Christ thrives in controversy when truth and grace jointly win. The goal of good controversy is not for you to win the debate—it is to represent the heart of Christ. Your accusers may not agree with your theological emphasis, but they can and must respect your humble attitude that accompanies your bold beliefs. Good controversy clarifies privately but loves publicly. It embraces grace and truth.

"But avoid foolish controversies and genealogies and arguments and quarrels about the law, because these are unprofitable and useless" (Titus 3:9).

Related Readings: John 13:1; Acts 15:1-41; 1 Timothy 6:4

MIND MARGIN

Do not conform to the pattern of this world, but be transformed by the renewing of your mind. Romans 12:2a

———◄●◄●►●►———

The human brain is not meant to operate at full capacity all the time. The Lord never sleeps or slumbers, but the minds of mere mortals must. If thinking never turns off, like an idling car engine, it eventually runs out of gas. Creativity is crushed under the weight of worry or having to work out urgent issues. A mind requires rest, just like the body, soul, and spirit. Thus, wise are those who don't mind resting their minds.

We are creatures of habit who have become addicted to the screens of modern society. Phones aggressively capture the attention of our eyes and ears. They only let go of their grip when they are turned off. Computers save us time, only to consume our time with necessary and needless information. Like an addict who must have another hit or drink, so we become inebriated with access to endless digital knowledge. Virtual conveniences like music and movies on demand can demand our affections above the heart of God.

"Whatever is true, whatever is noble, whatever is right, whatever is pure, whatever is lovely, whatever is admirable—if anything is excellent or praiseworthy—think about such things" (Philippians 4:8).

Related Readings: Daniel 10:12; Mark 8:33; 12:30; Romans 15:5-6

SIMPLIFIED LIVING

I know what it is to be in need, and I know what it is to have plenty. I have learned the secret of being content in any and every situation. Philippians 4:12a

Certainly life can be complicated: graduate school, work, relational conflict, wealth, economic downturns, job loss, health loss, and the loss of a loved one. But life from the Lord's perspective is not meant to be rushed and out of control. An individual who is perpetually on the go can go right past God's best. A heart that traffics exclusively in the high-occupancy lane of life will run itself ragged. Thus, the wise slow down and simplify.

Could it be that busyness is keeping us from relational integrity with Jesus, family, and friends? Perhaps the Lord is leading us to prayerfully unclutter our lives for His kingdom's purpose. How can we adjust our lifestyle, so we are freed up to better love others? Like a fisherman who slowly untangles a bird's nest of line, Christ can help us unwind our complicated lifestyle. Our simplified living will increase the quality of our lives and possibly extend our lives. Indeed, the Lord liberates our lifestyle to seek first His kingdom and His righteousness.

"Two things I ask of you, LORD; do not refuse me before I die: Keep falsehood and lies far from me; give me neither poverty nor riches, but give me only my daily bread" (Proverbs 30:7-8).

Related Readings: Job 27:10; Psalm 37:4; Matthew 19:29; Colossians 1:11

OCTOBER 4

LIMITED UNDERSTANDING

I have much more to say to you, more than you can now bear.
John 16:12

———◦◦◦———

The Holy Spirit holds back understanding until a disciple's maturity can handle its ramifications. Too much information can confuse. Thus, through a tender process of gradual illumination, the Spirit of God shows sincere Jesus followers what they need to know, when they need to know. This is why infant faith does not have the capacity to comprehend like seasoned faith. The Lord gives discernment to those He can trust. For example, a 10-year-old is not prepared to drive a car. Physically and emotionally they are not ready, nor have they practiced and applied their motor skills behind two tons of steel. It is deadly for them and others to give a child a car.

Thus, we are at the mercy of our master Jesus to give us what we need in His timing. We can sulk in impatience, or we can serve in anticipation. Preparation precedes illumination. Furthermore, be a patient teacher in your relationships; don't overwhelm them with so much information and responsibility that they give up. The wise wait to share wisdom, until another is ready to receive wisdom. Understanding comes to those who remain faithful to the learning process.

"I gave you milk, not solid food, for you were not yet ready for it. Indeed, you are still not ready" (1 Corinthians 3:2).

Related Readings: Psalm 85:13; Romans 8:14;
1 Corinthians 2:10-11; 1 John 2:27

SELF-RELIANT

Remain in me, as I also remain in you. No branch can bear fruit by itself; it must remain in the vine. Neither can you bear fruit unless you remain in Me. John 15:4

———————◆———————

I struggle with self-reliance. I wrongly assume that unless I make things happen at work or home, it will not get done. Or, I falsely flatter myself that my ability to problem solve is the solution to the professional and personal issues I face. But, in reality there are too many "I's" in this equation. It is not about what I can do but what Jesus has already done. He is the reliant one. The Lord longs for me rest in Him and allow Him to grow His fruit.

Self-reliance is a stumbling block when it short-circuits the Spirit's work. Impatience takes matters into its own hands and misses out on seeing the power and glory of God at work. We are better off when we invite others into our thinking and our feelings of inadequacy. Wise are we to admit our weaknesses and confess our mistakes rather than projecting an image of having it all together. Health issues, emotional pain, and spiritual emptiness bring self-reliance to its knees.

"Therefore, anyone who rejects this instruction does not reject a human being but God, the very God who gives you his Holy Spirit" (1 Thessalonians 4:8).

Related Readings: Ezekiel 36:27; Romans 5:5; 2 Corinthians 1:22; Galatians 4:6

PHYSICAL INTIMACY

The marriage bed must be a place of mutuality—the husband seeking to satisfy his wife, the wife seeking to satisfy her husband. 1 Corinthians 7:3, The Message

Our marital duty is neither to demand sex nor endure sex; rather see it as an expression of love and respect. We have the unique privilege to connect with our spouses at a spiritual, emotional, and physical level in ways no one else can. Physical intimacy is a privilege reserved for marriage. Done well, it takes time and planning. Yes, there are those spontaneous intimate rendezvous, but we all need to be intentional in learning to understand our spouse's needs and desires. When we emotionally connect and communicate throughout the day it often leads to physical intimacy at night.

The richest and most fulfilling physical intimacy flows out of emotional intimacy. When a husband and wife connect emotionally with their feelings, they are better primed to connect physically. Indeed, physical intimacy is more than a transaction; it is a relational process that often finds its highest expression in the event of two becoming one. Women who deny their husbands for an unreasonable time can unwittingly signal disinterest and disrespect. Men who rush past the emotional needs of their wives miss engaging their need for security, attention, and respect. Thus, prayerfully seek to love your lover in ways that are meaningful to them.

"How beautiful you are, my darling! Oh, how beautiful! Your eyes are doves. How handsome you are, my beloved! Oh, how charming! And our bed is verdant [lush]" (Song of Solomon 1:15¬16).

Related Readings: Genesis 4:1; 25:21; Song of Songs 2:14, 4:16; 1 Peter 3:7

PRODIGAL CHILDREN

Eli's sons were scoundrels; they had no regard for the LORD.
1 Samuel 2:12

———◆◆◆———

Prodigal children produce heartache and humility in the heart of their parents. They also break the heart of God. Some, who have had the best of parents, have been the worst of sons or daughters. How can an ungrateful child grow up in a home full of grace and loving discipline? One reason is found in a heart that listens to unwise voices and is drawn by emotional duplicity. Satan's foolish ploys easily sway kids into reckless living.

Even homes where Jesus is loved and worshiped as God can see their little one grow up with no regard for the Lord. It doesn't make sense to us that one sibling serves the Lord gladly, while the other has contempt for Christ. However, this is the laboratory of free will where the Holy Spirit allows us all to linger. We all have the choice of good or evil. In fact, even more disturbing, some put on a facade of faith that is later exposed as adults. So, if you are away from the Lord, come home to the sweet acceptance of Jesus and your parents.

"When he came to his senses, he said… 'I will set out and go back to my father and say to him: Father, I have sinned'" (Luke 15:17-18).

Related Readings: Genesis 45:14-15; Leviticus 26:40; Hebrews 10:26; 2 Timothy 4:11

GOD KEEPS PROMISES

And now, LORD God, keep forever the promise you have made... Do as you promised. 2 Samuel 7:25

———•◆•———

The Lord keeps His promises—He never has and never will break a promise. He promises to forgive, so He forgives liberally. He promises to give grace in time of need, so He gives abundantly. He promises to love, so He loves lavishly. He promises Satan's defeat, pain and joy in childbirth, toil in work, safety, danger, His presence, heaven, hell, judgment, rewards, wisdom, foolishness for fools, and a Savior in Jesus Christ.

God's promises concerning Christ are profound: born to a virgin woman, from the line of Jacob, who inherits David's throne, Spirit-filled, and the righteous king with a forerunner. He will be rejected, bear our sins and die like a criminal. He will be born in Bethlehem, be appointed to preach, and be full of unfailing love and faithfulness. He is God's good news, who brings resurrection, new life, and is the fulfillment of all God's promises. His best promise is salvation by faith in Jesus, which begins at conversion and continues in Christ. Jesus saves you for His glory and for His purposes. He promises you, so you can trust in His Word.

"From the descendants of this man [David], according to promise, God has brought to Israel a Savior, Jesus" (Acts 13:23, NASB).

Related Readings: Psalm 106:12; Joshua 21:45; Luke 1:45; Romans 15:8

OCTOBER 9

USED BY GOD

So the king did not listen to the people, for this turn of events was from God, to fulfill the word the LORD had spoken to Jeroboam. 2 Chronicles 10:15a

———————◆◆◆———————

Sometimes the Lord uses negative situations to get His positive results. What looks like a serious mistake on the surface turns out to be an opportunity for the Spirit to succeed. The Lord can use unruly people and a crisis of faith to carry out His game plan. One person's blunder in judgment becomes an open door for Jesus to walk through, showing Himself up close and personal. A turn of events can turn into the way God uses.

We are wise not to fight against God; we should wait on the validation of His will and way. If we rush to rescue a person, we may be delaying the inevitable. The Holy Spirit directs the hearts of men and women. It's with our humble heart we hear from the Spirit the steps we need to take. So, be bold in speaking up for what's right, even if it will fall on deaf ears. The Holy Spirit is using you to fulfill the Word of the Lord.

"Leave these men alone! Let them go! For if their purpose or activity is of human origin, it will fail. But if it is from God, you will not be able to stop these men" (Acts 5:38b-39a).

Related Readings: 2 Chronicles 11:4; Ezekiel 12:28; Acts 13:27; Romans 15:18

OCTOBER 10

HUMBLED BY HEALTH

So he [Naaman] went down and dipped himself in the Jordan
seven times, as the man of God had told him, and his flesh was
restored and became clean like that of a young boy.
2 Kings 5:14

Softening happens when sickness seizes the body. There is a
sensitivity and tenderness of heart that may have been dormant
in the behavior of a controlling Christian. But a body under fire
from illness is asking to let go of control and cling to Christ.
At first there may be an angry reaction, then acquiescence to a
sense that God's got it—He is in control. Faith in the face of
fiery trials is the fruit of humility. Sickness is an invitation to
submission to Jesus.

Yes, there are acts of obedience that accompany a life
smothered by a cloud of uncertainty. As we walk in humility,
we listen for the Lord's voice. He speaks through His Word, His
teachers, His preachers, His children, and experts in treating
physical ailments. Prayer and modern medicine are a powerful
partnership in producing positive outcomes. A humbled heart
creates clarity of mind for wisdom in decision-making. Humility
invites healing.

"Jesus reached out His hand and touched the man. 'I am
willing,' he said. 'Be clean!' And immediately the leprosy left
him" (Luke 5:13).

Related Readings: Job 14:22; Psalm 38:6-8; Proverbs 17:22;
Mark 7:37; 3 John 1:2

BUSINESS AS MISSION

Paul went to see them [Pricilla and Aquila], and because he was a tentmaker as they were, he stayed and worked with them. Acts 18:2b-3

Business is an excuse to be an excellent example of a Jesus follower. It is a professional platform to perform good deeds and exhibit integrity in business interactions. The sacred and secular are partners in business—a kingdom mission models actions that speak louder than words. When work exceeds the industry standard, people begin to ask "Why?" Indeed, a company that acknowledges Christ as the owner is positioned for God's favor. Do the values of our company mirror the heart of Jesus? Are honesty, humility, and hard work embraced as everyday virtues to live out? Are team members quick to serve, find solutions, and give positive feedback?

If our work culture reflects the character of Christ, we will attract team members with the character, competency, and chemistry to grow His company. Great people are not motivated by money alone, but by a mission much greater than themselves. Greatness comes to a company with a greater purpose. Therefore, give time off for team members to invest in their marriages and travel on mission trips. Grow leaders who will pour into their teams. Dedicate your company to Christ. He will determine your steps for success.

"In their hearts humans plan their course, but the LORD establishes their steps" (Proverbs 16:9).

Related Readings: Exodus 32:16; Jeremiah 31:33;
1 Thessalonians 2:9; 2 Thessalonians 3:8

OCTOBER 12

HOPELESS TO HOPEFUL

There is hope in your future, says the Lord.
Jeremiah 31:17a, NKJV

In Christ there is hope; outside of Christ there is no hope. Those focused on heaven find hope; those focused on earth find hope illusive. A life lived by faith is hopeful, but a life lived in fear is hopeless. Hope is not just the outcome of an optimist, it is the fruit of those whose security is in their Savior Jesus Christ. Moreover, money messes with the mind as it demands full allegiance to the almighty dollar in exchange for false hope.

However, we discover authentic hope and freedom in our submission to Christ as Lord and Master of our fate. Deep abiding hope is not a strategy but a reality when we bow in reverent obedience to God. He does not tease His children with pseudo promises; on the contrary, our heavenly Father gave what was most precious to Him, His Son, so we could become sons and daughters of the Most High. Praise God, for hope is His gift when we focus by faith on Him.

"He who did not spare his own Son, but gave Him up for us all—how will he not also, along with him, graciously give us all things?" (Romans 8:32)

Related Readings: Ecclesiastes 9:4; Jeremiah 17:13; 1 Timothy 4:10; Colossians 3:1-4

GRACE IN VAIN

As God's co-workers we urge you not to receive God's grace in vain. 2 Corinthians 6:1

There is a vanity associated with someone who has been saved by the grace of God, but does not appropriate the grace of God. Ironically, they believe in Jesus for the forgiveness of their sins, but they do not behave like they believe. Pride has a way of working itself back into the good graces of a life that is not governed by God's grace. Humility, on the other hand, flourishes in the hothouse of a heart that appreciates and applies God's grace.

We are all in danger of forgetting how faith in Christ changed us and brought us into a place of grace. The flesh forges ahead of faith and facilitates graceless living. Before we know it we are back to bad habits, putting grace on the back burner of our belief. Hence, we need reminders of the transformational work of the Holy Spirit that seizes the heart of a life in submission to almighty God. Grace empowers a humble heart. Praise the Lord that we, the redeemed, are a container and dispenser of God's grace. You are a cherished co-worker with Christ—His grace grows in your humble, teachable heart.

"But He gives a greater grace. Therefore it says, 'God is opposed to the proud, but gives grace to the humble'" (James 4:6, NASB).

Related Readings: Proverbs 3:34; Matthew 22:12; 1 Corinthians 3:9; 15:2

CONTENT WITH GOD

You have put gladness in my heart, more than in the season that their grain and wine increased. Psalm 4:7, NKJV

———◆◆◆◆◆———

There is a gladness God gives that cannot be generated by the world. His Spirit brings a smile to a face that faces fiery trials. Jesus gives joy in a job loss or the jettison of an opportunity. The Lord puts gladness in the heart of His children when they hurt or do not feel well. His wellspring of cheerfulness comes in a close relationship with Christ. Indeed, when mortality rubs shoulders with immortality, there is an abiding enjoyment.

Happiness based on circumstances comes and goes based on the whims of the world, but God's gladness is consistent. We can be sad at the state of our affairs and still be glad in God. Grief and joy coexist in Christ as He mourns and rejoices with us. A heart in touch with Jesus needs His truth and comfort. If we obsess over obstacles out of our control, we strive in discontentment: sad. When we leave the results to God we are content: glad. Above all else, because God has made you glad, your gladness is a gift you give back to Him.

"This is the LORD, we trusted in him; let us rejoice and be glad in his salvation" (Isaiah 25:9b).

Related Readings: Psalm 68:3; 69:32; Joel 2:23; Acts 13:48

OCTOBER 15

ALONENESS FEEDS FEAR

The Lord God called to the man, and said to him, "Where are you?" He said, "I heard the sound of You in the garden, and I was afraid." Genesis 3:9-10a, NASB

———◆———

Fear accompanies the feeling of aloneness. Like a child attending a new school, people who are alone can be anxious and unsure. Aloneness attacks celebrities flush with fame and single parents reeling from a ravaged relationship. Indeed, isolation increases when someone chooses to isolate themselves from relational risk. Hesitation to venture out to engage community can cause a crisis of faith. It is not good to be alone.

Ironically, a person can feel lonesome even while surrounded by people. Close proximity to a caring community does not guarantee the sense of belonging. Are you suffering from the feeling of insecurity in your aloneness? Have you drifted from connection with concerned confidants or deserted spiritual disciplines? Do you acknowledge the Lord's pursuit of your affections? His desire is to flush out your fear and replace it with faith. So, stay enlisted in the Lord's service— experience His miraculous works of grace. Invite into your life God's love and feel His warm embrace. Christ followers are not alone—you are a part of His body, created for companionship.

"The LORD God said, 'It is not good for the man to be alone'" (Genesis 2:18a).

Related Readings: Job 7:19; Psalm 102:7; Ecclesiastes 4:8, 11; John 8:16, 29; Romans 14:7

WISE DECISION-MAKING

Then the king gave his ruling: "Give the living baby to the first woman. Do not kill him; she is his mother." When all Israel heard the verdict the king had given, they held the king in awe, because they saw that he had wisdom from God to administer justice. 1 Kings 3:27-28

Wise decision-making is not accidental but intentional. There is a humble understanding for the need of the Lord's insightful solutions to very serious issues. Wisdom comes over time to those whose priority is wisdom hunting. Like a patient outdoorsman who looks for the best places and times to bag game, so seekers of wisdom are always in search of scriptural trophies of truth. Wise decision-making works for humble seekers.

Wise decision-making is necessary for a life that leverages the Lord's favor. The Almighty is on the lookout for those who align with His agenda. He is wisdom—He offers wisdom—He blesses wisdom. So, wise are we to daily look to God for His game plan. We especially need wisdom when we have conflicting conclusions to consider. Are you facing a dilemma that is life or death? If so, ask Jesus to tell you the wise thing to do.

"But the wisdom that comes from heaven is first of all pure; then peace-loving, considerate, submissive, full of mercy and good fruit, impartial and sincere" (James 3:17).

Related Readings: 1 Kings 3:9; Daniel 1:17; Matthew 7:7; James 3:13

HUMBLE LISTENING

Speak, Lord, for your servant is listening. 1 Samuel 3:9

———————

Humble listening is both science and art. It is science, because there are common occurrences in effective communication. Eye contact, emotional engagement, and comprehension all contribute to listeners who truly understand. Humble listening is also an art, because people are different in their experiences, their ability to clearly communicate, and limitations based on the biased interpretation of their own feelings. Therefore, as humble listeners we see ourselves as servants seeking to truly understand another's heart and mind.

We listen to their words for inflection of emotion. We may sense excitement in a high-pitched voice, or anger in a tone of defensiveness. Fear floods out of shaky speech, and apathy is evident in monotone words with a deadpan face. Compassion comprehends these indicators of the heart. Yes, humility diagnoses emotions. Lastly, people or institutions in authority over us are a mouthpiece for our master Jesus. His established authorities are boundaries for our protection and progress. So, listen to and obey the law of the Lord and the law of the land. Indeed, humility is slow to speak, quick to listen, and always ready to serve.

"I waited while you spoke, I listened to your reasoning; while you were searching for words, I gave you my full attention" (Job 32:11-12a).

Related Readings: Psalm 34:11; Proverbs 10:19; John 5:24; James 3:3-12

OCTOBER 18

HUMILITY FINDS FAVOR

Now Moses was a very humble man, more humble than
anyone else on the face of the earth. Numbers 12:3

Humility finds favor with God and man. Because of their
trustworthy temperament, the spirit of the humble solicits trust
and blessing. Like honey attracts a bee, so the Lord's heart is
drawn to the humble. It is a sweet exchange when the Holy Spirit
fills a submissive soul. There are no downsides in taking the
road of authentic lowliness. It is the path less trodden, because
its route encounters roadblocks, mix-ups—even ridicule.

However, our humble hearts are the hinges that swing open the
door of God's grace. Greater grace requires greater humility—
especially in face of unfair criticism. The Holy Spirit is our
defense attorney, retained on our behalf, by our heavenly Father.
He will bring to light the truth and discredit the dishonest. The
Lord lays bare man's motives. Our humility is a prescription of
choice to combat pride. It cleans our spiritual veins of vanity's
vestiges. So, never forget where He's brought you from and
where He wants to take you. Your humble heart in the eyes of
the Lord prepares you for His blessings.

"He mocks proud mockers but shows favor to the humble and
oppressed" (Proverbs 3:34).

Related Readings: Job 5:11; Matthew 23:12; Ephesians 5:21;
1 Peter 3:8

GOD'S ALREADY PROVIDED

He [Jesus] replied, "You give them something to eat." They answered, "We have only five loaves of bread and two fish."

Luke 9:13

God is not passive in His provision. He aggressively applies His resources directly to the needs of His children. His works are outside the small box of unbelief. The Lord's faithfulness flourishes where the soul fluently speaks the language of faith. The Holy Spirit traffics freely on the highway of a trusting heart. Man's natural eye limits the Lord's supernatural supply, but an eternal gaze engages His possibilities. Sometimes we find ourselves in situations where it seems we lack the Lord's provision. The resources right in front us look like they are limited.

Can Christ be creative with what He has already given us? Yes of course, if we are obedient to follow His directives. Faith says yes to God's "what," even when His "how" is unclear. Many times God has already provided for His children. The provision may seem disguised in its unconventional appearance, but nonetheless it is still very near. He is building your trust to make you trustworthy with His blessings. Like mighty vessels that cross deep channels of water, so you are the Lord's vessel to deliver His unfathomable blessings. Perhaps His provision is you!

"Jesus looked at them and said, 'With man this is impossible, but not with God; all things are possible with God'" (Mark 10:27).

Related Readings: Psalm 62:10; Ephesians 6:10; 1 Timothy 6:17; 1 Peter 4:11

DEAD HEROES

Therefore, since we are surrounded by such a great cloud of witnesses, let us throw off everything that hinders and the sin that so easily entangles. Hebrews 12:1a

---

Dead heroes are the most dependable, because they are not in a position to mess up. Their legacy had been sealed in death, and now they speak from the influence they left behind. Dead heroes inspire with their memory of love, wisdom, and perseverance. They have stood the test of time, having stood with courage in the face of adverse conditions even to the point of death. Dead heroes bring love and faith to life.

We think about Abraham and our faith is energized. We mull over Moses and humility grips our heart. We read about David and come away with courage to be accountable. Solomon soaks our minds with wisdom and Hannah moves our hearts to pray. Naomi inspires encouragement and Ruth instills obedience. These heroes of the faith facilitate faithfulness to our Lord Jesus. Heroes arouse hope. Ultimately, Christ's example inspires us to endure in doing what's right. His Spirit empowers us in service for Him. Jesus is our hero who was momentarily dead but is now alive in us. We look to heroes who give us life in Christ!

"By faith Abel brought God a better offering than Cain did… And by faith Abel still speaks, even though he is dead" (Hebrews 11:4).

Related Readings: Genesis 31:53; 2 Kings 14:3; Psalm 25:15; John 13:15; 1 Corinthians 9:24

PROMISE TO GOD

A man said to him [Jesus], "I will follow you wherever you go." Luke 9:57

Christ takes seriously the commitments of His children. Indeed, faith is not a flippant force that fluctuates based on feelings. Rather it is a righteous resolve that is the result of a devoted disciple of Jesus. A promise made to God is an exclamation mark of a sold-out life. It is at this crossroad of commitment that disciples are exposed as authentic followers or impostors. This lofty vow of loyalty to the Lord believes in the Cross and takes up a cross. Will we follow Jesus wherever He goes?

What if He asks us to go with Him into vocational ministry—will we follow Him? What if He asks us to go with Him to forgive a friend—will we follow Him? What if He asks us to go with Him and die to our dreams—will we follow Him? What if He asks us to go with Him to use our relationships, finances, and resources for His kingdom—will we follow Him? Our "yes" to our new life in Him means "no" to our old life. It's not how we start with Jesus but how we finish with Jesus that counts. So, by faith we promise to follow Him wherever He goes.

"Whoever wants to be my disciple must deny themselves and take up their cross and follow me" (Mark 8:34).

Related Readings: Isaiah 42:1; 48:16; 50:7; Luke 14:27; Romans 8:36

UNCONTROLLABLE DECISIONS

So when the Midianite merchants came by, his brothers pulled Joseph up out of the cistern and sold him for twenty shekels of silver. Genesis 37:28

There are decisions made by others that directly affect those in the wake of their influence. It may be a father who abuses alcohol or a mother who is unfaithful. Children may find themselves caring for their mom and dad prematurely because of their parents' unwise financial decisions. A decision of a boss to pass over a more qualified person affects that individual and related team members. Decisions out of our control are not to control us but cause us to trust Christ's control.

So, how will we react when we are directly impacted by another's detrimental decision? Will we let go of control when decisions are made out of our control? Joseph could have become a victim, spending his whole life attempting to avenge his abusive treatment, but instead he chose to fear God and forgive man. We are wise to give over to God those who've harmed us with their irresponsible actions. As we decide to let go of control of decisions out of our control, the Holy Spirit takes control. So, recognize Christ's control and rest in His secure, peaceful presence.

"But Joseph said to them, 'Don't be afraid. Am I in the place of God? You intended to harm me, but God intended it for good'" (Genesis 50:19-20a).

Related Readings: Matthew 8:26; Philippians 3:20-21; 4:11; 1 Thessalonians 5:18

WORTHY TO FOLLOW

Even if you had ten thousand guardians in Christ, you do not have many fathers, for in Christ Jesus I became your father through the gospel. 1 Corinthians 4:15

Spiritual fathers and mothers are necessary for growing disciples of Jesus. These are mature believers who have experienced bumps, bruises, and brokenness over their lifetime of following the Lord. They know what it means to enjoy God's grace and peace, and they know how to give Him the glory in their success. These seasoned saints don't pretend to know it all; on the contrary, they are diligent students in the school of faith.

Wise are we to be on the lookout for mature believers who are worthy of following. Their humble heart attracts our hearts, and their keen mind challenges our thinking. It is out of our mentor's engagement with Jesus that they are able to parent us in the faith. We only imitate those who first imitate Jesus. Whom do I follow who will make me wiser tomorrow? Grow in your love and obedience to the Lord and others will want to follow you. As a spiritual parent, model well love and obedience to God. Imitate Jesus and you are worthy to follow.

"You became imitators of us and of the Lord, for you welcomed the message in the midst of severe suffering with the joy given by the Holy Spirit" (1 Thessalonians 1:6).

Related Readings: Deuteronomy 18:9; 2 Kings 17:15; 2 Thessalonians 3:9; 3 John 1:11

NOT ABOUT ME

Love must be sincere. Hate what is evil; cling to what is good.
Be devoted to one another in love. Honor one another above
yourselves. Romans 12:9-10

I often forget that it's not about me. Humility reminds me that
it's first Him, then them, and finally me. I struggle with keeping
myself off the throne of my life. Only one king can reign over
a surrendered soul and that's my Savior Jesus. Yet, daily, my
old life seeks to dethrone the Lord with its selfish whims and
spiritual disengagement. Fortunately, by faith through grace, I
am able to resist the flesh's foolish coup to overtake Christ.

Love wins only when we use it as our spiritual strategy of choice.
Devotion to one another in love is irresistible to the recipient and
extremely fulfilling to the dispenser of grace. But, sometimes it
seems easier to be devoted to the Lord than to another human
being. Yet, devotion to each other need not be fickle when
unconditional love is the motivation. Devotion loves deeply.
Indeed, our unselfish devotion is the fruit of unconditional love.
You know it's not about you, when you gain joy and define JOY
by: Jesus—Others—You.

"Now that you have purified yourselves by obeying the truth
so that you have sincere love for each other, love one another
deeply, from the heart" (1 Peter 1:22).

Related Readings: Psalm 133:1; Proverbs 14:31;
1 Thessalonians 4:9; Hebrews 13:1

LIQUID LOVE

Jesus wept. John 11:35

———◆———

Tears are evidence of a kind and caring heart. They are the nectar of God that brings sweet support to another suffering soul. Moist eyes make a friend feel understood and accepted. It is this tenderness of spirit that seizes a hurting heart and won't let go until it lingers long in love. Tears create crevices of comfort where words will never lodge. Indeed, liquid love is possible for anyone whose heart has been touched by the love of Jesus. Weep for injustice, cry over sin, and ask the Lord to glorify Himself out of your tears.

When our tear ducts have dried up, our heart may have shriveled up. When we are too strong to cry, we may have become too weak to really care. When the tears of others make us uncomfortable, we may be comfortable in our own self-reliance. However, when we comprehend the compassion of Christ and see His wet eyes of love for us, we weep. He weeps over our loss; He cries for our comfort; He hurts over our hurt. He weeps for us. Perhaps you ask forgiveness with moist eyes of contrition or embrace a loved one with a comforting caress. Your liquid love speaks volumes when words won't work.

"When Paul had finished speaking, he knelt down with all of them and prayed. They all wept as they embraced him and kissed him" (Acts 20:36-37).

Related Readings: Nehemiah 1:4; Job 30: 25; Psalm 137:1; Luke 22:62

YOU MATTER

For you are a people holy to the LORD your God. Out of all the peoples on the face of the earth, the LORD has chosen you to be his treasured possession. Deuteronomy 14:2

———◆◆◆———

You matter. You matter because you're made in the image of God. You are a blueprint of a beauty birthed out of heaven. Your physical makeup is beautiful because the eye of your beloved beholder is your heavenly Father. Your intellectual capacity is attractive because in Christ you know the mind of Christ. Your emotional energy is engaging because you are accepted and loved by God. You matter because your master Jesus says you matter.

You matter. You matter because you are chosen by the Lord—you are His treasured possession. Jesus wants you to be with Him like a coach who recruits athletes; He has picked you to be on His team. He calls the plays and He expects you to excel in the position suited for your skills, gifts, and experiences. You matter most to the Lord of Hosts. Since Jesus Christ thinks the world of you, He laid down His life for the world on your behalf. You have been given much in your faith journey, so God expects much. Thus, you matter in helping others know they matter.

"The Spirit of God has made me; the breath of the Almighty gives me life" (Job 33:4).

Related Readings: Numbers 16:22; Malachi 2:15: Colossians 3:12; 1 Peter 2:9

OCTOBER 27

TAUGHT BY GOD

Now about your love for one another we do not need to write to you, for you yourselves have been taught by God to love each other. 1 Thessalonians 4:9

God the Father is a tender teacher of truth to His children. God the Son, Jesus, is a teacher who taught with clarity and authority when He walked on earth. And God the Holy Spirit is a teacher who reveals to the heart of humans the hidden secrets of heaven. Indeed, followers of Christ are schooled in the academy of understanding the Almighty's ways. Wise servants of the Lord stay enrolled in His school for a lifetime of learning.

If we cease to learn from God, we cease to grow in our faith and obedience. We remain a student as we remain in Him. We learn the language of heaven as we learn to listen to the Holy Spirit's promptings in our heart. We comprehend Christ when we first receive Him by faith into our life, as we study His life, and as we seek to emulate His example. Are you learning from Jesus how to love like Jesus? Your curriculum in love includes unconditional love, brotherly love, and romantic love. Therefore, be thorough in your studies of Christ. You get an A+ when you learn and apply His truth.

"It is written in the Prophets: 'They will all be taught by God'" (John 6:45a).

Related Readings: Isaiah 54:13; Jeremiah 31:33; 1 Corinthians 2:13; 1 Peter 2:21

SIN OF OMISSION

If anyone, then, knows the good they ought to do and doesn't
do it, it is sin for them. James 4:17

———◄••►———

What is a sin of omission? A sin of omission is passive
permission for wrong. It does nothing when something needs
to be said or done. It gives a pass to people or situations that
require sticky confrontation. Sometimes the silence of good
people makes them bad people. Their inertia of integrity
condones unrighteous conduct. A sin of omission can be more
damaging than a sin of commission. A quiet friend can be worse
than a loud enemy.

We who are people of the Lord's light know better than those
who grope in darkness. The bar of behavior is higher for those
of us who believe in Jesus. Thus, we do not have the option of
the proverbial ostrich to place our informed heads in the sand
of irresponsibility. Omit sins of omission, and you will move
beyond immaturity and ignorance. It takes courage and faith
to become an overcomer of omission. Be quick to confess and
repent of subtle sins, and be slow to seek selfish avoidance.
Good people who do nothing invite sin's influence to infiltrate
the culture. So overcome errant omissions with courageous
faith that commissions righteousness.

"Jesus said, 'If you were blind, you would not be guilty of sin;
but now that you claim you can see, your guilt remains'"
(John 9:41).

Related Readings: Deuteronomy 22:1-4; Ezekiel 33:31;
Proverbs 21:13; 1 John 3:16-18

PROCESSING GRIEF

But you, God, see the trouble of the afflicted; you consider their grief and take it in hand. The victims commit themselves to you; you are the helper of the fatherless. Psalm 10:14

———◆———

Grief is a God-given emotion that processes sorrow related to a loss. It can be the loss of a loved one to death or the death of a vision. Loss associated with finances, health, a pet, a job, divorce, or relocation contributes to extended sorrow. Moreover, nations grieve corporately over war, mass murder by a maniac, and the death of a revered national leader. Grief calls for a pause to pray and reflect on what's important. Sorrow seeks out a Savior.

Heaven's desire is to fill the hole in our hearts with hope. Indeed, sorrow slows us down to meditate on what really matters: Jesus, family, friends, spiritual, physical, and emotional health, church, fellowship, evangelism, discipleship, and God's game plan for our lives. Grief gets us to God so that we take Him seriously. The spiritually serious are eventually able to smile. Our mourning turns into trust in Christ, and He is able to restore our joy and hope. What anguish empties, faith fills. We serve emotional and physical needs so they will embrace their spiritual need. Grief needs God.

"My eyes are dim with grief. I call to you, LORD, every day; I spread out my hands to you" (Psalm 88:9).

Related Readings: Psalm 31:9; Proverbs 14:13; John 16:5-7; 20-22; 1 Peter 1:6

PEDESTAL OF PRIDE

So, if you think you are standing firm, be careful that you don't fall! 1 Corinthians 10:12

A pedestal of pride looks down on other inferior souls. It is a position of self-worship that threatens integrity and influence. Like a drug, pride is addictive and impairs good judgment. If it could be packaged as a pill in a prescription bottle, the label would read, "Warning: taken too often in large doses may lead to a great fall, even death."

If we build a monument in our minds to ourselves, we are on a pedestal of pride. This self-imposed idolatry acts like a monarch who expects blind loyalty and unquestionable submission to everyone under his or her authority. If we don't wake up from this narcissistic dream, it will turn into a hellish nightmare. Relationships will be wrecked, reputations will be ruined, and respect will be absent from those who mean the most. However, a prayerful posture dethrones pride and replaces it with humility. The Lord lifts us out of the slimy pit of pride and sets us on His solid rock of righteousness. Pride has no place in the personality of a child of the King. You are the workmanship of God's grace, mercy, and love.

"He lifted me out of the slimy pit, out of the mud and mire; he set my feet on a rock" (Psalm 40:2).

Related Readings: 1 Samuel 17:42; Psalm 18:27; Proverbs 16:18; Isaiah 13:11; Romans 12:16

INFLUENCE OF IMPURE SPIRITS

Just then a man in their synagogue who was possessed by an impure spirit cried out, "What do you want with us, Jesus of Nazareth?" Mark 1:23-24a

---

Jesus encountered evil in the synagogue and cast out the impure spirit from the man. Demons are not comfortable where Christ is taught and where the Spirit of God has a powerful presence. Unfortunately, some impotent churches have people who go through the motions with zombie-like spiritual energy. The enemy's influence has invaded their minds. Evil induces individuals to smile and be satisfied to live for themselves. Impure spirits lead people to live impure lives.

Therefore, make sure to not make light of the influence of impure spirits. If you embrace activities and entertainment that espouse evil, you expose yourself and your family to the influence of impure spirits. Even events enjoyed in fun and jest can open the door to the unintentional consequences of accepting the abnormal as normal. Your children can dress up and have fun without imitating witches, warlocks, spiritists, and the occult. Why dance with the enemy and risk defilement by his influence? Impure spirits cannot remain in the presence of Purity, the Lord Jesus.

"Do not turn to mediums or seek out spiritists, for you will be defiled by them. I am the LORD your God" (Leviticus 19:31).

Related Readings: 1 Samuel 28:3-9; Job 1:6-12; Mark 3:15; 1 Timothy 4:1; Revelation 9:20

NOVEMBER

Now all glory to God, who is able, through his mighty power at work within us, to accomplish infinitely more than we might ask or think. Glory to him in the church and in Christ Jesus through all generations forever and ever! Amen.

Ephesians 3: 20-21

NOVEMBER 1

GRACE MADE MAN

But by the grace of God I am what I am. 1 Corinthians 15:10a

―――――――◆◄►◆―――――――

A self-made man is the antithesis of a grace-made man. A self-made man becomes desperate for God on occasion, as when a crisis occurs—a grace-made man is continually desperate for God since he sees himself as a needy man. A self-made man struggles to give God the glory for his accomplishments, but the grace-made man is quick to give Christ the credit for his success. Grace brings out the best in humble hearts.

Furthermore, a grace-made man's work is led by the Spirit. Gratitude governs grace-based behavior into focused diligence. A man or woman motivated by the grace of God works for an audience of One. Their godly ambition has an eternal allegiance that no earthly boss can inspire. So, we work hard because God's grace is at work within us. Is your work and life a divine portrait of grace? If so, you are attractive; beautiful to behold. God's grace makes the man; man does not make the man. "T'was Grace that brought us safe thus far…and Grace will lead us home." ("Amazing Grace")

"For by the grace given me I say to every one of you: Do not think of yourself more highly than you ought, but rather think of yourself with sober judgment" (Romans 12:3a).

Related Readings: 1 Samuel 2:7; 2 Corinthians 11:23; Colossians 1:29; Philippians 2:13

SOCIAL JUSTICE

Therefore, as we have opportunity, let us do good to all
people, especially to those who belong to the family of
believers. Galatians 6:10

The Church of Jesus Christ has the opportunity and obligation
to serve in Jesus' name those suffering under the injustices of
society. Protecting the life of the unborn and elderly, providing
for widows and orphans, caring for the sick and dying, and
visiting those in jail or prison allow the church to engage the
culture. Compassion is not just a feeling but a meaningful effort
to get involved. A secular society needs a Savior to save its soul
of injustice.

Who is the church? It is both an institution and individual
believers who make up the Body of Christ. We are responsible
corporately and personally to serve society with good deeds
and with the good news of salvation in Jesus. Words without
works indicate a dead faith, and works without words comprise
an ashamed faith. The good news of Jesus goes to the heart for
salvation, the mind for renewal, and the body for purification.
Social justice for the Church is modeling Christ's actions of
preaching, teaching, giving, feeding, and clothing. We love
children and honor the elderly. As the Church grows in its
influence, the need for government lessens. Where the Lord
reigns above—justice rains down on society.

"Carry each other's burdens, and in this way you will fulfill the
law of Christ" (Galatians 6:2).

Related Readings: Deuteronomy 14:29; Isaiah 1:17;
Titus 2:14; Ephesians 2:19

PROTECT YOUR WIFE

For the husband is the head of the wife as Christ is the head of
the church, His body, of which He is the Savior.
Ephesians 5:23

———————◆◆◆◆————————

A wife is vulnerable to emotional exploitation. She needs her
husband's loving care and protection. Insensitive friends and
family can take advantage of her sweet and sensitive spirit.
So, a husband who takes seriously his role of protector is ever
vigilant to shield his bride from bad behavior. What was once
a blossoming flower of faith can wither under the assault of
rejection and disrespect. Thus, guard her heart with your strong
loving protection.

Every woman of faith prays for a godly knight in shining armor
who will bear the sword of the Spirit on her behalf. She longs
for a godly man who by faith walks in the fullness of the Spirit,
courageous and confident in Christ. Are you that husband? Are
you active in safeguarding your wife's mind, will, and emotions?
Is her spirit in safekeeping with you? Wife, your husband is
God's buffer against bad people. So rest; his role is to defend
you. Men, don't shrink back from stepping up for your woman.
Just like Jesus is the head of the church and gave Himself up for
His bride, so you do the same for yours. Love protects.

"For he guards the course of the just and protects the way of his
faithful ones" (Proverbs 2:8).

Related Readings: Proverbs 2:11; Malachi 2:16; John 17:11-
15; 1 Corinthians 13:7

SUPPORT YOUR HUSBAND

The LORD God said, "It is not good for the man to be alone. I will make a helper suitable for him." Genesis 2:18

Husbands have a God-given support system in their sweet spouse. Heaven has provided just the right wife for a husband to receive help. This divine strategy is a blessing because, left to himself, a husband is incomplete—he maintains at best. The Lord's plan gives a wife the opportunity to make her man feel confident and in control. Most of all, her love for Jesus is the fuel that fuels her faith in her husband. She is his best helper.

What if your husband is ungrateful and hard to please? Your model of unselfish support is a testimony to your trust in God. If your husband takes you for granted, pray the Holy Sprit will convict him of his need for appreciation. A supportive attitude attracts your husband to your heart. Trust the Lord to grow him in grace and gratitude. A woman of prayer wisely waits on God to work without rushing ahead with sincere solutions. As a husband, you may seem self-sufficient, but you need your sweetheart. You are one flesh with your bride, and you need her help. So, acknowledge your dependence on God and need for your wife's support.

"He who finds a wife finds what is good and receives favor from the LORD" (Proverbs 18:22).

Related Readings: Job 42:5; Proverbs 31:11; 1 Corinthians 11:9; 2 Corinthians 4:6

GOD OF SECOND CHANCES

"Let's have a feast and celebrate. For this son of mine was dead and is alive again; he was lost and is found." So they began to celebrate. Luke 15:23-24

God does not hold grudges. He is quick to forgive and anticipates receiving His children back from the foreign land of foolish living. Regret and pain may haunt the human heart, but heaven loves to love someone who is tired of trying to live without the Lord. Misery is the object of pity, thus the compassion of Christ is pregnant with possibility to a contrite and repentant heart. Once we tire of sin's consequences there is a righteous reunion we can expect from our loving heavenly Father.

God our Father can't wait to wrap us in His arms, weep over our return and rejoice with a great celebration. He saves His best for when we are ready to rest in Him. Christ's love removes our guilt by His grace. Are you in need of a second chance? Grace and mercy are not about what you deserve. They are about what your heavenly Father has already done for you in Christ. You get over your guilt by going to God in heart-felt repentance. He forgives you. Second chances mirror His mercy.

"See, I have taken away your sin, and I will put fine garments on you" (Zechariah 3:4b).

Related Readings: Malachi 3:17; Ephesians 2:1-9; 1 Timothy 5:6; 2 Timothy 4:11

GOD'S GLORY REVEALED

So Moses thought, "I will go over and see this strange sight—why the bush does not burn up." When the LORD saw that he had gone over to look, God called to him from within the bush, "Moses! Moses!" Exodus 3:3-4

The glory of God is revealed through humility, not pride. He chose a humble thorn bush, not a proud oak tree. It's to the lowly lovers of the Lord that He shows Himself in His regal righteousness. Indeed, the fire of the Holy Spirit burns brightly in a life combustible for Christ. The fire of faith will not be extinguished in a humble heart that burns for God.

It is not the places of honor that we seek, but the place of dependency we desire. The lower the status of self is relegated, the higher we look up to our Lord in reverence. Christ is within us for salvation and companionship, but He is above us for worship and praise. He is our confidant and our Lord—our Savior and our Master. We are His friend and follower. God's glory is your rear guard, your covering overhead, and your torch for Him to guide you. He reveals His glory in you and through you for His glory!

"Jesus replied, 'If I glorify myself, my glory means nothing. My Father, whom you claim as your God, is the one who glorifies me" (John 8:54).

Related Readings: Isaiah 6:8; Philippians 1:11; 1 Peter 1:7; 4:13

ECLIPSED BY GLORY

"**D**o not come any closer," God said. "Take off your sandals,
for the place where you are standing is holy ground."
Exodus 3:5

———————◆◆◆———————

There are seasons when a servant of the Lord Jesus will engage
the glory of God in an intense fashion. Yes, His glory is all-
encompassing, all the time, but these less frequent, intimate
encounters are especially revealing. God's glory goes to places
in the heart where humans fear to tread. Only by faith and
brokenness can a Christian experience this deep communing
with Christ in the middle of pain, uncertainty, prayer, worship,
and transition.

Moses, in reverent awe, worshiped God in His glory during
his burning bush experience. In humility he took off his shoes
and bowed in submission to his King of Glory! In these very
meaningful moments we listen for the voice of the Lord and we
do exactly what He says. If He says go, we go. If He says stay,
we stay. If he says wait, we wait. The voice of God does not
stutter, nor should our faith. We obey because His glory is our
guarantor. His glory eclipses our earthly challenges and invites
us to be called friend. Wow, what a privilege to walk with Jesus
and worship Jesus at the same time!

"The LORD would speak to Moses face to face, as one speaks
to a friend" (Exodus 33:11a).

Related Readings: Numbers 12:8; Matthew 5:8; John 15:13-
15; 1 John 3:2

SPIRITUAL LIVING

Since we live by the Spirit, let us keep in step with the Spirit.
Galatians 5:25

The Holy Spirit fuels spiritual living. This is where freedom resides and where fruit-bearing takes place. The flesh is pre-conversion to Christ living; it is reliance on self to seek security. The Spirit is post-conversion to Christ living; it is reliance on God to secure earthly and eternal security. The Spirit and the flesh conflict, but the flesh has been put to death by faith and the Spirit has come alive. Spiritual living submits to Christ. Spiritual living thrives as we daily surrender to Jesus.

The way we became a Christian—by grace through faith—is the same way we continue as a Christian. Yet, the flesh tries to flaunt its old habits as teasers for us not to trust God. But we know better—it's better not to boast in the flesh, but to be humbled by the Spirit. When we walk in the Spirit, we are empowered to bear the fruit of the Spirit. The Spirit brings wisdom when we consider ways that are unwise. The Spirit brings conviction when we begin to drift from our convictions. The Spirit brings comfort when we struggle with discomfort. The Holy Spirit is heaven's secret to spiritual living.

"So I say, walk by the Spirit, and you will not gratify the desires of the flesh" (Galatians 5:16).

Related Readings: Romans 8:3-5, 14; 2 Corinthians 5:17; Colossians 2:11; 1 Peter 2:16

FRUIT OF LOVE

But the fruit of the Spirit is love… Galatians 5:22a

———◆◆◆———

Love leads the list of nine character traits that constitute the fruit of the Spirit. Love, the greatest commandment, is God's gold medal for His children who run the race of faith. This authentic affection for the Lord and people sets the tone for the following eight character traits. Love is foundational, because it keeps motives pure and it builds trust that delivers truth. Like a loving mom, love looks for ways to give care and comfort.

Love gets behind enemy lines with the determination of a Navy Seal. It is the tip of a sharp arrow of virtue that pierces the hardest of hearts. Delicious love is an appetizer and entrée we can offer to hungry souls. It is attractive to acquaintances, and it retains friends. We love when we initiate interest, refrain from retaliation, give grace, and take responsibility. Love listens, gives, helps, forgives, perseveres, serves, and sacrifices. Love is a verb. We love someone who does not love us because our heavenly Father did this for us before we fell in love with Jesus. Our Spirit-filled fruit of love shares the gospel and our life. Our fruit of love is appetizing.

"Because we loved you so much, we were delighted to share with you not only the gospel of God but our lives as well" (1 Thessalonians 2:8).

Related Readings: Luke 6:31-34; 1 Corinthians 13:1-13; 2 Thessalonians 2:13; 1 John 4:19

FRUIT OF JOY

But the fruit of the Spirit is… joy. Galatians 5:22a

Joy is the juice that flows from the fruit of the Spirit. It is tasty, delightful, and delicious. Joy from Jesus gives strength for the journey, endurance to obey, and enjoyment to relationships. It offers hope for the future, optimism in the present, and reflects on pleasant memories from the past. Spirit-filled joy is a faith-filled attitude that is contagious. It converts frowns to smiles, cranks to encouragers, and inertia to energy.

Joy gives fuel to our faith and allows us to fuel the faith of others. It lights up a room with its genuine gladness and delights to hear another's heart. Indeed, our countenance stays soft and kind when joy, like emotional lotion, has been applied by the Spirit. Just as sunblock protects us from overexposure to harmful rays of light, so joy shields our soul from the lies of defeat and depression. Joy in Jesus generates gladness. Thus, be an agent of joy on behalf of Jesus. Perhaps that means you should take yourself less seriously and the Lord more seriously. Laugh at yourself, sing in the Spirit, and extend encouragement. A smiling soul molds the mouth.

"Worship the LORD with gladness; come before him with joyful songs" (Psalm 100:2).

Related Readings: Nehemiah 8:10; Psalm 19:8;
1 Thessalonians 1:6; 2:19; Philemon 1:7

FRUIT OF PEACE

But the fruit of the Spirit is… peace. Galatians 5:22a

———————◄•◦•►———————

Peace is an intuitive fruit of the Spirit. It is an inner sense that Christ is in control, even when external circumstances swirl with uncertainty. It is a calm that only the Spirit can create. Furthermore, a lack of peace protects from moving forward too fast or at all. It is a check and balance to impulsive emotional commitments or impetuous mental assent. Peace produced by the Spirit is not subject to shifting situations but to a stable Savior.

Spirit-filled peace leads us to become peacemakers, not just peacekeepers. We take the initiative to bring together two friends who may be in conflict, reminding them of the traits they admire in each other. Once we have peace with God, others, and ourselves, we can create a safe environment of acceptance. Peacemakers who sow peace reap righteous results. Above all, peace is found in resting in a right relationship with the Almighty. Chaos is replaced with calm. Trust and tranquility triumph over anxiety and striving. Guilt is gone, peace remains. Our risen Savior breathes peace into our lungs of faith. Peace with God brings the peace of God.

"Peace I leave with you, My peace I give to you; not as the world gives do I give to you. Let not your heart be troubled, neither let it be afraid" (John 14:27, NKJV).

Related Readings: Numbers 6:25-27; Job 22:21; Matthew 5:7; Romans 5:1; 15:13

FRUIT OF FORBEARANCE

The fruit of the Spirit is… forbearance. Galatians 5:22a

———•◄●●►•———

The Spirit's fruit of forbearance is much more than patience. It is choosing not to retaliate when wronged. It's extending terms to benefit another instead of demanding a justifiable immediate payment. Forbearance is the long-suffering the Lord has towards sinners who need Him. He knows that time away from Him eventually loses its luster and appeal. Do not buckle in unbelief under the pressures that threaten to crush your spirit.

By faith we are able to model God's great patience toward those who anger us, who deeply disappoint us. The Holy Spirit fills us with the fruit of forbearance so He can lengthen the fuse of our temper. The longer it takes for our temper to smolder under self-control, the more time we have to cool down. The Spirit's forbearance releases our vengeance to the Lord. There is not a drought of God's grace during hot summers of suffering. Critics will come and go. Hard circumstances are meant to soften our heart to grow a harvest for Christ. The fruit of forbearance in our life waters seeds in other searching souls. Thus, be a faithful fruit bearer of forbearance!

"Or do you show contempt for the riches of his kindness, forbearance and patience, not realizing that God's kindness is intended to lead you to repentance" (Romans 2:4).

Related Readings: Psalm 86:15; Proverbs 19:11; Colossians 3:12-13; Hebrews 6:12

FRUIT OF KINDNESS

The fruit of the Spirit is… kindness. Galatians 5:22a

———◄••••►———

Kindness comes for the Christian from the Holy Spirit's inner work of compassion that expresses itself in outward deeds. Random acts of kindness are divine encounters wrought to illustrate the kindness of God. Kindness is more than being nice; it is discerning another's point of pain and, with Spirit-led sensitivity, bringing them relief. A kind action may come in the form of a gift, a word of wisdom, a verbal prayer, an introduction, or an affirmation.

Because of God's great kindness He gave His Son Jesus to save sinners and grow saints. And for all who believe, He grants a seat to sit at His table as an adopted child of God. Yes, we are sons and daughters of the Most High! What a privilege to have access to our heavenly Father's vast resources of grace, wisdom, love, forgiveness, and holiness. His kindness leads us to repentance, guides us in character growth, and graduates us to heaven. Kindness comes from feeling accepted. Not everyone will affirm our kindness; some will use us, so react kindly to the unkind. The fruit of kindness heals and gives hope.

"But when the kindness and love of God our Savior appeared, He saved us" (Titus 3:4-5a).

Related Readings: Ezra 9:9; Hosea 11:3-4; Acts 4:9; 28:2; Romans 2:4; 11:22

FRUIT OF GOODNESS

The fruit of the Spirit is… goodness. Galatians 5:22b

———◆◆◆———

The Holy Spirit's fruit of goodness flows from the heart of God. It is pure in its essence, and it is sure in its application for good. Good is to God what bad is to evil—a reflection of its origin. Goodness is the expression of moral excellence found in any man or woman surrendered to the Spirit's control. It is virtue that bubbles up from a deep-seated belief that outside of Christ there is no good thing. His goodness reveals His glory to the world.

To say he or she is a good man or woman does not do justice to the depth of the fruit of goodness. It puts too much emphasis on the human element in being good. Goodness comes from God to do good for God. We are only good if our goodness is initiated by Christ and sustained by the Spirit. At salvation God's goodness floods our soul like a warm bath cleanses a dirty body. Goodness takes permanent residence when the Lord Jesus is the landlord of our life. He's all-good. Our goodness gives us the influence to change the culture. God is calling us to be an agent of change for His good!

"We constantly pray for you… that by his power he may bring to fruition your every desire for goodness and your every deed prompted by faith" (2 Thessalonians 1:11).

Related Readings: Exodus 33:19; Psalm 23:6; Romans 15:14; Hebrews 6:5

FRUIT OF FAITHFULNESS

The fruit of the Spirit is… faithfulness. Galatians 5:22b

———◆———

Faithfulness flows from the fruit of the Spirit's vine with divine fidelity. It is the ability to stay the course in a crisis or correct a corrupt circumstance. Faithfulness is a personal resolve to stay committed in marriage through "sickness and health, richer and poorer, and to death do us part." Faithfulness feels a compelling call from Christ to stay put in a career, especially when it's not easy, knowing perseverance leads to righteous rewards. Invite the Lord's faithfulness to you to facilitate your faithfulness to Him and others.

Are you at the crossroads of a commitment? Will you remain faithful, even though it is unfair and hard? It is easier to follow Jesus when He heals and forgives. It is harder to be a dedicated disciple when you are persecuted for your faith and demeaned for doing good. However, because Christ remained faithful to the Cross, on the Cross and after the Cross, you remain faithful to bear your cross for Christ. Make sure to keep your eyes on Jesus, not on the unfaithfulness of others. A friend's unfaithfulness, even betrayal, is your opportunity to remain faithful. Scared friends may scatter and an insecure family member may gossip, but you still model loyalty to those you love. Love is faithful in the face of unfaithfulness.

Related Readings: Psalm 91:4; Isaiah 38:18-19; 3 John 1:3; Revelation 13:10

FRUIT OF GENTLENESS

The fruit of the Spirit is… gentleness. Galatians 5:23

———◆◆◆———

Gentleness is the fruit of the Spirit that germinates from God. Indeed, the voice of the Lord is gentle, but weighty in worth. He does not scream in a defensive or demanding tone, rather He speaks with authority under control. Speech initiated by the Holy Spirit is not harsh, but helpful—not loud, but loving—not testy, but tolerant. The gentleness of Jesus grows in the soil of patience, from the seed of sensitivity, with the water of humility.

We know we are governed by gentleness when the cadence of our conversation is not high-pitched with rapid-fire reactions. There is respectful dialogue without angrily attacking another's motives. We prayerfully pronounce God's principles as a fellow lifetime learner, not with an "I have finally arrived," know-it-all attitude. Knowledge, wisdom, and discernment delivered with gentle force, carry influence and insight to the recipient. So lead, teach, and serve with the even keel of Christ. Always learn of Him and His meek and gentle heart. Your gentleness generates gentleness in others for God's glory. A gentle soul saves souls!

"But in your hearts revere Christ as Lord. Always be prepared to give an answer to everyone who asks you to give the reason for the hope that you have. But do this with gentleness and respect" (1 Peter 3:15).

Related Readings: 1 Kings 19:12; Proverbs 15:1; 25:15; Matthew 21:5; Philippians 4:5

FRUIT OF SELF-CONTROL

The fruit of the Spirit is… self-control. Galatians 5:23

Self-control is the temperate fruit that blossoms on the vine of the Spirit. It uses the gasoline of grace to govern the engine of a disciple's activity. Proper self-control is Spirit control, since the flesh can be determined and undisciplined without the horsepower of the Holy Spirit. Spirit-led self-control bows to no ego—it only surrenders to Christ. It is free from the desires and whims of the flesh. The body is a good servant, but a poor master.

The fruit of self-control breaks unholy habits and replaces them with holy habits. It is so much more than just having a disciplined temperament—it is a mindset that is mastered by Christ's preferences. We can't confuse self-reliance with the Spirit's self-control. Self-control relies on the Spirit's energy and insight to accomplish God's will. It is the difference between gutting out a bad circumstance without Christ and walking with Christ. When Christ controls us—we are capable of controlling our life. Self-control is the Spirit's work, but our cooperation is required. Ultimately, God is in control. He bears the fruit of self-control.

"For the grace of God has appeared that offers salvation to all people. It teaches us to say 'No' to ungodliness and worldly passions, and to live self-controlled" (Titus 2:11-12a).

Related Readings: Job 37:15; 1 Corinthians 7:9; 9:25-27; 2 Peter 1:6; Titus 2:5

THE ONLY WAY

Jesus answered, "I am the way and the truth and the life. No one comes to the Father except through me." John 14:6

———— ❖ ————

Faith in Jesus Christ is the only way to God. There are many types of experiences and various expressions of worship and religious tradition, but Christ is the "only name under heaven where mankind must be saved" (Acts 4:12). Heaven comes from Jesus, not a denomination. He is the Son of God who died for the sins of humanity. His death on the cross created a bridge between God and man. No one gets to the Father but by Him.

Jesus is grace—His gift of heaven is not earned or deserved. Jesus is forgiver—no one can forgive sin but Him. Jesus is God—when we see Him we see the Father. Jesus is King—we bow to no one else in awe and worship. Jesus is the one and only true God—no other gods share His glory and fame. Jesus on earth was fully man and God. He wept, walked on water, healed the diseased, taught, resurrected the dead, and rose from the dead. The most compelling apologetic is your life transformed by Christ. He is the only way to God and an abundant life. Trust Him.

"For there is one God and one mediator between God and mankind, the man Christ Jesus" (1 Timothy 2:5).

Related Readings: Matthew 1:21; John 1:4; 14:9; Acts 10:43; Ephesians 2:18

ONE ANOTHER

So we, who are many, are one body in Christ, and individually members one of another. Romans 12:5, NASB

Committed followers of Jesus are called to community, not seclusion. Jesus had His disciples, Paul had the church; even monks have brothers in the monastery, and nuns have sisters in the convent. Men and women of faith are not islands of isolation, but a beautiful Body of Christ intricately woven together by God's grace. Just like a physical body relies on a variety of organs and appendages, so the spiritual body is interdependent. Christ calls us to one another. We need one another. Yes, we are complete in Christ, but we are incomplete without a Christ-centered community.

When Christ called us, He called us to Himself and to His body of believers. Spiritual growth slows absent engagement with other sincere souls. We are part of a worldwide movement of faith and good works initiated by the Spirit through the Church of Jesus Christ and His disciples. Our vision radically expands when we are part of a mission much bigger than ourselves. We need one another to know one another and to be known. We need one another because God says so. Religion is not solitary. When we are with other followers of Christ, we are encouraged, prayed for, and held accountable.

"And let us consider how we may spur one another on toward love and good deeds" (Hebrews 10:24).

Related Readings: Joel 2:15-17; Matthew 28:20; Acts 1:14; Hebrews 3:13

DEVOTED TO ONE ANOTHER

Be devoted to one another in brotherly love.
Romans 12:10a, NASB

Disciples of Jesus are devoted to Christ, but they are also devoted to each other. Devotion to divinity brings about devotion to humanity. There is a worldwide fraternity of faith and a sorority of salvation that enjoys a brotherly and sisterly love for one another. For some Christians intimacy with other believers is much more real than their relationship with blood relatives. Those washed in the blood of Christ can be soul mates in the faith. Our dependable devotion during difficult times is refreshing to the recipient. So, we refresh often!

We see this devotion when we mess up and another spiritual comrade helps us through our sticky situation. We lose our job, and they help us network a new beginning. We suffer, and they suffer with us; we rejoice, and they rejoice with us. The kinship with other Christ followers is a humbling benefit of being a believer, but it does require fidelity both ways. Our devotion back to believers is a signal of loyalty and love—it provides security. Be a dedicated disciple by remaining in Him. Devotion to Jesus Christ brings about devotion to one another.

"Before God you could see for yourselves how devoted to us you are" (2 Corinthians 7:12b).

Related Readings: 1 Kings 15:3; Ezekiel 44:29; Luke 16:13; 1 Timothy 6:2

HONOR ONE ANOTHER

Honor one another above yourselves. Romans 12:10b

⚬⚬⚬

To honor is to give preference. It is the act of extending to another the first opportunity. Giving preference is more than good manners; it's preferring another person's needs over our own personal needs. For example, deferring to another's choice for a meeting time and location or allowing a person to go ahead in line shows respect and courtesy. Honor is incubated in a heart of humility. It is the art of serving someone else, even at personal expense.

We can disrespect the process, but still honor the person. We may have been left out of the decision-making loop at work, but we can still honor those who made decisions that disturbed our work. How do we honor them? Honor does not gossip or make disparaging remarks about those who brought us despair. Honor thinks the best and does not assume the worse. Honor values the relationship over being right. It looks for potential in others. The greatest honor is to serve God and people above ourselves. As we honor others, the Lord honors us.

"But when you are invited, take the lowest place, so that when your host comes, he will say to you, 'Friend, move up to a better place.' Then you will be honored" (Luke 14:10).

Related Readings: Proverbs 22:4; John 12:2, 26; Acts 13:48; 1 Corinthians 12:23-26

GRATITUDE SHOWS UP

Godly men buried Stephen and mourned deeply for him.
Acts 8:2

———— ••◆•• ————

When a life has been well spent and invested in the kingdom of God, admirers show up to pay honor at their homegoing to heaven. The godly show up to honor the death of the godly. It is gratitude to God that compels Christ followers to attend the funeral of another faithful brother or sister in the faith. Mourning comforts the one suffering loss and shows appreciation for the loved one's life. Gratitude shows up to empathize with the shaky souls left behind.

If we are grateful for someone, we show up for the important milestones in their lives. Graduations, school plays, art lessons, surgery, sonograms, athletic events, dance recitals, grandparent's day, an open house, retirement, or a friend's big birthday are all events to attend and express support and gratitude. Attendance communicates appreciation. Our body may be weary, but our spirit compels us to be there for those who need us to care. We are motivated by appreciation because of the Lord's great love toward us. We can't outgive Christ, but we can express our gratitude to Him by showing up on His behalf.

"So we cared for you. Because we loved you so much, we were delighted to share with you not only the gospel of God but our lives as well" (1 Thessalonians 2:8).

Related Readings: Isaiah 30:18; Luke 18:1; 2 Corinthians 12:15; 1 John 3:16

GRATITUDE SPEAKS UP

One of them, when he saw he was healed, came back, praising God in a loud voice. He threw himself at Jesus' feet and thanked him. Luke 17:15-16

Gratitude cannot keep quiet. Like a giddy fan at their favorite sporting event, emotions explode in cheers over a well-executed play. Heartfelt thanksgiving has to escape and express itself to those who contributed to this cause for joy. If verbal gratitude is withheld, then those who remain silent miss out on bringing public praise to God. Ultimately, Jesus is behind every good gift, and often He uses His people in the process of blessing.

An outcast of society becomes an insider with God through thoughtful and verbal thanksgiving to Him. Do you still exhibit a humble attitude of gratitude, or have you graduated beyond gratefulness? In fact, the more you grow in the grace of God, the more thankful you become. You show up and speak up with thanksgiving. At work you thank your team leader for employment and trust God with opportunities for advancement. Open wide your mouth with words of thanksgiving, and watch the Lord do wonderful works around you. Gratitude speaks up to its Savior!

"We have enjoyed a long period of peace under you, and your foresight has brought about reforms in this nation. Everywhere and in every way, most excellent Felix, we acknowledge this with profound gratitude" (Acts 24:2-3).

Related Readings: Psalm 147:7; Jonah 2:9; Romans 16:4; Colossians 4:2

THANKFUL PRAYERS

We always thank God for all of you and continually mention you in our prayers. 1 Thessalonians 1:2

———————◆◆◆▸———————

Prayers of thanksgiving bring a smile to the face of God. He delights in hearing His children express to heaven gratitude for their sisters and brothers on earth. Jesus expects His followers to not just tolerate one another but to celebrate each other's uniqueness. A prayer of thanksgiving for another needy soul grows a heart of love for souls. Consistent prayers of gratitude get God's attention and move His heart to bless, forgive, and love.

We all need prayer: prayer for wisdom, prayer for solutions, prayer for healing, prayer for forgiveness, prayer for reconciliation, prayer for salvation, prayer for God's will, prayer for strength, prayer for faith, prayer for courage, prayer for work, and prayer for patience. How grateful we soon become when we reflect on friends who lift us to the Lord with passionate petitions. We thank God for those precious souls who pray for our soul's care.

"We ought always to thank God for you, brothers and sisters, and rightly so, because your faith is growing more and more, and the love all of you have for one another is increasing" (2 Thessalonians 1:3).

Related Readings: Nehemiah 11:17; Philippians 4:6; 1 Timothy 2:1

PRAYERS OF GRATITUDE

I always thank my God as I remember you in my prayers, because I hear about your love for all his holy people and your faith in the Lord Jesus. Philemon 1:4-5

Do you thank Christ regularly for those whose faith is on fire? Are you grateful to God for the grace of God that is ever growing in your community of faith? Those who boldly bear a beautiful banner for Jesus need our serious prayer support. The enemy rages against the righteous who are engaged in eternal issues: justice for the poor, education for the ignorant, church planting, job training, discipleship, and food for the hungry.

Your grateful prayers to God garner goodwill for those executing God's will. Thank Him for their trust that perseveres through persecution. Thank Jesus for those who share Jesus with words and deeds. Thank your heavenly Father for the fathers and mothers who model compassion, love, leadership, and the nurturing of their children. Thank Him for single adults who hope in Christ and who serve unselfishly in His name. Thank Him for the great faith of those who influence you to remain faithful to Christ. Gratitude prays!

"We always thank God, the Father of our Lord Jesus Christ, when we pray for you, because we have heard of your faith in Christ Jesus and of the love you have for all God's people" (Colossians 1:3-4).

Related Readings: Romans 1:8; Ephesians 1:15; Philemon 1:4-5

THANKFUL FOR THANKSGIVING

Cry out, "Save us, God our Savior; gather us and deliver us from the nations, that we may give thanks to your holy name, and glory in your praise. 1 Chronicles 16:35

A nation that stays on its knees in thanksgiving to God enjoys the blessings of God. Sophistication is never meant to substitute ingenuity for the Spirit's power. Modern conveniences are meant to be a catalyst for Christ's love to be leveraged worldwide. When a country dedicates a holiday—holy day—in remembrance of the Almighty's favor, the citizens of that nation remember their true originator and sustainer. The faith of our forefathers in our heavenly Father is a gift that keeps giving to this day. So, we remind our children of the context of their country's Christian roots.

We are a blessed people because of the godly people who went before us under the authority of almighty God. We stand on the shoulders of other saints who believed boldly in the bodily resurrection of Jesus Christ and the working of His power that fueled their faith, their patriotism, their life, their work, and their relationships. We are compelled to be thankful for our ancestors' blood, sweat, tears, resolve, and trust in God. So today, thank God for a day of Thanksgiving, and from a grateful heart give all nations an opportunity to know His love!

"I thank and praise you, God of my ancestors" (Daniel 2:23a).

Related Readings: Exodus 3:15; Micah 7:7; Colossians 3:17; 1 Thessalonians 2:13

LIVING IN HARMONY

Live in harmony with one another. Do not be proud, but be willing to associate with people of low position. Do not be conceited. Romans 12:16

Relational harmony comes from humility. Yes, there are times for confrontation and clarity, but a chronic state of conflict is not healthy. Pride drives disharmony, but humility disarms discord. Fighting is not the forte of Jesus followers. A world caught up in conflict needs a safe, secure, and stable environment. Are you tempted by Satan to slight, even slander, another brother or sister in Christ? Words that sow discord reap division. Has gossip caught you in a lie? If so, humble yourself and ask your offended friend for forgiveness.

Or, if you have been talked about behind your back, don't pay back. Instead, pray for those who threaten harmony at home or work. Be a life-giver and generous giver full of mercy, grace, and forgiveness. Be a harmonizer, not a demonizer. Be a team player, not a stubborn troublemaker. You are a connecter for Christ. So, connect first with your heavenly Father; then you can connect with other Christ followers. Harmony brings heaven to earth.

"'Love your neighbor as yourself.' If you bite and devour each other, watch out or you will be destroyed by each other" (Galatians 5:14b-15).

Related Readings: Psalm 133:1; Jeremiah 32:39; Ephesians 4:1-6; Philippians 4:1-3

LOVE ONE ANOTHER

Let no debt remain outstanding, except the continuing debt to love one another, for whoever loves others has fulfilled the law. Romans 13:8

There is a debt of love owed between believers in Jesus Christ. It's wise to be debt free, but the debt of love is never paid off. Love is a mortgage we take out to our landlord Jesus to pay back on His behalf. It is an interest rate of integrity based on our consistent interest to love well. Indeed, love is an appreciating asset that never declines in value. We experience true riches when our wealth is measured in how well we love one another. The love of Christ for us constrains us to love in Jesus' name. His love does not harm—it heals.

The job description of Jesus followers is love. The qualified candidate is a child of God who regularly receives the love of their Heavenly Father and who then loves freely from the overflow of their heart. Like showering, sleeping, and eating, love becomes the habit of your heart. Because gratitude grips your soul, your love for others spontaneously erupts in enthusiastic generosity. You love much because you have been forgiven much by Jesus.

"Therefore, I [Jesus] tell you, her many sins have been forgiven—as her great love has shown. But whoever has been forgiven little loves little" (Luke 7:47).

Related Readings: John 15:12; Romans 13:10; Colossians 3:14; 1 John 4:10-11

ENCOURAGE ONE ANOTHER

Therefore encourage one another and build each other up, just as in fact you are doing. 1 Thessalonians 5:11

Courage in Christ is a gift Christians have to give one another. It is a boldness of belief bent on bettering others. Daily life drains courage from a person's heart, but believers are able to fill with encouragement what unrighteousness removes with discouragement. Saintly support comes when a person is aware that someone knows and cares about them. There is an emotional engagement that flows from an inner desire to be there for a needy friend.

Our encouragement is an ambassador from almighty God. We represent Jesus to His followers and to those who have not come to faith. It's when people see Jesus in our actions and attitudes that they are drawn to personally know Him. Yes, our encouragement is a conduit for Christ! We give a cup of courage in Jesus' name, and the thirsty recipient tastes that the Lord is good. Most do not complain of too much encouragement, but many quietly crave more. We are encouraged by Christ so we can encourage another. Encouragement gives courage!

"Finally, brothers and sisters, rejoice! Strive for full restoration, encourage one another, be of one mind, live in peace. And the God of love and peace will be with you" (2 Corinthians 13:11).

Related Readings: Job 16:5; Act 14:22; 1 Thessalonians 4:18; Hebrews 3:13

ACCEPT ONE ANOTHER

Accept one another, then, just as Christ accepted you, in order to bring praise to God. Romans 15:7

Acceptance sets the tone in a trusting relationship. It ascribes value by making a friend feel special, especially if someone struggles with wounds from past rejection and hurt. Acceptance is an antidote for guilt and regret. It looks to bring meaning in the moment and doesn't dwell on former failures. It creates a non-judgmental, safe environment. Like a compassionate nurse, it listens with empathy. Acceptance feels no discrimination or bias.

Who is hungry for your approval and acceptance? Is it a child, a parent, a friend, a co-worker, or fellow Christ follower who needs to feel your warm words of delight in them? To not be an included team member is emotional torture. Passive rejection can be worse that blatant rejection. Indeed, an accepting attitude says, "I believe in you," "I need you," "I am for you." You give others the benefit of the doubt. A person who feels approval has nothing to prove. When you love someone with conflicting standards, they tend to ask, "Why me?" Kindly say, "Why not you?"—that will bring praise to God!

"The one who eats everything must not treat with contempt the one who does not, and the one who does not eat everything must not judge the one who does, for God has accepted them" (Romans 14:3).

Related Readings: Psalm 101:3; John 6:27; Acts 15:8; 1 Thessalonians 2:13

DECEMBER

Therefore, as you received Christ Jesus the Lord, so walk in him, rooted and built up in him and established in the faith, just as you were taught, abounding in thanksgiving.

Colossians 2:6-7

DECEMBER 1

SERVE ONE ANOTHER

You, my brothers and sisters, were called to be free. But do not use your freedom to indulge the flesh; rather, serve one another humbly in love. Galatians 5:13

———————•••••———————

Soldiers in Christ's army enlist to serve. They serve at their Savior's pleasure and they unselfishly serve fellow servants of the Lord. Servants of Jesus are first responders to the needs that afflict or attack the Body of Christ. There is no waiting to be drafted, because salvation in Jesus assumes service. Like America and apple pie is Christian and service. Serving others is an extension of love, a platform for humility, and an expression of Jesus.

Love is the motivation of Christ-centered service. Because we love, we volunteer at church, in the parking lot, in the nursery, or lead a small group. We clean up the kitchen after a meal because we love. We manage the home finances, wash clothes, cook, do yard work, help a child with homework, visit a sick friend, give a gift, and write a caring note because we love. Love must serve—our service says I love you. So, serve others for Christ's sake and watch Him work. You serve Jesus by serving others!

"Each of you should use whatever gift you have received to serve others, as faithful stewards of God's grace in its various forms" (1 Peter 4:10).

Related Readings: Deuteronomy 10:12; Jeremiah 35:15; Matthew 6:24; 1 Peter 4:11

ADMONISH ONE ANOTHER

I myself also am convinced that you yourselves are full of goodness, filled with all knowledge and able also to admonish one another. Romans 15:14, NASB

Admonishment is a gentle but firm warning. It is best received when the words are delivered clearly and directly in relationship well oiled by trust and love. A recommended idea is optional, but an admonishment is a strong suggestion. It implores an individual by almost demanding. Yes, a brother or sister in Christ admonishes another to protect them from foolish friends or an unwise choice. Blessed are we to have men and women in our lives who feel the freedom to warn us. Those who have traveled the road of life longer know where to tread lightly or not at all.

It is a blessing, not a curse, for us to have someone who cares enough to tell us the truth. A messenger who means well should not be dismissed but welcomed. Be grateful for a reproving word, an honest assessment, or direct warning. Some are not ready, so don't waste your words on fools. Ask the Spirit to lead you into conversations that cultivate a heart where a seed of admonishment grows a tree of wisdom. Invite admonishment and admonish the teachable.

"It is better to heed the rebuke of a wise person than to listen to the song of fools" (Ecclesiastes 7:5).

Related Readings: Psalm 141:5; Proverbs 13:1, 25:12; Colossians 1:28; 3:16; 1 Thessalonians 5:12

PRAY FOR ONE ANOTHER

Pray for us that the message of the Lord may spread rapidly and be honored, just as it was with you. 2 Thessalonians 3:1b

———————————

Prayer for one another is a spiritual secret weapon. It rocks the devil's world, wins over a lost world, and brings peace in this world. Prayer for another is a necessary ingredient in the recipe for successful living. A prayer investment is an eternal investment. Prayers for healing, prayers for wisdom, prayers of praise, and prayers to courageously spread the gospel all acknowledge the Lord's priorities. Indeed, prayer promotes God's agenda.

Moreover, our prayers for others change us. When we implore Christ to heal the illness of a sweaty browed, small child, our heart grows tender. When we ask God to give a friend wisdom in a crucial decision, we grow in wisdom. When we pray to the Lord of the harvest to send forth laborers, the Spirit directs us to share the good news of Jesus Christ. Prayer is a platform that produces righteous results for the giver and the receiver. A supplication to your Savior for suffering saints brings fear to its knees and elevates faith and hope front and center. Thus, ask for prayer and offer prayer for God's glory. Earnest prayers encourage.

"So Peter was kept in prison, but the church was earnestly praying to God for him" (Acts 12:5).

Related Readings: Acts 1:14; Romans 15:13; 30-31;
1 Thessalonians 4:1

DECEMBER 4

ESTABLISHED BY GOD

And David knew that the LORD had established him as king.
1 Chronicles 14:2a

———————

God establishes people for His purposes. What He establishes no man or movement can stop. Establishments energized by the Holy Spirit enjoy momentum that propels them forward in faith. For example, a church or ministry freshly challenged with a God-sized vision and a unified mission will move forward by God's grace. A leader led by the Lord will persevere through rough patches because his motive is for the sake of God's people.

Where has God established you? Are you honored to be at home for the sake of your family? Your faithfulness now in disciplining, training, coaching, and mentoring your child will pay a lifetime of dividends in their adult experiences. Does the Lord have you in an influential role at work? Your ability to see the bigger picture of service to the people is what will sustain you to lead well. God established you for His people. What He establishes, He sustains and blesses. He accomplishes His will through what He has established—thus make sure the flashing neon sign on your life reads: ESTABLISHED BY GOD!

"The children of your servants will live in your presence; their descendants will be established before you" (Psalm 102:28).

Related Readings: 2 Samuel 5:12; Psalm 89:4;
Colossians 1:23; Hebrews 8:6

DECEMBER 5

GOD RELIANT

Very truly I tell you, the Son can do nothing by himself; he can do only what he sees his Father doing, because whatever the Father does the Son also does. John 5:19

———————

The ultimate expression of humility is reliance on almighty God. He is the source of significance, and He provides strength for life's journey. Jesus Himself confessed that He depended on His heavenly Father as a model of what to do. Just as Jesus looked to His Father, so His followers look to their heavenly Father. Obedience does not act alone. Activity for the Lord is best achieved when accompanied by a blueprint from God.

Our self-reliance gets in the way of our God reliance. Anger, will power, and intellect are the fruit of self-reliance. Patience, trust, and humility are the fruit of God reliance. We honor our heavenly Father when we first ask Him how to solve a problem or how to love the unlovely. Our imitation of Christ's actions is an indicator of humble reliance. We rely on God when we share the gospel in the power of the Holy Spirit and trust the results with Him. Pray as if everything depends on God, then work passionately as unto the Lord.

"For I have always been mindful of your unfailing love and have lived in reliance on your faithfulness" (Psalm 26:3).

Related Readings: 1 Kings 2:4; Psalm 86:11; Proverbs 25:19; Matthew 26:39

356

DECEMBER 6

CALLED TO WAIT

So Samuel took the horn of oil and anointed him in the presence of his brothers, and from that day on the Spirit of the Lord came powerfully upon David. 1 Samuel 16:13

———————

The calling of God includes seasons of waiting in faithful service. David was anointed and experienced the power of God, but it was over twenty years before he became king. Public responsibilities require private experience and success. The Lord's calling starts with a thorny crown of commitment and grows into a shiny crown of respect. The flesh wants to influence the masses prematurely, but the Spirit is patient to pay the price of wise waiting before proceeding.

We have the opportunity to be faithful where the Lord has us. His power is prevalent through our humble prayers and our quiet acts of random kindness. Jesus doesn't discount small deeds done in His name. Thus, whatever we do, we do all for the glory of God. We visit the elderly, care for the dying, rescue the unrighteous, carry one another's burdens, and shepherd the flock of God— all for Him. We win while we wait because Christ is positioning us for influence. We work faithfully as we wait and watch Him work!

"I come against you in the name of the LORD Almighty, the God of the armies of Israel, whom you have defied" (1 Samuel 17:45b).

Related Readings: Psalm 130:5-6; Proverbs 20:22; Isaiah 26:8; Lamentations 3:24-26; Jude 1:21

DECEMBER 7

BUDGET YOUR TIME

There is a time for everything, and a season for every activity
under the heavens. Ecclesiastes 3:1

There is enough time to do God's will, thus He desires a
stewardship of time. Just as money can be overspent, so can
time. The twenty-four hours in a day, the seven days in a week,
and the fifty-two weeks in a year need budget restraints. Some
days may go by slowly, but years seem to fly by quickly. A life
well spent and prayerfully invested pays dividends for a lifetime
and into eternity. But, a chronically reactive life wakes up one
day weary, wondering, "What have I done?"

Therefore, we are wise to lay out a life plan and adjust it
over time. We prayerfully modify our calendar regularly so
overcommitment does not overcome us. It is much better to
have fewer obligations than to find ourselves emotionally and
physically spent—unable and unwilling to follow through.
Time is a treasure from heaven that needs close attention and
protection. We number our days, so at the end of each day, we
are satisfied that we were successful for God. By God's grace
we manage our calendar or it will manage us. We trust the Lord
to lead us along His timetable.

"I am the LORD; in its time I will do this swiftly" (Isaiah
60:22b).

Related Readings: Job 14:5; Psalm 39:4; 90:12; Luke 1:20;
Acts 17:26

DECEMBER 8

GIFTED BY GOD

Now about the gifts of the Spirit, brothers and sisters, I do not want you to be uninformed… There are different kinds of gifts, but the same Spirit distributes them. 1 Corinthians 12:1, 4

One of Satan's schemes is to keep God's children ignorant or confused concerning spiritual gifts. However, His gifts are what empower followers of Jesus to carry out His will. The Great Commission, to make disciples, and the Great Commandment, to love God and love people, are implemented best by the Spirit's inspired gifts. There are a variety of gifts, but they originate and are distributed by one Holy Spirit. Gifts come from God.

Like the multicolors of a rainbow make a compelling commercial for God, so His diverse gifts glorify Him. We are gifted by God for the glory of God. Moreover, we are gifted as a gift to the Body of Christ. Our spiritual gifts are for service, not self. They are for the good of the whole, not just the benefit of one. A gift's manifestation is wrongly employed if the result leaves observers in awe of a person. Spiritual gifts glorify God when used by humble and wise users. Your unique giftedness is Christ's canvas of you. A world wakes up to watch your gifts glow for God. Use your gifts from God to serve others.

"Each of you should use whatever gift you have received to serve others" (1 Peter 4:10a).

Related Readings: Romans 12:6-8; 1 Corinthians 12: 8-10, 28; Ephesians 4:11

GIFT OF MERCY

If it is to encourage, then give encouragement; if it is giving, then give generously; if it is to lead, do it diligently; if it is to show mercy, do it cheerfully. Romans 12:8

———————•◄●►•————————

The gift of mercy is compelled to be compassionate. Its sensitive spirit hurts when others hurt and rejoices when others rejoice. Merciful followers of Jesus find great satisfaction in alleviating suffering and applying God's grace to a wounded heart. Their tears of concern flow freely; they are pained to see others in pain. The merciful can be soft-spoken and gentle in disposition. Behind the scenes they do quiet acts of kindness. They know how you are doing without asking.

We all need those gifted with mercy to give us comfort in our time of need. We need their unconditional love when we don't feel loved. We need their affirmation when we don't feel affirmed. Just like our sympathetic Savior brings empathy to our empty soul, so those gifted in mercy empathize with our emptiness. By God's grace be quick to forgive and slow to anger. Look at those who are stuck in selfishness with sympathy. Indeed, pity people who are trapped in the pit of pride. Pursue the apathetic with authentic love—mercy initiates.

"But the wisdom that comes from heaven is first of all pure; then peace-loving, considerate, submissive, full of mercy and good fruit, impartial and sincere" (James 3:17).

Related Readings: Psalm 6:2, 9; Isaiah 55:7; Matthew 23:23; Jude 1:2

GIFT OF ADMINISTRATION

And God has appointed in the church, first apostles, second prophets, third teachers, then miracles, then gifts of healings, helps, administrations, various kinds of tongues.
1 Corinthians 12:28, NASB

The gift of administration likes for people, projects, and processes to be properly organized. Efficiency and effectiveness energize those with this gift. They keep chaos at bay by bringing consistency and calm to a work or home culture. This supportive gift takes time to plan and then implement the plan. Gifted administrators understand the long-term needs and define the short-term steps needed to accomplish future goals. They are intentional with strategic initiatives.

Those who keep us in line logistically bless us with sustainable systems. It may be a financial manager who is tedious in stewarding income and expenses at work or home. The budget is their accountability partner. They give daily oversight to the proper allocation of resources and are able to discern positive and negative trends. They pay rich dividends in fiscal wisdom. If administration is your gift, be patient when people do not live up to your standards or execute precisely your expectations. Your administrative gift uniquely places you in a place of significant influence!

"Do you see someone skilled in their work? They will serve before kings; they will not serve before officials of low rank" (Proverbs 22:29).

Related Readings: 1 Chronicles 24:19; Daniel 2:49;
2 Corinthians 8:20

GIFT OF TEACHING

If it is serving, then serve; if it is teaching, then teach.
Romans 12:7

———————————

Gifted teachers love examining, interpreting, and explaining Holy Scripture. They can instruct in their area of expertise, but they especially enjoy bringing out the meaning of the Bible. Context is critical for teachers, because the integrity of rightly dividing the word of truth is fundamental. Teachers love to ask what the reader was thinking and experiencing. Why did the Holy Spirit inspire that exact Hebrew or Greek word? Teachers thrive on knowing the "why" behind the word.

If you are a Spirit-filled teacher you embrace the need for dependency on God in understanding His intended message. The same Holy Spirit that originally inspired the penning of the Bible's profound writings is the same Holy Spirit who illuminates its meaning to modern-day teachers. Your teaching gift positions you to perceive God's heart through your humble heart. Beyond an academic exercise is a divine encounter. The best teachers are students of the Spirit's teachings. So, teach out of your weakness whatever the Lord's teaching you and you will never need to search for content. Be humble, be bold, be honest, admit mistakes, and never stop learning. Teach to make God smile.

"But the Advocate, the Holy Spirit, whom the Father will send in my name, will teach you all things and will remind you of everything I have said to you" (John 14:26).

Related Readings: Ephesians 4:11; Romans 2:21; 2 Timothy 4:3; Hebrews 5:12

GIFT OF EXHORTATION

Or he who exhorts, in his exhortation; he who gives, with liberality; he who leads, with diligence; he who shows mercy, with cheerfulness. Romans 12:8, NASB

An exhorter encourages others in the ways of God. They have a genuine desire for their brothers and sisters in Christ to grow in Christlikeness. Therefore, application of biblical truth is the basis of their motivation toward maturity. For the exhorter, information without application leads to spiritual inoculation. Growing in grace is much more than hearing what's required of a disciple; it's doing the right things the right way. The exhortation gift provides a roadmap for righteous living.

Every follower of Jesus needs an exhorter for encouragement and accountability. We need to know that someone really knows and understands us. They know us so well that they can tell when we are not doing well. They ask us questions that are to the point but delivered with patience. The gift of exhortation gives us courage to continue and warns when to turn around. Exhorters praise our strengths and protect us from our weaknesses. We are wise to invite exhorters into our life. One simple "I love you" from Jesus lingers in your heart. Thus, be exhorted in the Lord and then exhort others to the Lord.

"Finally then, brethren, we request and exhort you in the Lord Jesus" (1 Thessalonians 4:1, NASB).

Related Readings: Proverbs 1:8; Philippians 4:4; 1 Timothy 5:1; Hebrews 13:1, 22

GIFT OF GIVING

If it is to encourage, then give encouragement; if it is giving,
then give generously. Romans 12:8a

Those with the gift of giving find great joy in contributing to a
compelling cause or investing in a needy individual. They are on
the lookout for opportunities where the Lord is at work. Givers
can't wait to give. They may even feel guilty or a little anxious
if they cannot connect a kingdom need with their time, talent,
or treasure. Those with the gift of giving believe, since God has
mightily blessed them, they have the privilege and responsibility
to participate in generosity.

You can be a gifted giver with a lot of money or with little
financial resources. It is a heart liberal toward helping others
that motivates your acts of giving. You are thrifty and love to
save to have additional surplus for lost souls and to feed and
clothe the poor, not to spend on yourself. You understand that
the remedy for greed is generosity. The best medicine for
selfishness is becoming big hearted toward other hurting hearts.
You are free to give because God has freely given to you. Jesus
gave you true riches.

"For you know the grace of our Lord Jesus Christ, that though he
was rich, yet for your sake he became poor, so that you through
his poverty might become rich" (2 Corinthians 8:9).

Related Readings: Psalm 68:9; Luke 21:4; 2 Corinthians 8:12;
9:7; Philippians 2:6-8

GIFT OF LEADERSHIP

If it is to lead, do it diligently; if it is to show mercy, do it cheerfully. Romans 12:8b

---

Gifted leaders are first and foremost good followers of God. They recognize the gift giver as their authority, so they do not lord over others—rather they submit to the Lord. Because the leader respects Christ, he or she respects those they lead. Because they love the Lord, they love their team. Because they serve Jesus, they serve those who serve with them. Yes, a gifted leader is able to influence and educate a group toward an agreed upon goal. Leaders have followers.

Are you called to lead but feel inferior? If so, seek your confidence in Christ. Go to the resourceful one for reassurance. Resistance does not mean you are a bad leader; on the contrary it may be a validation that you are moving in the right direction. Indeed, some struggle with change—it threatens their security. So, stay the course and lead prayerfully, patiently, and lovingly. Trust the Spirit's small voice that affirms your actions—God is with you. Be intentional and prayerful to train up faithful men and women who will train others. You steward your leadership best by birthing other leaders!

"And David shepherded them with integrity of heart; with skillful hands he led them" (Psalm 78:72).

Related Readings: Exodus 32:21; 1 Samuel 18:16; Isaiah 48:21; 1 Timothy 6:11-12; 1 Corinthians 1:10

GIFT OF EVANGELISM

So Christ Himself gave the apostles, the prophets, the evangelists, the pastors and teachers, to equip His people for works of service. Ephesians 4:11-12

Every follower of Jesus can and should be a witness of His amazing grace, but there are some specifically gifted to share the gospel. The good news of salvation from sin in Christ somehow makes its way into the conversations of an evangelist. These bold believers are compelled by the love of God to share the love of God. This gift of evangelism cannot be silent about the need for a Savior. Because their conversion to Christ was transformational, they pray for all to come to know Him.

Many of us became believers because of the message we heeded from an evangelistic messenger. Maybe we heard on the radio, "You must be born again." Perhaps a visiting preacher at church proclaimed Christ's death on the cross as the payment for our sin. A friend may have asked us about our assurance of going to heaven when we die. Reading the Bible, the fiery faith of the apostles may have ignited your faith. Use your gift of evangelism to equip the saints of God to do the work of God. Your experience and passion are a bridge to help other believers share Jesus.

"Keep your head in all situations, endure hardship, do the work of an evangelist" (2 Timothy 4:5).

Related Readings: John 3:14-15; Acts 13:46; Romans 1:2, 16; Galatians 3:8; 2 Timothy 1:8

DECEMBER 16

MADE TO MAKE

For we are His workmanship, created in Christ Jesus for good works, which God prepared beforehand that we should walk in them. Ephesians 2:10, NKJV

God makes things beautiful so, in turn, they can make things beautiful. For instance, an artist who has tasted the grace of God is able to take a blank canvas and create a complex and attractive expression of Christ's love. Architects make plans, builders make houses, homeowners make warm homes, and chefs make meals. Senators make laws, technicians make systems, leaders make decisions, and gardeners make gardens. What are you making for your Maker? Perhaps it includes loved ones who love the Lord and people, a legacy of wise living, eternal financial investments, and relationships built on respect and unselfish service.

You are God's wonderful workmanship created in Christ for good works. Yes, He molds you with messy circumstances, painful processes, and daily discipline. Your spiritual formation in Christ is not always easy, but it is fulfilling. Indeed, Jesus doesn't make any junk. The last words of Christ to us, His disciples, were to make disciples. Ask God in whom you should invest your time to help make them a mature disciple of Jesus. Disciple-making invites the power and presence of Christ. Model for them how their Maker wants to make them a disciple-maker.

"Therefore go and make disciples of all nations" (Matthew 28:19a).

Related Readings: Isaiah 49:6; Acts 1:8; Ephesians 4:24; 2 Timothy 2:2; Titus 2:14

FREE FROM WORRY

Do not be anxious about anything, but in every situation, by prayer and petition, with thanksgiving, present your requests to God. Philippians 4:6

Worry is a weight that is self-imposed. It uses up today's strength on tomorrow's concerns. Worry worries most when others don't seem worried. It feels the responsibility to be anxious on behalf of friends who are not engaged in anxiety. A fearful person may even get mad because other people are not concerned enough. If left unchecked, worry crushes confidence and grows into an all-consuming fear and faith killer. Worry becomes dramatic and ignores intimacy with Christ.

The remedy for worries is to give them to God for His safekeeping. Like a secure vault inaccessible to man, lock up your worries in the Lord's bank of trust. Your salvation is His safe deposit box of eternal security. Because you trust Him with the eternal, You can trust Him with the temporal. Worry given away stays at bay, but worry held on to controls you. Anxiety is a discontent master that is never satisfied with future preparations—the worst is assumed. Thus, leave your worries with Jesus. Your Savior soothes your soul with His sweet presence.

"In His great mercy He has given us new birth into a living hope through the resurrection of Jesus Christ from the dead" (1 Peter 1:3).

Related Readings: Jeremiah 17:3; Psalm 139:23-23; Matthew 6:25-34; 1 Timothy 4:10

DEALING WITH DISAPPOINTMENT

Then you will know that I am the LORD; those who hope in me will not be disappointed. Isaiah 49:23b

Everyone deals with disappointment—some more than others. These letdowns vary in scope: another year with no raise at work, a friend's forgetfulness, a lost opportunity, a teenager's poor choices, a missed deadline, a relative's financial woes, a boss's oversight, an injured body, or unexpected dental work. In this world troubles abound, but in Christ, His peace is profound. Yes, disappointment is a fact that forces us to make appointments with Jesus. He doesn't disappoint.

Moreover, disappointments left unattended lead to disobedience. The hole in our heart is meant to grow our dependency on God. He brings wholeness and holiness to a lacerated soul. The Lord heals hurt feelings when we offer forgiveness. Yes, disappointment feeds selfishness when we don't get our way. So, we allow our trust in Jesus to trump testy relationships. We adjust our expectations to His concerns. Appointments with God help us to deal with disappointment. He gives us rest when we are restless. He gives us calm when there is calamity. He gives us peace when there is chaos. He gives us trust when there is distrust. Jesus never disappoints.

"My soul, wait silently for God alone, for my expectation is from Him" (Psalm 62:5, NKJV).

Related Readings: Job 6:20; Psalm 5:3, 22:5; John 6:60-71; 2 Corinthians 8:5; James 1:6-8

RELY ON GOD

Indeed, we felt we had received the sentence of death. But this happened that we might not rely on ourselves but on God, who raises the dead" 2 Corinthians 1:9

———◆◆◆———

Children of God have the privilege to rely on the only one who raises the dead. He raised His Son Jesus from the dead, and today He still brings life from death. Indeed, even a dead relationship He can bring back to life. A dead deal—He can resurrect. A dead end job—He can breathe life into with opportunities and new ideas. A dead marriage—He can call forth like Lazarus, and by His grace remove the grave clothes of bitterness and unforgiveness. God gives life—He is reliable!

Our Lord and Savior Jesus Christ is reliable because His track record is 100% trustworthy. It is when we rely on ourselves that our faith becomes stale and irrelevant. However, when we choose to chase after the comfort of Christ, we are comforted. When we wait and seek out His wisdom before we react, we are protected. When we bow in humble worship of the Almighty, we avoid worshiping at the altar of our ego or economics. We rely on God, because He is totally reliable. The Holy Spirit is our sherpa to guide us into His will!

"Stop trusting in mere humans, who have but a breath in their nostrils. Why hold them in esteem?" (Isaiah 2:22)

Related Readings: : Jeremiah 17:5-7; Psalm 108:12; John 5:21; Romans 4:17

CHOSEN TO WAIT

Then the Lord said, "Rise and anoint him; this is the one." So Samuel took the horn of oil and anointed him in the presence of his brothers. 1 Samuel 16:12-13

———————

Whom God chooses He uses, but His initial lessons are learned in the incubator of waiting. David was anointed to be king, but he would wait over 20 years before he became king. God's game plan was to grow his leadership, humility, and intimacy with Him before he experienced the honor of ruling over the entire kingdom. Indeed, every follower of Jesus can be filled with the Spirit by faith, but the fullness of the Spirit may lead to obscurity, not fame; submission, not authority.

We are called to be faithful where we are and not to be preoccupied with promotion and recognition. The favor of the Lord is what eventually wins out, not our winsomeness or persuasiveness. So we wait—not in self-pity but in self-denial. We wait and learn not to carry the weight of the world on our shoulders but to cast our cares on Christ who has overcome the world. A season of limitations is a time to tap into the Lord's limitless resources. Embrace waiting while God molds you into His image bearer. God chose you to wait on Him.

"Keep yourselves in God's love as you wait for the mercy of our Lord Jesus Christ" (Jude 1:21).

Related Readings: Psalm 130:5; Micah 7:7; 1 Corinthians 1:7; Hebrews 9:28

BUSY FOR GOD

But Martha was distracted by all the preparations that had to
be made. Luke 10:40a

———————•◄═►•———————

Busyness can breed a bad attitude. It creates an expectation
that everyone should be involved in hyperactivity for the Lord.
Unfortunately, what started out as sincere service for Jesus
becomes a demanding spirit cloaked in spiritual slogans. The
graceless pace of a busy person is worried and upset at God that
more people don't have their same sense of urgency. Because
busyness has no mental, emotional, or spiritual margin, it misses
the Lord's bigger priority of prayer. It's tired.

It is not what we do for God that matters most—what matters
most is what God does through us. If we lunge through life, we
hit and miss finding Jesus, but if we sit at His feet with patient
expectation, we can hear His voice. Christ doesn't call us to
neglect our health, our family, and our friends in the name of
good activities. Truly knowing God begins with being with
Jesus. Once we sit at His feet, we are able to look up to His
face. In stillness His Spirit fills us with peace. Grace provides a
sustainable pace to serve with God, not just be busy for God.

"God looks down from heaven on all mankind to see if there are
any who understand, any who seek God" (Psalm 53:2).

Related Readings: 2 Chronicles 15:2; Psalm 27:4, 100:3;
Philippians 3:13-14; 2 Peter 3:8-9

APPOINTMENTS WITH GOD

Sow righteousness for yourselves, reap the fruit of unfailing love, and break up your unplowed ground; for it is time to seek the LORD, until he comes and showers his righteousness on you. Hosea 10:12

Appointments with God honor God. When He is scheduled daily, it shows He is your priority. Some people clamor to get on a celebrity's calendar, yet Christ is accessible 24/7. Indeed, Jesus, the most iconic person of all time, is available to engage any interested individual at any time. Almighty God has no handlers or gatekeepers—He is easily reachable by faith. So, why are we reluctant to schedule time with eternity? Are we really too busy to pray?

In life we have appointments for activities that really matter to us: haircuts, exercise, doctors, dentists, mechanics, job interviews, breakfasts, lunches, dinners, and dates. Why not schedule time with our Savior, so we feel accountable to meet with Him? We would certainly not miss an appointment with Jesus any more than we would stand up our hair stylist. Time that has been calendared makes it easier to say, "I have another commitment." Give Him your undivided attention with no multitasking or distractions. Create a calm place to be quiet before your Lord. Begin the day by feeding your soul; then your fullness of faith will feed other starving souls.

"This is what the LORD says to Israel: 'Seek me and live'" (Amos 5:4).

Related Readings: 1 Samuel 1:19a; Psalm 5:3; Zephaniah 2:3; Mark 1:35

MODEST MEANS

She gave birth to her firstborn, a son. She wrapped Him in cloths and placed Him in a manger, because there was no guest room available for them. Luke 2:7

Jesus came into the world in a modest manger with parents who had modest means. Mary and Joseph were long on love but short on financial resources. But, in God's economy, a family first needs faith in their Provider and not in the provision. A family who prays together has a higher probability of staying together. A home rich in relational depth experiences true riches. Modest financial means can liberate one's love for the Lord.

You may receive a cool reception from those who feel superior because of their self-proclaimed social status. Some look down on the work of your hands because their hands have not been soiled by sweat and physical labor. Pride breeds a smug countenance while humility births a kind and compassionate face. Indeed, modesty makes room for humility. Give over to the Lord your modest means, and He will multiply it for His glory. Your limited time He redeems with creative opportunities; your humble finances He stretches beyond a strict budget, and your rich relationships He makes richer. Dedicate your modest means to your master Jesus, and, like the fish and loaves, He will multiply (Matthew 14:19).

"Whoever can be trusted with very little can also be trusted with much" (Luke 16:10a).

Related Readings: Exodus 16:17; Proverbs 16:8; Luke 19:17; 1 Corinthians 12:23

NIGHT BEFORE CHRISTMAS

So Joseph also went up from the town of Nazareth in Galilee to Judea, to Bethlehem the town of David. Luke 2:4

———————◆◆◆———————

It was the night before Christmas, and Jesus, who was from the line of David, was to be born in the city of David. He was coming not as a king but as a Savior to shepherd the souls of hurting humanity. In God's eyes His Son had always been and always would be. But, to mankind the birth of Jesus was the defining moment in history (His story!). Calendars began to divide time: BC (before Christ), AD (Anno Domini: in the year of our Lord).

In a similar way we define our conversion to Jesus as a new birth into His kingdom. The calendar of our soul is clearly categorized as before Christ and after Christ. The night before our new birth we were lost in our sins. But at the daybreak of our faith, we stepped into the light of forgiveness. Yes, Jesus was born into the world to seek and to save the lost. He was born so we could be born again. Have you made room for your Lord Jesus at the inn of your soul, or is He in the hay barn of your heart? Christmas Eve is a celebration of Christ's joy to the world!

"With joy you will draw water from the wells of salvation" (Isaiah 12:3).

Related Readings: Deuteronomy 20:7; Isaiah 9:6; Daniel 6:4; John 4:14; 7:42

GOD WITH US

All this took place to fulfill what the Lord had said through the prophet: "The virgin will conceive and give birth to a son, and they will call him Immanuel." Matthew 1:22-23

———◦◦◦———

Wow! The Creator came to dwell with His creation. The all-knowing One came to teach teachers and students limited by their lack of knowledge and understanding. The ever-present One came to comfort hurting people stuck in their suffering. The all-powerful One came to serve weak people, empowering them with His Spirit. The Almighty sent His only Son Jesus into the world, fully God and fully man. Yes, the Word became flesh!

God is with us to face down our fears by faith. God is with us in our hurts, applying His healing balm of grace. God is with us in our transitions to grow our trust in Him. God is with us in our uncertainty. God is with us when we feel His presence and when we don't feel Him near. God is with us and for us for His glory. Christ is with us to comfort us in our pain and encourage us to persevere. He is with us, and He is in us to work through us. Christmas celebrates God with us in the birth of His Son Jesus.

"And surely I [Jesus] am with you always, to the very end of the age" (Matthew 28:20b).

Related Readings: 1 Kings 8:57; Isaiah 8:10; Psalm 46:11; Acts 10:41; Ephesians 2:6

FALSE RELIGION

Not everyone who says to me, "Lord, Lord," will enter the kingdom of heaven, but only the one who does the will of my Father who is in heaven. Matthew 7:21

———◦•◦———

There is a false religion that is absent of authentic faith in Jesus Christ. A person who lacks a real relationship with the Lord can know all the right words to say, but they do not know the Word that became flesh. This fake follower of Jesus may mislead other church members, but they can't deceive the ultimate judge—almighty God. A desperate plea after death does not change an eternal conclusion determined in life. A false faith fails.

Therefore, we are all wise to examine our hearts and ask the Holy Spirit to validate our conversion to Christ. It is the Spirit of our heavenly Father that drew us to Himself and it is the same Spirit of God that affirms our faith. We don't pass from death to life by just living in a household of faith—we come to Christ by taking hold of faith. Our transaction of trust in Jesus seals our soul's fate to be with Jesus. He keeps us secure. So, confess Jesus as Lord now, and there will be no doubt about your confession later.

"If you declare with your mouth, 'Jesus is Lord,' and believe in your heart that God raised him from the dead, you will be saved" (Romans 10:9).

Related Readings: Hosea 8:12; Romans 8:16; Ephesians 1:17; 1 John 3:24

INTENTIONAL LIVING

Hanani, one of my brothers, came from Judah with some other men, and I questioned them about the Jewish remnant that had survived the exile. Nehemiah 1:2

Intentional living is meaningful living. It is an invitation to significance. Intentional living inquires where God may be working and then works to serve there. It's a wise balance between peering into the future at what can be accomplished, with focus in the present on what needs to get done next. Intentionality separates good leaders from great leaders, average parents from exceptional parents, and mediocrity from excellence. Greatness insists on intentionality.

Nehemiah was set for life. He had significant influence with the most powerful person on the planet. However, his heart was set on helping his people. He traded affluence and comfort for modesty and discomfort. Yes, intentional living is willing to let go of current success and replace it with lesser notoriety. For example, intentional parenting may require a pause in our career advancement to come home for a season until the children leave home. Faithfulness is deliberate. Most of all we ask Jesus to lead us in His process. Intentional living anticipates God.

"He [Moses] regarded disgrace for the sake of Christ as of greater value than the treasures of Egypt, because he was looking ahead to his reward" (Hebrews 11:26).

Related Readings: 1 Samuel 3:9; Psalm 37:4; John 15:4-5; Ephesians 6:13-15; Colossians 3:23

SPIRITUAL GROWTH PLAN

I have hidden your word in my heart that I might not sin against you. Psalm 119:11

Scripture memory is a spiritual growth plan against sin, Satan, and self. It is also God's primary method of conforming us into the image of His Son, Jesus Christ. We all are privileged to renew our minds with the truth of Scripture and to cleanse our hearts with the purifying Word of God. Perhaps we commit to memory a verse a week related to what we are experiencing in life. Over the course of a year we will hide fifty-two nuggets of spiritual nourishment within our soul. Thus, when needed, the Spirit brings to mind what has been deposited deep within our hearts.

We may not be the best at memorization, but we do seem to remember what engages our affections. Our ability to retain sports statistics and other details related to interests or hobbies should be trumped by the truth of Scripture. Sure, some have the uncanny ability to recite back word-perfect even paragraphs of content. We need not be intimidated but work within our God-given abilities. Let's start off the new year with a systematic plan to retain the Word of the Lord.

"The LORD continued to appear at Shiloh, and there he revealed himself to Samuel through his word" (1 Samuel 3:21).

Related Readings: Psalm 19:14; Jeremiah 15:16; Matthew 4:1-11; John 1:14; Ephesians 6:17

FINANCIAL MANAGEMENT PLAN

The man who had received five bags of gold went at once and
put his money to work and gained five bags more.
Matthew 25:16

———————

Money manages people or people manage money. Money is a
productive servant but a dreadful master. Thus, a financial plan
is necessary to organize assets around a system to spend, give,
and save. Simple processes offer checks and balances to keep
the checkbook balanced, avoid debt, pay taxes, stay accountable
to not overspend, be generous, and prepare not presume on
the future. Our heavenly Father entrusts us with His material
blessings to be wise managers.

Perhaps you start by recording all your expenditures over a
month. Watch closely how much it takes you to live; save receipts
from everything: coffee, gasoline, books, magazines, food,
eating out, medical, house, and car repair. Store the amount of
the receipts on a budgeting app or spreadsheet. This discipline
to attend to details gives you a realistic understanding of what
it costs to live. For example, you may have to choose between
private education now for your child or a college fund for later.
Don't put unrealistic pressure on your family to do both if it
erases your financial margin or dips into debt. A financial plan
is freedom.

"The plans of the diligent lead to profit as surely as haste leads
to poverty" (Proverbs 21:5).

Related Readings: Proverbs 15:22, 25:28; Luke 12:16-21;
14:28-30; 1 Timothy 6:6-10

PHYSICAL CARE PLAN

Do you not know that your bodies are temples of the Holy Spirit, who is in you, whom you have received from God? You are not your own. 1 Corinthians 6:19

The Holy Spirit has such a high regard for our body that He makes His residence within us. Our body, His temple, is His holy habitation. We wouldn't desecrate a church with unholy influences, nor should we mistreat the temple of the Spirit with unhealthy influences. It is our spiritual responsibility to nourish and care for what God owns and allows us to inhabit. We seek to make wise decisions in our physical care plan since God's Spirit lives within us.

What does it mean for us to feed and care for our body as Christ does the church? For one, He cherishes and nourishes the church, His Body, with what is necessary for its growth, holiness, and happiness. In the same way we love our body by submitting it to a healthy diet and regular exercise. Hence, we grow to love, respect, and enjoy ourselves as God does. Our physical care plan can include healthy meals at home, a workout partner, and a competent, caring physician.

"Husbands ought to love their wives as their own bodies... After all, no one ever hated their own body, but they feed and care for their body, just as Christ does the church" (Ephesians 5:28-29).

Related Readings: 1 Samuel 7:6; Daniel 1:15-16; Psalm 139:14; Matthew 4:2; Acts 14:23

RELATIONAL INVESTMENT PLAN

To Titus, my true son in our common faith: Grace and peace from God the Father and Christ Jesus our Savior. Titus 1:4

———◆◆◆———

Relational investments compound into eternity. Yes, loving people takes time, effort, and perseverance, but the dividends pay off handsomely. For example, we can regularly read a children's Bible to our little one and not see immediate character change, but hopefully over time they will accept the Scripture as God's wisdom and love letter to them personally. Or, our efforts to encourage a friend may be frustrating, but at least they know we love them unconditionally.

Who needs your intentional attention in this season of life? A co-worker? A relative? A neighbor? Relational involvement is messy, so ask the Lord for His grace, patience, and forgiveness to fill your soul. Go the extra third and fourth mile to serve, even if someone takes advantage of your goodwill. Better to take the risk to love than to hide your affections from a hurting heart. If you receive a cold shoulder for your care, keep a warm heart. Love is the best relational investment. Be grateful and give more than you receive in all relationships. Your relational investments will grow into true riches!

"A new command I [Jesus] give you: Love one another. As I have loved you, so you must love one another" (John 13:34).

Related Readings: Genesis 13:8; Luke 16:11; Acts 2:44-45; Ephesians 5:2; 1 Peter 1:22

SCRIPTURE INDEX

TITLE INDEX

HOW TO BECOME A DISCIPLE OF JESUS CHRIST

"Then Jesus came to them and said, "All authority in heaven and on earth has been given to me. Therefore go and make disciples of all nations, baptizing them in the name of the Father and of the Son and of the Holy Spirit, and teaching them to obey everything I have commanded you. And surely I am with you always, to the very end of the age" (Matthew 28:18-20).

Holy Scripture gives us principles related to becoming a disciple and to making disciples:

1. BELIEVE: "That if you confess with your mouth, "Jesus is Lord," and believe in your heart that God raised him from the dead, you will be saved" (Romans 10:9).

Belief in Jesus Christ as your Savior and Lord gives you eternal life in heaven.

2. REPENT AND BE BAPTIZED: "Peter replied, "Repent and be baptized, every one of you, in the name of Jesus Christ for the forgiveness of your sins. And you will receive the gift of the Holy Spirit" (Acts 2:38).

Repentance means you turn from you sin and then publicly confess Christ in baptism.

3. OBEY: "Jesus replied, "If anyone loves me, he will obey my teaching. My Father will love him, and we will come to him and make our home with him" (John 14:23).

Obedience is an indicator of our love for the Lord Jesus and His presence in our life.

4. WORSHIP, PRAYER, COMMUNITY, EVANGELISM AND STUDY: "Every day they continued to meet together in the temple courts.They broke bread in their homes and ate together with glad and sincere hearts, praising God and enjoying the favor of all the people. And the Lord added to their number daily those who were being saved" (Acts 2:46-47).

Worship and prayer is our expression of gratitude and honor to God and our dependence on His grace. Community and evangelism is accountability to Christians and compassion for non-Christians. Study to apply the knowledge, understanding and wisdom of God.

5. LOVE GOD: "Jesus replied: " 'Love the Lord your God with all your heart and with all your soul and with all your mind.'This is the first and greatest commandment" (Matthew 22:37-38).

Intimacy with Almighty God is a growing and loving relationship.We are loved by Him, so we can love others and be empowered by the Holy Spirit to obey His commands.

6. LOVE PEOPLE: "And the second is like it: 'Love your neighbor as yourself "
(Matthew 22:39).

Loving people is an outflow of the love for our Heavenly Father.We are able to love because He first loved us.

7. MAKE DISCIPLES: "And the things you have heard me say in the presence of many witnesses entrust to reliable men who will also be qualified to teach others" (2 Timothy 2:2).

The reason we disciple others is because we are extremely grateful to God and to those who disciple us, and we want to obey Christ's last instructions before going to heaven.

MEET THE AUTHOR:
BOYD BAILEY

Photography By: Crocker Photo

Boyd Bailey, the author of Wisdom Hunters devotionals, is the founder of Wisdom Hunters, Inc., an Atlanta-based ministry created to encourage Christians (a.k.a wisdom hunters) to apply God's unchanging Truth in a changing world.

For over 30 years Boyd Bailey has passionately pursued wisdom through his career in fulltime ministry, executive coaching, and mentoring.

Since becoming a Christian at the age of 19, Boyd begins each day as a wisdom hunter, diligently searching for Truth in scripture, and through God's grace, applying it to his life. These raw, 'real time' reflections from his personal time with the Lord, are now impacting over 100,000 people in 86 countries across the globe through the Wisdom Hunters Daily Devotion email and 11 devotional books.

Boyd received his Bachelor of Arts from Jacksonville State University and his Masters of Divinity from Southwestern Seminary. He and Rita, his wife of 30 plus years, live in Roswell, Georgia and are blessed with four daughters, three sons-in-law who love Jesus, two granddaughters and three grandsons. Boyd and Rita enjoy missions and investing in young couples, as well as hiking, reading, traveling, working through their bucket list, watching college football, and hanging out with their kids and grand kids when ever possible.

WISDOM HUNTERS RESOURCES BY
BOYD BAILEY

DAILY DEVOTIONAL
Sign up for free Daily Devotional emails at **WisdomHunters.com**

E-BOOKS & PRINT BOOKS
available at **WisdomHunters.com**

Download the free WisdomHunters App for
tablets & mobile devides on iTunes & Google Play.